Teaching Virtue

Teaching Virtue

The Contribution of Religious Education

EDITED BY
MARIUS FELDERHOF
AND PENNY THOMPSON

BLOOMSBURY

LONDON · NEW DELHI · NEW YORK · SYDNEY

Bloomsbury Academic

An imprint of Bloomsbury Publishing Plc

50 Bedford Square	1385 Broadway
London	New York
WC1B 3DP	NY 10018
UK	USA

www.bloomsbury.com

First published 2014

British Library Cataloguing-in-Publication Data
A catalogue record for this book is available from the British Library.

ISBN: HB: 978-1-4725-2291-7
PB: 978-1-4725-2253-5
ePDF: 978-1-4725-2222-1
ePub: 978-1-4725-2810-0

Library of Congress Cataloging-in-Publication Data
A catalog record for this book is available from the Library of Congress.

Typeset by Deanta Global Publishing Services, Chennai, India
Printed and bound in India

CONTENTS

NOTES ON CONTRIBUTORS

Jeff Astley is Honorary Professor in the Department of Theology and Religion at the University of Durham, UK, where he has taught since 1981. He is also a visiting professor at Glyndwr University, UK, and York St John University, UK. For over 30 years he was Director of the North of England Institute for Christian Education and is an ordained Anglican priest. He is the author or editor of over 35 books on Christian education, practical theology or religious faith. His publications include *The Philosophy of Christian Religious Education* (1994), *Theological Perspectives on Christian Formation* (1997), *Choosing Life?* (2000), *Children, Churches and Christian Learning* (2002), *Exploring Ordinary Theology* (2003), *Exploring God-talk* (2004), and the *SCM Studyguide: Christian Doctrine* (2010). He may be contacted at jeff.astley@durham.ac.uk.

L. Philip Barnes is Reader in Religious and Theological Education at King's College London, UK, where until recently he was Programme Director for the MA in the topic of Religious Education. He has published widely on religious education. He is the joint editor of *Learning to Teach Religious Education in the Secondary School: A companion to school experience* (2008) and editor of *Debates in Religious Education* (2012). He is the author of *Education, Religion and Diversity: Developing a new model of religious education* (2014) and the joint author of *Does Religious Education Work? A Multi-Dimensional Investigation* (2013) and of *Religious Education: Educating for diversity* (2015). He may be contacted at philip.barnes@kcl.ac.uk.

David Carr is Emeritus Professor at the University of Edinburgh, UK, and currently Professor of Ethics and Education at the Jubilee Centre for the Study of Character and Values at the University of Birmingham, UK. He is the author of three books and the editor or co-editor of several major collections of essays on the philosophy and ethics of education. Of his numerous philosophical and educational papers and book chapters, many have been concerned with aspects of virtue ethics and, more recently, with the value of art and literature for the education of moral character. He has a long-standing interest in religious education and has published several articles on the topic. He may be contacted at david.carr@ed.ac.uk.

Marius Felderhof is Executive Director of the Museum of World Religions, UK, and Honorary Senior Research Fellow and former Senior Lecturer in Systematic and Philosophical Theology in the Department of Theology and Religion at the University of Birmingham, UK. He has published many articles concerning various aspects of religious education and was the drafting secretary for the Agreed Syllabus for Religious Education adopted unanimously by the Birmingham City Council in 2007. He is the author of *Revisiting Christianity, theological reflections* (2011) and edited *Religious Education in a Pluralistic Society*, (1985) and co-edited with Penny Thompson and David Torevell, *Inspiring Faith in Schools* (2007). He may be contacted at m.c.felderhof@bham.ac.uk.

Rod Garner is an Anglican priest, writer and theologian. He is Vicar of Holy Trinity, Southport, Diocesan Theologian for the Anglican Diocese of Liverpool, UK, and Hon. Canon of Liverpool Cathedral, UK. Prior to ordination he was a Group Personnel Manager in the pharmaceutical industry. He has served in urban communities combining parish ministry with a varied remit as a theological educator. He has written and contributed to several books and his recent publications include *On Being Saved: The Roots of Redemption* (2011) and *How to be Wise: growing in discernment and love* (2013). He may be contacted at holytrinitysouthport@gmail.com.

Joseph Houston is Visiting Professor at St. Andrews University, UK. He retired in 2004 as Professor of Philosophical Theology in Glasgow University, UK; from 1966 he taught variously in the Departments of Logic, Philosophy, and Theology, and was Dean of the Divinity Faculty from 1985 to 1988. For a decade (1996–2007) he also worked for the Scottish Qualifications Authority as an examiner, and on curriculum revision for Sixth Year Religious, Moral and Philosophical Studies in Scotland. He was an editor of the *Scottish Journal of Theology* (1976–86). He is the author of *Reported Miracles: A Critique of Hume* (1994), editor and contributor to *Thomas Reid* (2004), he has also published articles in philosophical and theological journals. He contributed a chapter to *Inspiring Faith in Schools*, ed. Felderhof, Thompson and Torevell (2007). He may be contacted at joseph.houston@hotmail.com.

Penny Jennings is a former public school Head of Religious Education in the UK, Section 23 Inspector of Anglican primary schools, and researcher in religious education. She has a PhD in Theology and Religious Studies (University of Wales, Bangor, UK) entitled *The impact of different approaches to religious education on the spiritual and moral development of year nine and year ten pupils (2003)*. This research was quantitative, employing questionnaires for heads of religious education and Year 9 and 10 pupils in community schools across Cornwall, the county where Dr Jennings lives.

To facilitate assessment of the impact on teachers and pupils of the new 2007 Birmingham Agreed Syllabus of Religious Education, the research was expanded (2009–12) to be more appropriate to Birmingham's more ethnically diverse school population, and also extended to include a primary school research population. Dr Jennings may be contacted at penny.jennings@btinternet.com.

William K. Kay is Professor of Theology at Glyndŵr University and Professor of Pentecostal Studies at the University of Chester, UK. He is a former Senior Lecturer in the Department of Education and Professional Studies at King's College London, UK. He has published widely on religious education, often using empirical methods to verify or challenge contemporary orthodoxies and has been involved in RE syllabus development in Wales. He is on the editorial board of the *British Journal of Religious Education*. His most recent book is *Pentecostalism, a very short introduction* (2012). He may be contacted at william.kay@trinity.oxon.org.

D. Ieuan Lloyd is Honorary Research Fellow of Birmingham University, UK, in the School of History and Culture. He taught philosophy and philosophy of education at Birmingham from 1978 to 1990 and philosophy from 1990 to 2000 at the University of Swansea. He is the author of *Philosophy and the Teacher* (1976) and contributed chapters or articles to *The Possibilities of Sense*, (2002) to *Inspiring Faith in Schools* (2007) and to the *Journals of Curriculum Studies*, of *Religious Education*, of *Philosophy of Education*, and *Teodicea Oggi*. His main interest is in the philosophy of Wittgenstein. He has been an executive member of the British Society for the Philosophy of Religion and Secretary to the National Committee of Philosophy (now BPA). He may be contacted at rarebooks@worcester74.freeserve.co.uk.

Penny Thompson is a freelance writer and retired teacher of religious education with experience of teaching in comprehensive schools in Sefton, Merseyside, UK. She is the author of *Whatever Happened to Religious Education* (2004) and, with Brenda Watson, a co-author of *The Effective Teacher of Religious Education* (2007). Together with Marius Felderhof and David Torevell she co-edited *Inspiring Faith in Schools* (2007). She has had articles on religious education published in journals such as the *British Journal of Religious Education* and the *Journal of Beliefs and Values*. She is a member of Liverpool and Knowsley SACREs, (UK) and may be contacted at penelopethompson@btinternet.com.

Brenda Watson is a freelance writer on education and especially religious education. She taught in schools and Didsbury College of Education and her books include *Education and Belief* (1987), *Truth and Scripture* (2004), and, with Penny Thompson, *The Effective Teaching of Religious Education* (2nd edition, 2007). She edited *Priorities in Religious Education: A Model for the*

1990s and Beyond (1992) and, with Elizabeth Ashton, *Society in Conflict: the Value of Education* (1994). Author of many articles and chapters in books, her most recent articles have been in the *Journal of Beliefs and Values* and in the philosophy journal *Think*. She is currently working on a project concerning Democracy, Values and Education, and may be contacted at bgwatson@waitrose.com.

FOREWORD

Bhai Sahib Bhai Mohinder Singh,
Guru Nanak Nishkam Sewak Jatha,
Birmingham, UK

Parh-ay sun-ay kiaa hoee, jou sehaj na miliou soee
– Sri Guru Granth Sahib, p. 655

What use are the rituals of reading, studying and listening, if inward peace, wisdom and understanding are not attained?

Vidiyaa veecharee ta paroupkaree
– Sri Guru Granth Sahib, p. 356

Contemplate upon and come to understand religious wisdom, and you will become magnanimous and altruistic in character.

We talk these days of living in an interconnected world, a global village, and recognize the need to take shared responsibility to address myriad, geographically diverse problems, which inevitably have an impact on us all. As I have engaged with issues over the years, such as working towards the UN's Millennium Development Goals, the practice of faith has constantly reminded me that our search for sustainable outward solutions starts with addressing our inward human condition. It encompasses our own development spiritually, morally, socially and culturally. It involves creating social and educational conditions to positively nurture and uplift the self, to activate and magnify virtues latent within it.

From a Sikh perspective, the virtues of compassion, love, contentment, courage, humility, integrity and forgiveness are not our own, but God's gift to us. To kindle them and overcome *haumai*, the selfish ego, leads us to resonate with the divine presence and 'live in God's image', (to use a Christian term reflected in Sikh teachings). Faith develops this connectivity with the Divine within the self. It provides a vital compass to navigate the complexities of the inward challenges we face as humans and impacts on the quality, direction and sustainability of our outward endeavours. In our efforts to build a better world, our collective heritage of religious wisdom deserves our most serious interest and attention.

This brings us to the subject of this book, highlighting the specific contribution religious education has to make to the teaching of virtue.

Introduced in these chapters is an approach formulated through the 2007 locally agreed syllabus for RE in Birmingham (UK), based on the fostering of spiritual and moral dispositions. It prompts us to rethink ways of 'learning about' religions with the intention of meaningfully 'learning from' them. In a world where the local is global and global is local, it offers scope to explore the contribution of different faiths to this collective enterprise. By asking critical questions about educational purpose and process, the Birmingham experience will be pertinent to debates about the future orientation of RE just at the point when this school subject stands at the crossroads in various countries. Moreover, it goes some way, I feel, to help both those who teach and those who are taught to live well and deeply.

The perception that more explicit attention be given to the formal teaching of virtue is undergoing a revival (e.g. 'Schools fail to teach morals', The Sunday Times, London, June 2013). School is, of course, only part of the education of the self. Our nine months in the womb after conception, formative experiences in the home and our early social exposure play a critical role. If virtues are innate within us, their flourishing involves the less tangible aspects of learning through everyday human interaction, beyond academic study. Practical initiatives to support individuals and families, school and neighbourhood communities as well as influential guiding institutions are therefore part and parcel of the story.

The word *Sikh* means learner and the word we use for faith is *dharam*. It is the living of life, ever-conscious of its overarching and more infinite context, framed by questions of where we have come from, where we are going and what we are here to do. Virtues, values, dispositions and ethics lie implicitly at the heart of education; religious education brings their importance into focus and religious life demands their practice, to shun shallowness and hypocrisy, cultivate an abundance of love, unflinching trust, selfless sacrifice and an incessant spirit of optimism. As the Sikh 'anthem', interpreted in English below, reminds me, human life is too precious and too short to ignore religion's role in propelling the human impulse to live a virtuous and worthy life.

> Empower me, God, to never shy away
> From doing what is good and right
>
> May I, thus, become fearless in facing life's battles,
> Inside and around me, with resolute belief in victory
>
> May my mind then learn;
> Yearning only to praise Your infinite goodness
>
> And so, may I relentlessly continue
> To do all that is good and right,
> Until my very last breath.

English interpretation of 'Deh Shiva' composed by the tenth Sikh Guru

ACKNOWLEDGEMENTS

Behind the creation of this book lie two particular sources of inspiration.

First we wish to acknowledge the faithful work of those contributors who have met annually since 2004 with the purpose of bringing philosophical and theological insights to bear on the practice of religious education. It has been a great encouragement to us that they have returned every year and now contributed to this, our second full length book. In a book with so many individual contributors it can be difficult to achieve coherence. To the extent that this is not the case here we are indebted to this group. We would like to thank Gladstone's Library, Hawarden (formerly St Deiniol's), Cheshire, UK, who looked after us on these occasions and supported our endeavour. One of our colloquia was funded by the University of Birmingham, UK, and we thank both institutions for their support and the tolerance of colleagues.

Second we acknowledge the contribution of the City of Birmingham, UK, which recently took the bold step of creating a new trend in religious education. In 2005, it convened an Agreed Syllabus Conference under the able leadership of Mr Guy Hordern, MBE which devised a new syllabus that focused on cultivating pupils with 24 dispositions to which the many different religious traditions present in the City could contribute. We in effect selected eight of their dispositions and wish to express our thanks to the City and Mr Hordern for the earlier work done. We hope that others will have the insight to follow in their footsteps and to this end offer this book as a way of deepening understanding and modelling a way to live that can inspire our pupils to live well.

We were also much encouraged by the Sikh community in Birmingham and GNNSJ Gurdwara, ably led by Bhai Sahib Bhai Mohinder Singh, which in founding their Sikh free schools made the dispositions central to their educational work. It was the work done by members of those schools which helped to provide some suggestions using Sikh material. To that end I would particularly like to thank Mr. Ranjit Dhanda, the principal of the schools in question.

We are also grateful to Elizabeth Ashton for her review of, and insightful comments on, the exemplars. Elizabeth was, for over 19 years, a classroom-based primary teacher and latterly appointed to the University of Durham, UK, in the School of Education as Lecturer in Religious and Moral Education.

Marius Felderhof
Penny Thompson

Introduction

Marius Felderhof

In Plato's dialogue, *Euthydemus,* two teachers (Euthydemus and Dionysodorus) claim to have given up on instructing the young in the most important and traditional skills in ancient Athens.

Euthydemus states:

'We no longer bother with those matters, Socrates. We treat them as peripheral.'

I [Socrates] was astonished. 'If you treat such important matters as peripheral,' I said, 'then what on earth can your main occupation be? It must be pretty impressive. Tell me please.' 'Virtue, Socrates', he said. 'We think that we are the finest and quickest teachers of virtue alive.' (Plato 1987, 273D, p. 318)

Socrates reacts pretty sceptically to their educational ambition. Two questions need to be answered first. Is virtue something that can be learnt? And second, are you the best teachers to teach it?

We too are in a time of educational change and are proposing that education should have the teaching of virtue and the development of character at its core. Perhaps we too deserve a dose of Socratic scepticism. But Plato through the Socratic voice was not indifferent to teaching virtue but raised philosophical questions about what this meant and how it was to be done. It demanded a close scrutiny of what the key human virtues are, together with an examination of the appropriate pedagogy and a consideration of whom the right persons are to deliver such objectives. We are not so immodest as Euthydemus as to claim that 'we are finest and quickest teachers of virtue alive' but we agree with Plato that these matters are at the core of education and therefore seek to invite our readers to consider the kind of issues this agenda generates for teachers generally, but for Religious Education teachers in particular. In effect we wish the conversation which began some 2,500 years ago to continue.

To contribute in a modest way to Plato's agenda, this book intended primarily for people with an interest in Religious Education has been divided into four different elements: (a) chapters that relate to the theory of RE, (b) chapters that reflect on and characterize some of the important virtues and dispositions in the context of religious life, (c) sections that set out how this characterization might inform and become part of RE lessons, and finally (d) some indication in the appendix of the reception of such an approach to RE. These different elements in the book are, of course, interrelated and interdependent and are the outcome of work done over a period of years by practitioners, educationalists, theologians and philosophers in a series of colloquia. We believe that this range of expertise is necessary at a minimum to get right such a complex activity as Religious Education. Ideally, practice should direct theoretical enquiry and theory should inform practice. This approach to RE with the communication of dispositions and virtues at its core is not untried. Experience of its positive reception is offered as encouragement to experiment and to take it further.

Some of the earlier work of the colloquia, which led to this particular volume, was published in a book *Inspiring Faith in Schools* and provides further discussion of related issues not addressed here. But how might this present book be used? With most books one would normally begin reading at the beginning and work one's way through to the end. However, in this book many of the chapters can stand on their own two feet – even as we seek to build an overarching picture of an approach to RE that meets the ambitions of different stakeholders: pupils, teachers, parents, politicians and faith leaders. Any teachers reading this book could as usefully look at an idea for an RE lesson and then read some of the thinking that inspired it. Thus, one might plan the lesson on courage on the basis of the proposed ideas and then enrich your thinking and planning with the philosophical reflections which courage and the teaching of courage generated. Lastly, one might turn to the theories on RE and virtues which underpin the whole approach of teaching virtues, such as courage, to begin with. Examples of how teachers in Birmingham, UK have tried to deliver RE with a focus on dispositions or virtues may be found on their website www.faithmakesadifference.co.uk/landing#node-99 where a whole primary and secondary school lesson has been filmed from start to finish. One was filmed in Marsh Hill Primary School and the other in Frankley Community High School. These were followed by filmed reviews and observations from teachers, Initial Teacher Trainers and the City's Faith Leaders.

Some justification for teaching virtues is called for. Currently most RE advice in Britain today encourages one to teach 'about religions and secular philosophies' in the hope that young people will reflect on them, and in doing so, acquire a set of attitudes such as open-mindedness, tolerance and respect for others. Whether such a set of attitudes is forthcoming in teaching *about* religion is an open question. It may have less to do with the content of what is taught than with how it is taught and with the dispositions and intentions of the teacher. In this book we believe that whatever young people are to gain personally *from* their RE in school (e.g. the inspiration to virtue) should be in the forefront of teachers' thinking and planning. Once they have this goal in mind they should then draw on the treasury of religious faith to realize their goal. This treasury of faith is, of course, much more extensive than that provided by the history and traditions of Christianity. The contributions of the other 'principal' religions in Britain and in the wider world are substantive and not to be neglected, most especially with young people who have their family roots in those traditions.

Some teachers may complain, 'Is this focus on virtues and human dispositions not just moral education?' One answer is that RE must be *at least* a form of moral education. No doubt religious life concerns more than moral matters. For example, it cultivates the aesthetic interests that human beings have with religious music and art. But were any religious practice and belief to be amoral or immoral that would be a serious criticism and grounds for reforming or abandoning it. With moral interests and goals in mind one has a way of getting to the very heart of religious life. These interests and goals are something that all religions share. One will begin to appreciate the different religious traditions when one studies the moral insights that each brings to the religious market place, their different emphases, their different priorities, and their strategies for encouraging and supporting people in their efforts to achieve the ideals that claim their loyalty. Any disagreements between the religious traditions on what ought to be done, or on what kind of persons we should seek to be, are then serious disagreements that require some resolution. That would be truly interesting and informative for life, and would give young people real pause for thought!

There is something peculiar about a *religious* education that makes 'religions' its focus of study. It appears to suggest that the state of being religious is in essence to be interested in the phenomena of religions, that is, in what people think, believe and do in different places and in different times. But this does not follow and is clearly not the case. One only has to look at what some of the prophets in the Hebrew Scriptures had to say. Their complaint on the whole was not that people were not interested enough in religion. In fact, the people engaged in a whole host of religious practices, celebrations, sacrifices, but all without moral seriousness. Thus the prophet Amos attributes the following words to God (chapter 5, verses 21–24)[1]:

I hate, I despise your feast days, I will not smell in your solemn assemblies. Though you offer me burnt offerings and your meat offerings, I will not accept them: neither will I regard the peace offerings of your fat beasts. Take thou away from me the noise of thy songs: for I will not hear the melody of thy viols. But let judgment run down as waters, and righteousness as a mighty stream.

Or listen to the words of the prophet Micah (chapter 6, verses 6–8)

> Wherewith shall I come before the Lord, and bow myself before the
> high God? Shall I come before him with burnt offerings, with calves of a
> year old? Will the Lord be pleased with thousands of rams, or with ten
> thousands rivers of oil? Shall I give my firstborn for my transgressions,
> the fruit of my body for the sin of my soul? He hath shewed thee, O man,
> what is good; and what does the Lord require of thee, but to do justly,
> and to love mercy, and to walk humbly with thy God?

Or finally the words of the prophet Hosea (chapter 6, verses 4–6):

> O Ephraim, what shall I do unto thee? O Judah, what shall I do unto
> thee? For your goodness is as the morning cloud, and as the early dew
> goeth away. Therefore have I hewed them by the prophets; I have slain
> them by the words of my mouth: and thy judgements are as the light that
> goeth forth. For I desired mercy and not sacrifice; and the knowledge of
> God more than burnt offerings.

The appeal is not for costly ritual, for example, the extreme of sacrificing
one's own children, but for justice, mercy and humility. They set aside
externals which are empty without an intimacy with the Divine or with
whatever is sacred. Those who think about life with a religious intent can
never be overly fascinated with rituals and the externals of religions; such a
fascination attributes to these practices and beliefs a significance they cannot
bear *in their own right*.

If this is the burden of the message of Judaism, any acquaintance with
the parable of the Good Samaritan will tell one that the same message is
repeated in the Christian scriptures (and I have no reason to believe that other
religious traditions take a different view): the parable effectively states that
courage, compassion, mercy and love, for someone traditionally despised,
comes before 'religious' commitments.

St Augustine defined the essence of sin as a condition of being curved in
upon the self. To suggest that the religious intent is the condition of being
enthralled by religion (and its practices) is to attribute to religions precisely
the narcissistic condition St Augustine encourages us to resist. In contrast, the
healthy religious interest is in being focused on whatever is other, that is, on
one's God-relationship with its moral and spiritual demands. The difference
is precisely this: *religion* is what human beings do, believe and think, all of
which may or may not be interesting, profound or trite, rational or irrational.
Religious *faith*, on the other hand, as explained in the chapter by Jeff Astley,
is of a different order; in coming to recognize something as Good or Holy,
one is simultaneously under an authoritative claim that demands trust and
obedience in response, which is in essence what religious *faith* is Religious
education in these terms is to help people of all ages to discover what is

authoritative and good and thus to cultivate the ears to hear and the eyes to see what is demanded from them in life, together with attention to the insight, support and encouragement that religious practice offers.

It is possible that we are mistaken in thinking that the emphasis in the term 'religious education' is on the word 'religious', perhaps it should be on the word *education*. The problem is that the reference to 'education' among the professional educators can be used as a distancing device, insulating the young from serious engagement with religious life and its claims, including moral claims, which actually demand a response from the young. More positively, the change from religious *instruction* in the British '44 Education Act to religious *education* in the '88 Education Reform Act also has the effect of marking a change in the style of teaching on the part of teachers from a form catechesis to a form that is more open.

Now what education is or should be at the different stages of human development needs to be carefully examined. What is clear is that at no stage can it ever be value free. It is more a question of *which* values are to be transmitted rather than some vacuous neutrality. In dealing with young people there is no room for moral cynicism, as if anything goes, or to suppose that the good is only a matter of what we happen to decide it is. If we were to take such a path we would offer the young no defence against such vicious ideologies as Nazism or against an Apartheid political agenda. Adults have a responsibility to give the young a lead on what they believe really matters and why it matters, and in the context of RE showing what it is that is valued in religious life. Giving the young a lead on this is not the same as dictating to them and even less of bullying them; they can make no moral decisions on that basis, nor will they learn what it is to take a moral decision. The same is true of religious life. One cannot *make* a person religious without betraying what it means to be religious. At best, in dialogue with the young one can show what is inspiring and what, if anything, is repellent about religious life.

And that there is something offensive about religious life is self-evident from the religious traditions themselves. To take some Christian examples: why should one assume that 'taking up one's cross' and following Jesus is either an easy or an attractive option? According to the gospel (Matthew, chapter 19, verses 16–22), Jesus invited the rich young ruler to sell all that he has and to follow him, and he just could not bring himself to do so. His wealth was simply too important to him to do that. Many contemporaries today would not blame him in the least and would rationally make the same response. There are always good reasons for not taking religious commands or invitations seriously; otherwise there would be no temptations, no religious doubts, no dark nights of the soul, no backsliding, no difficult decisions and no apostasy. What these thoughts show is that it is necessary to debate and discuss what religious education means, or should be, today in Britain or elsewhere, hence Part 1 of this book sets the stage for getting on with the job.

The first chapter seeks to emphasize the importance of a future orientation in RE and how this might affect one's pedagogical strategies. Brenda Watson sets out the basic commitments that any RE must exhibit in a plural and secular society. Philip Barnes examines the state of RE and its relationship to moral education in Britain, emphasizing the importance of locating the latter within RE. David Carr provides background information on virtue ethics, exploring its character and roots in western culture.

There is a complaint that may be generated by Part 2 of this book with its discussion of key dispositions and virtues. Why these particular virtues and not others? To which there is a simple response: there are indeed others, those virtues which have been selected are mere illustrations of what any serious application to religious education may require and to assist teachers on the way. However, the choice of virtues was not entirely arbitrary and they do have a significant historical pedigree in the West. We began with honesty because we regard it as foundational for any sustainable spiritual and moral development. Self-deception and dishonest teaching will ultimately undermine any religious education. As for the remainder, if an essential failure is to be self-enclosed then we must struggle to be attentive to others, to their needs and interests. And look to the creation of just relationships between people. This struggle will inevitably require courage and an expectant spirit. Temperance and wisdom bring our cognitive capacities and self-awareness to bear on our life contributing a balance and moderating influence. Finally, a faithfulness and constancy is necessary if one is to make any progress on the path of life. One should not be deflected too readily by criticism and opposition but remain true to the ideal which beckons. One might also note that the traditional cardinal virtues (wisdom, justice, courage and temperance) reflected the different faculties or aspects of a person so that together they manifest the *whole* person and contribute the key dimensions of a spiritual and moral integrity.

A further complaint might be: Are the selection of virtues and the authors not influenced too much by the Western tradition? It would indeed have been helpful to have had more suggestions and reflections from other traditions. The book would then have become a good deal thicker! But experience has found that agreement on the various dispositions and virtues is not all that difficult to achieve with people of a different religious tradition. It is hard to find a religious tradition that does not believe in courage, justice, wisdom, and so on; indeed, secular humanists also share them. It is the task of unpacking these dispositions and virtues that provides the challenge. Other religious traditions may have wished to add resources or may have had different views as to which virtues should have priority. However, the essence of religious education seems to lie in showing what the *religious* contribution might be to the spiritual, moral, social and cultural development of pupils and society. Once we are clear on its spiritual and moral purpose then we can turn to the second stage of *which* religious traditions one selects for this purpose in one's lessons. This choice will be largely influenced by the children in the classroom and the makeup of the community which the school serves. It will inevitably vary from country to country, from place to place and from school to school. In Britain the law requires RE to be in the *main* Christian and to take account of the other principal religions in Great Britain without specifying which, or how many, and without explaining what it means to take account of them. These are decisions which according to British law are for each Local Agreed Syllabus Conference, or in the case of faith schools, for the board of education of the local diocese or for the relevant authority of Sikh, Muslim or Jewish schools *et al* to make. We can only draw attention to what in our judgement good RE might look like in *any* school, anywhere, and set out some of the principles which inform it.

The appendix of this book shows where this approach to RE has been tried, and with what success. Whatever is true and good are not normally decided by taking a vote or by testing its popularity. However, the strength of the commitment to this approach within RE in Birmingham, which is one of Britain's largest religiously plural Cities, may be an indication that this moral understanding of RE addresses a perceived need. The Birmingham 2007 Syllabus has been strongly supported by the City's Faith Leaders, by its politicians, by teachers and head teachers in its schools. It has been incorporated in the RE of Church of England schools and has been put at the heart of the Sikh free schools. But more importantly it has led to a real engagement by pupils with the issues that all religious traditions seek to address, namely, with the endeavour of learning to live well and deeply.

Note

1 Quotations are from the King James authorized translation of 1611.

References

Bible, The Authorised King James Version.
Plato (1987), *Early Socratic Dialogues* (with various translations and introductions) Penguin: Harmondsworth.

PART ONE

Orientations

CHAPTER ONE

The prospective nature of Religious Education

Marius Felderhof

CHAPTER OUTLINE

This chapter seeks to show that the widespread accepted aims and aspirations for religious education can be both misleading and subversive of religious life. It shows how the character and very nature of the intellectual enquiry can be destructive of religious sensibilities. There is a difference between *talking about* and *doing*. Religions above all command and require action. And actions are prospective with a vision of the future; also, actions presuppose intentions and consequences, and hence an ethic. It is further argued that a value-based syllabus for RE must be democratic, child and society centred, and strongly focused on human flourishing in moral and spiritual terms. Treating pupils as agents or as persons makes a number of pedagogical demands with cognitive, affective and conative dimensions. In RE such person-centred education means cultivating dispositions. Freedom and the future will feature large in its pedagogy.

Introduction: The aims of RE (Religious Education)

The history of Religious Education in England and Wales has shown some remarkable transformations in the subject, not all of them welcome. These transformations reflect the changing aims and aspirations for the subject in British society. It is perhaps worth stopping to think about whose aims and aspirations they are because people do not always concur. Are they the aims of the professional educationalists or 'RE community'? academics? parents? pupils? politicians? faith communities? the wider society? These stakeholders, I believe, have their own distinct expectations and interests. The professionals have a tendency to complain that the others do not understand their aims and objectives for the subject and are inclined to ascribe this supposed lack of understanding to failures in communication rather than to a climate of disagreement (See the Religious Education Council review of RE 2013). But the differences between the professionals and the other stakeholders are real and telling.

Given the widespread acceptance in Britain of the Non-Statutory National Framework for RE (2004) it must seem obvious to many professional RE teachers and theorists in Britain today that all the major religious traditions should be taught 'in depth', fairly and equally. Perhaps for the sake of inclusivity the advice (p. 12) is that one should also include a number of 'minor' religions. Better still. We should also introduce a serious study of secular philosophies. The aim appears to be to present them impartially as so many alternative 'worldviews' that people around the world have embraced and presumably might still reasonably embrace. Young people are then sent away with the guidance to think, evaluate the evidence and to make up their own mind as to which 'worldview' reflects their position. Alternatively, the young might formulate their own world view in the light of such study for their own use. Putting aside the issues of whether teachers have the requisite curriculum time, resources or even the knowledge to pursue such a policy of teaching so many 'religions and beliefs', there are other deeper concerns that parents and faith leaders might have about the professional educators' ambitions for the subject. These concerns are not always well articulated but they are rooted in a deep unease, which believes that those particular aims and objectives of RE are subversive of religious life and somehow miss its essence.

Subverting religiousness

The potential for subversion may be a matter of indifference to some professional religious educators since some have taken the view that it is not their business to either encourage or support religious faith, their duty is solely to teach about it. In their eyes the value that RE has is not to be found in religious faith itself but in the impact the subject of RE has on children. There is a subtle but important shift of emphases here from the value of religious faith to the value of the school subject. The latter is deemed by some to be independent of the merit of religious faith. Note how some RE theorists write about 'teaching Religious Education' rather than teaching or cultivating religious sensibilities. In the past, and possibly still present among parents and politicians, there is a belief that the merit of religious faith and the presence of the subject on the curriculum were connected. Religious faith is itself what is of value and this provides the reason that it is a subject on the school curriculum. That the subject of RE can separate itself from the value of religious life and may even have within it the potential to subvert religious faith has possibly not fully dawned on the non-professional stakeholder.

It is worth considering how the subject can and does subvert religious faith, that is, how teaching about the various religions 'in depth' could somehow become subversive of religious life or miss the essence of religious life. Initially this may just be a hunch based on the many pupils and adults who, having engaged in Religious Studies, have been led to abandon their faith or have failed to live more deeply, morally and spiritually speaking. There is then no necessary connection between religious studies and moral and spiritual development. To examine the issue further with any clarity requires an understanding of the nature of religious life and within it, the role of reflection. In the first instance this is to engage in the activity known as 'theology', something that is open to people of all ages and ability, since it attempts to show reflectively what one's religious faith means to one. This at least appears to be the task set by St Anselm when he defined theology as 'faith seeking understanding'. In effect, it suggests a method where one begins with the life of faith, critically examining it in order to show its sense (or potentially its contradictions or nonsense) and what it demands from us. The outcome of such an agenda should unashamedly be a deepening of life as an activity. A related attempt is found in the philosophy of religion developed by D. Z. Phillips under the influence of Wittgenstein where the reflection is guided closely by what religious people actually say and do. He refrains from measuring it against some other preconceived framework and expectations.

Phenomenology, as it was first developed by Husserl and later applied by Ninian Smart to RE in Britain, tried to show what a religion was without too many preconceptions. In its approach, it tried to set out how the religion appears to us, letting the phenomenon speak for itself without evaluating it against one's already existing understanding of the world. The aim is to describe religions as accurately as possible. As a movement this methodology proved to be enormously influential and popular within British RE. The phenomenological exercise is a very disciplined activity which never quite succeeds in its endeavour. There is a failure in the methodology which has something to do with the fact that when we are dealing with appearances, they are appearances to us. This engagement of the enquirer with the object of his or her interest is something so-called 'objective' studies systematically seek to leave out of the picture. Yet the relationship with the self will always intrude on the determination to let the phenomena speak for itself. In some respects this reminder (of the inescapable 'to us') is a blessing in disguise since a religious faith is itself precisely about the person's actions and reactions in the medium of life. The voice of engagement that speaks from faith, and to faith, as a consequence, cannot be heard by the secular person without calling upon a great deal more self-awareness and without a cultural critique of the society in which we live and in which we have a share. Secular culture has a way of dulling religious sensibilities precisely because it fails to think reflexively on what we are doing and becoming as individuals and as a society. One feature of these dulled sensibilities is a failure to recognize that the religious voice speaks to us inescapably at some point in the imperative mood rather than in the indicative mood of description. Hence, for example, the listeners said of Jesus that he spoke as one having authority. The question is, 'what does it mean to be confronted by authority?', especially an authority that makes claims or demands on the self.

Parents sometimes express their unease about a perceived subversion of faith in RE by saying, 'I am an "X" so why are you teaching my child about religion "Y." My child does not know enough about "X"'. It is all too easy to dismiss this as an expression of prejudice or intolerance as religious educators sometimes do. Parents perceive that the teaching about another religious tradition may be a distraction from the more important task in hand, namely of showing young people what they should live for and what they should live by, the kind of knowledge they have gained from their own religious tradition in the past. Educators have responded to this implied criticism: 'Our teaching is precisely aimed at communicating a set of attitudes and values. The teaching about religions other than their own is to encourage pupils to become more open minded, tolerant and to develop a respect for others.' But if this is the response then other considerations offer themselves. Parents might still legitimately wonder why so much time is spent on differing religions and secular philosophies. Could those particular goals of open-mindedness, tolerance and respect for others not have been achieved more easily and more readily by teaching young people from within their religious tradition a version of the golden rule of treating others as they would be done by? Or if speaking to children from a largely Christian tradition, would it not be enough to encourage them to love their neighbour as themselves, with the caveat that 'loving' is much more demanding than 'tolerating' or 'respecting'? It seems strange to suggest that open-mindedness, tolerance and respect was only available to human beings once they began to gather information about a number of faiths other than their own.

S. Kierkegaard, the nineteenth-century Danish philosopher, expressed somewhat differently the awareness that studying a religion at depth, even sympathetically, may be subversive of its religious sense. For example, he stated that to defend Christianity is already to have betrayed it. In effect one's relationship to the object of faith has changed the moment one begins to talk *about* it rather than to see it as a challenge to living it. He lampooned the behaviour of theologians who study the writings of the apostles 'objectively' and who do what religious educationalists not infrequently invite pupils to do in learning about religions. Thus Kierkegaard writes these words through the mouthpiece of a pseudonymous H.H:

> The divine authority of [an apostle] should in fact be the sure protection which safeguards the teaching, and preserves it at the majestic distance of the divine from impertinent curiosity, instead of which the doctrine has to be sniffed at – in order that the people may discover whether it was a revelation or not; and probably in the meanwhile God and the Apostle have to wait at the gate, or in the porter's lodge, till the learned upstairs have settled the matter. The man who is called ought, according to divine ordinance, to use his divine authority in order to be rid of all the impertinent people who will not obey, but want to reason; and instead of that men have, at a single go, transformed the Apostle into an examinee who appears at the market with a new teaching. [Of the difference between a genius and an apostle, p. 147f.]

The key words here are authority and impertinence. People become 'impertinent' because of the relationship to the object of faith, by the nature of the enquiry and the criteria by which one judges the matter. If one confronts an authority (whether the authority is God, apostle, parliament or police, etc.) the issue is obedience or disobedience. People have a great capacity for disobedience. They will find an excuse not to obey by shifting the grounds to the point of reflection, for example, thinking about the felicity or infelicity of the wording of the command, or with some such evaluation. As Kierkegaard expressed it, 'To honour one's father because he is intelligent is impiety' (p. 153). No doubt children will assess their parents. Their parents will have their particular strengths and weaknesses, but honouring does not follow from such assessments. To do this one needs no reasons other than to recognize that the person is one's parent; in fact, giving reasons subverts the very foundations of honouring in much the same way that to give reasons for loving another person subverts the relationship of love. If someone were to ask, 'why do you love your wife?' the only appropriate response is simply to say that you do. To give reasons, such as, she is rich, intelligent, humorous or beautiful, is to show that you do not love her or have been misled into thinking these reasons would, or should, matter to loving.

The issue at stake here is that it is possible to subvert the religiousness in the subject of RE simply by the character of the enquiry. To treat one's religion as one world view among others is already to show it is no longer what commands and binds (as the derivation of the word 'religion' suggests). Instead, one has put oneself in the position of authority as someone who will evaluate and judge whether the religion measures up to one's own standards. Whatever is true and good commands because it is true and good, not because one has decided for oneself what one will consider to be true or what one will take to be good. In short, to come to see that something is true and good is to acknowledge that it has a deep claim on oneself.

It is no coincidence that Kierkegaard's two minor treatises were prefaced by his pseudonym, H.H., as being only 'of essential interest to theologians' (ibid., p. 73). He wished them to reconsider the way in which they did their 'theologising' in the nineteenth century. In the first treatise, Kierkegaard begins by describing a child who was brought up in the Christian religion not because he was taught various things about Jesus and angels but because he is brought into a relationship to a picture of the crucified Christ. It was a picture that came to have an increasing grip on him in his life. He lived by it. He did not talk about it. Kierkegaard discusses the difference.

> Every man understands very well that to act is something far greater than to talk about it; if, therefore, he is resolved that he will do it, he does not talk about it. What a man talks about in connection with a proposed action is precisely that wherein he is not sure of himself. When a person prevails upon himself with ease to give ten dollars to the poor, so that it seems to him a natural thing, and he finds (here we have it!) that it is nothing to talk about – he never talks about it. But perhaps you may hear him talk about his intention of giving a thousand dollars to the poor – alas! The poor will have to be content with ten. (ibid., p. 83)

The theologian is essentially the man who thinks and talks about giving a thousand dollars. In his presence, the poor starve. For Kierkegaard, theologians are those who only chatter about life. If anything, the nineteenth-century theologian is created not by virtue of his faith or engagement with life but from a process of objectifying religions, a process that is an expression of his alienation and doubt. One may conclude that as a result, such theologians no longer really understand the religious life that begins and ends in action. This seems to be the message of his two short treatises.

It is not difficult to translate the nineteenth-century theologians into a twenty-first-century setting. The danger is that RE teachers, clergy, theologians and philosophers of religion just talk about religion without ever understanding that it commands and requires actions. To address this risk of mere talk, one might put the task of living and doing to the fore. A focus on the cultivation of dispositions, a tendency to act in particular ways, is one such effort. This option has been explored in the 2007 Birmingham [UK] Agreed Syllabus (see website address above in the introduction p. 2). It sets out to recapture religious sensibilities by seeing the task of living well to be the essence and major point of religious life. In doing so it also reconnects with the real concerns of other stakeholders in education.

Other stakeholders in education

The potential for subverting what other stakeholders value and what they may believe to be important with respect to RE requires one to reflect briefly about what their aims and hopes for the subject might be. It is clear that politicians, parents and faith communities often have very different expectations from RE in contrast to the RE professionals who seek to talk about a whole range of religions and beliefs. Politicians, for example, analyse the present state of society and diagnose what must be done to secure a better future for their society. Their quest for power is the power to direct society to this future and (some might think cynically) in the process enhance their own significance and status. Unsurprisingly, politicians look for cohesion in society and a disciplined focus on all the potential outcomes of schooling that are helpful to a flourishing society. Educating young people means enabling them to stay healthy, to be safe, and to contribute economically and in other ways to a future society.

Parents seek the best for their individual children by ensuring they develop according to a parental vision of what it means to be a good person, or of what constitutes a good life. They too make judgements about what skills their offspring will need for their own 'good' or to prepare them for a 'good' future in society. Parents will exercise their influence in diverse ways from the moment their offspring are born. They show what life can be through their example, their ideals, through their conversations with their children, through the bonds they form and through the organization of their family life. They may even try to manipulate the future of their children by pressurizing schools to deliver what they believe will offer their offspring the best future.

Faith communities also seek to exercise power and influence in the sphere of education – a most important factor being their spiritual and moral vision of what constitutes a good life and a good community. If this is widely shared, it is inherently persuasive, but faith communities have also devised their own programmes and institutions to develop young and old more actively according to that vision. Thus, subordinate to the overarching commitment to their vision of the good, faith communities have made practical attempts over the centuries to realize that vision, for example, through its worshipping activity, through their support for family life,[1] through political influence, through their contributions to the *agora*, that is, the public square where people discuss and interact, or through the maintenance and governance of various institutions, including their own schools, colleges and universities.

The impact of the past and future

A feature that we should observe at this point is that whether we are speaking of pupils, politicians, parents and faith communities, we find that they are essentially future orientated in their engagement with educational institutions. Parents and pupils will think about what the children will become or what they will do. Politicians will think about what will become of society and their role in it. Faith communities likewise will think about future transformations, that is, about matters such as 'sanctification' and the *eschaton* (the final end), both for individuals and for the whole human species, if not for the whole of creation, through their overarching narratives.

Teachers, in contrast, are much more likely to be absorbed by processes of transmission, by 'core' or 'essential knowledge' to be mastered and 'skills' that, culturally speaking, have already been acquired and that must be learnt anew by each generation. They tend to be absorbed by subject content that has already been ordered, and by familiar skills that must be practised. In this respect teachers may be more readily preoccupied by the present and past rather than the future. Teachers do, of course, have aims and objectives but on a day-to-day basis these aims are less often couched in terms of what pupils or society will become or ought to become, or what a subject discipline might become through their teaching or how their school as an educational community might change through what they do. Their pedagogical aims and objectives are more mundane; their main concerns are things which in themselves are already known and about which the pupils are to be examined to test whether they have mastered them.

In brief, the preoccupations and interests in schooling of teachers and educationalists, on the one hand, and those of other stakeholders, on the other hand, are in general terms tensed differently – the past and present versus the future. Educationalists, without a conscious effort, are inclined to see their subject matter predominantly retrospectively while the concerns of other stakeholders are predominantly prospective in nature. Any RE that represents the interest of parents, politicians and faith communities will need to recover its orientation to the future. We should conclude this section with three simple points.

Shared responsibilities

First, it should be noted that the vicissitudes of education generally, and of Religious Education in particular, are not the sole responsibility of the professional educator. It is shared, and necessarily democratic, if everyone is to have a legitimate stake. The educational enterprise may well reflect a shifting power balance of the different parties, and the relative influence of their visions or expectations from schooling. These expectations may be changing, for example, as reflected in the secularization of society or in the increasingly utilitarian approach to education or in the discourse about the role of schools in meeting society's need to be economically competitive. In times of change it is all the more important to confront the expectations.

Professional educators, above all, will need to take account of the existing and changing expectations. On the presumption that other stakeholders will always have a deep interest in schooling, it would be a fundamental mistake for professional educators to operate with the view that they know best and that it is solely up to them to determine the character of schooling. An approach without public consultation would be unwise not least because they will then carry sole responsibility for possibly failing to meet the implicit agenda and expectations of the others, expectations the professionals may not share. In a time when RE professionals busily tell politicians about the success and the high regard in which British RE is held internationally, the census figures reveal an increasing number in the population who avow no religious affiliation whatsoever. Politicians, parents and faith communities may regard the increase as symptoms of failure in RE. There are clearly differences in expectations concerning the benefits to be derived from RE. But before any accusations of failure in RE are to be accepted, there must be agreed criteria on which the judgements are based.

It has been to the great benefit of Religious Education that the British 1944 Education Act institutionalized the interplay of the different interest groups – (though pupils and parents are only indirectly represented) – and required these different interest groups to reach a unanimous agreement on an appropriate syllabus for the subject, with its defined aims. The usual impact of formalizing the discussion is an agreement in expectations. The negotiations normally lead to consensus and to moderation, avoiding extremism and idiosyncrasies. Further, where the input is genuinely from different sources and interests, and not monopolized by any one group at the expense of others, it is more likely to lead to a more nuanced and comprehensive syllabus. This joint ownership by the RE profession, faith communities and the political leaders of the wider community can offer individual teachers in the classroom grounds for confidence and an authority to teach, which they otherwise would not have in what is normally a contested field.

Subject centred or child and society centred?

Second, teachers may be tempted to be predominantly focused on already known subject content, on known pedagogical processes, on personal learning styles, or on how learning might be assessed against known criteria, or indeed how they themselves are assessed as individuals or as schools. Pupils, parents, politicians and faith communities are more likely to be focused on what the child or society will become as a result of the educational process. To them the secularization of society will be considered a pertinent issue, possibly revealing a process in which critical values are being lost or acquired. In some respects parents, politicians and faith communities are in an important sense, more deeply child-centred and society-centred because they are focused on what they are becoming. They are implicitly and singularly concerned with the well-being of children, and on what it means to flourish as a human being and as a community, and then on what we, personally and collectively, have to do to realize those goals.

Moral and spiritual

Third, a prospective education, as distinct from a retrospective education, is more likely to be deeply moral in being focused on the practical activity of living, that is, on what we have to do to conform to our personal and collective good. With moral and spiritual goals as ultimate ends clearly to the fore, the educational enterprise will be absorbed by matters that are valued for their own sakes and less likely to be distracted by the cultivation of utilitarian skills as an exclusive concern of education. Skills, for example, 'thinking skills', in themselves may be amoral. It is how, with what intentions and with what consequences one uses these skills that bring them into the moral sphere. Similarly, schooling as the transmission of known information is not yet to be engaged in a moral or spiritual exercise. Descriptions of what was and is purported to be the case, scientifically or historically, only enter the realm of the moral and spiritual when persons seek, or fail to seek, to be accurate, truthful and honest with such descriptions. It is the relationships that are formed, the goals that are adopted, the actions taken and the character of persons and society created that together propel us into the moral and spiritual sphere.

It should also be noted that all moral and spiritual education is genuinely inclusive since everyone has a stake in his or her own personal and collective good. In contrast, for the purposes of their spiritual and moral formation not everyone needs to have an advanced mastery of music, foreign languages, or, dare one say, mathematics and science, as desirable as all these things may be in their own right. There is in this sense no core curriculum without which one cannot achieve one's moral and spiritual good. If education is about the 'spiritual, moral, social and cultural development of pupils ... and of society' (the British 1996, Education Act), then a religious education that is explicitly guided by moral and spiritual ends will be at the heart of the educational enterprise. A religious education that loses sight of these ends will risk becoming a minority interest.

Prospective education, agency and the whole person

If one is to incorporate the future into one's educational practice, one must begin by seeing the pupils primarily as free agents with an inherent capacity to act to realize that future. There must be a presumption that there is a fundamental difference between a future and fate. The future is intrinsically open and provides the air for responsible living. It presupposes possibilities and promise, whereas fate suggests a predetermined end about which one can do little.

The decision to treat pupils as agents with a future can be radically countercultural in the current climate. Apart from the pressures of a superstitious popular culture that consults astrological charts to see what is in store for us, there are some forms of scientific culture that appear to presuppose a mechanistic world-picture in which all events are causally determined. This world-picture, reflected in behaviourist psychology and associated educational thinking, supposes it is a matter of so much input in order to achieve a predicted output. Such a world-picture gives one no room to breathe as an agent. Perhaps there is a limited place and use for such thinking but it cannot be a basis for religious education that thinks in terms of responsibility. Cultivating agency requires a different framework of thought and different pedagogical practices.

A most debilitating feature of a popular 'phenomenological' approach to RE in schools is its 'spectatorialism'; another word might be, its 'voyeurism'. It fits in with a dominant and emergent feature of Western intellectual life that fails to be reflexive by ignoring the conscious self that constructs the world (Barrett 1987). This in turn generates a pedagogy which consists fundamentally in looking at religion from a distance; it is descriptive, and often backward looking. This is not, of course, what naturally interests young people. Young people are preparing for life, so they are essentially forward looking, practising the roles they will have, (e.g. through their play), and equipping themselves with the skills they will need in adult life. With a prospective agenda they need to engage their imagination[2] as much as their memory. What religious educational pedagogy needs is an alternative approach that treats children and young people as 'do-ers' who are self-aware or as actors and agents in the world.[3] Once the fundamental shift has been made in which the development of young people and society is the main purpose of religious education, and turns religious traditions into a means to that end, one can begin to think about a different style of teaching.

Educating children and young people as persons who have names,[4] doers, engaged with the business of living and living well, demands certain basic requirements and a recognition of certain basic facts. First, while persons do reflect and think, they are also more complex than this. To drive this point home Dunlop opens his book, *The Education of Feeling and Emotion*, with these words:

> If we were asked to describe the sort of person we would be most frightened of, we might well think of a man whose intellectual powers were outstanding and properly trained but who had no 'heart' and no feelings. Such a person, we might think would be capable of any enormity. Indeed, we might well be tempted to say that he was not a person at all but a non-human monster in human form. Science fiction writers and horror film makers have long known how to exploit such facts. They testify to the absolutely central importance of emotion and feeling in human life. (Dunlop 1984, p. 1)

So in addition to thinking, pupils must also be presumed to feel and act; they develop skills and form relationships with others. In the absence of a more widely established and defined view of what a person is, it makes sense to presuppose that a person is a self-in-relation, with cognitive, affective and conative[5] faculties, and with a capacity for developing certain skills. In recognizing this complexity there is no suggestion that one can isolate one aspect from the other (Black 2011, p. 170), except as an academic exercise; the faculties co-inhere, interrelate and inter-depend in a person. This may in fact be the case more than we realize. David M. Black reports:

> A human organism, including its brain, develops from the event of conception, responds hugely to affective experience and education, . . . Gerald Edelman (1992) has shown that the structure of the brain is only to a limited extent determined by the genes; the fabulously complex pattern of synaptic connections (a thousand million of them, 10 to the power of 15, by the end of the first year of life) is fine-tuned and changes continually in response to *the affective environment* in which the baby or child find themselves. (Black 2011, p. 15) (emphasis added)

The point of acknowledging this complexity of the person is to insist that our emotions,[6] desires and our will need educating as much as our minds.

The fact that these faculties co-inhere in the person means that even with the cognitive pursuit of understanding and knowledge we may fail in our endeavour, not because we do not think logically or methodically enough. It may be that, as Wittgenstein suggests, a failure to understand is due to a lack of will, or alternatively due to *akrasia*, a weakness of will. Perhaps, our lack of understanding might even be, as traditional Christian thought held, due to a perverse will. If so, it is our will that needs educating and reform for 'it is the will, rather than the reason, that introduces value into the world' (Janik and Toulmin 1996, p. 195).

In addition to the will, our emotional life may equally get in the way of understanding our world well; we may be too hard-hearted or too sentimental; we may fail to love the natural world sufficiently to appreciate it well. We may lack the necessary empathy or sympathy to grasp a human situation. Nor can we come to knowledge without recourse to others with whom we share a language and a tradition of thought, or to strangers who can give us access to new concepts and other modes of thinking.

The recognition that education must be concerned with the whole person may be acutely worrying to some people. They may reason: Does this not give too much power to schools, and indirectly to the state, in determining the future character of our children and of our society? Indeed it would, if the operative word is 'determining'. Teaching virtue presupposes that we are teaching persons as Professor Carr shows in Chapter 4. The recognition that we are educating persons with a will and an affective life prevents any conception of education as a process in which young people acquire knowledge and understanding simply by applying the appropriate stimuli and reinforcement mechanisms. Teaching persons, or 'managing learning' (as some would have it), is not mechanistic but means engaging the wills and feelings of pupils as well as their minds, recognizing their freedom and developing their responsibility, that is, recognizing their subjectivity. These simple observations about teaching should ensure a pedagogy that does not admit bullying or the artificial manipulation of pupils. Persons need visions of the future; they need imagination; they need inspiration and examples of what they could be. The traditional pedagogy by which this was achieved, involved among others, creating art and music, sharing narratives, reading novels, employing dialogues, using dramas, performing rituals, relying on metaphors, and engaging in conversations – all of which are designed to recognize and enhance human subjectivity with its supposition of freedom and responsibility. The cultivation of persons and their virtues excludes dishonest manipulation. Where the manipulation of people succeeds, one has not created responsible, virtuous persons but one has successfully de-humanized them or treated them as objects to be used.

The Birmingham (UK) experience

The recognition that pupils are doers led the Agreed Syllabus Conference (2005–07) in Birmingham (UK) to speak of developing 24 dispositions in pupils, that is, the tendency to act in characteristics ways. They included the following: 'being imaginative and explorative; appreciating beauty; expressing joy; being thankful; caring for others, animals and the environment; sharing and being generous; being regardful of suffering; being merciful and forgiving; being fair and just; living by rules; being accountable and living with integrity; being temperate, exercising self-discipline and cultivating serene contentment; being modest and listening to others; cultivating inclusion, identity and belonging; creating unity and harmony; participating and willing to lead; remembering roots; being loyal and steadfast; being hopeful and visionary; being courageous and confident; being curious and valuing knowledge; being open, honest and truthful; being reflective and self-critical; being silent and attentive to, and cultivating a sense for, the sacred and transcendence'.

Within a context of RE, religious traditions were expected to show how their religious life, practices and beliefs contributed to the end of cultivating such dispositions. This task brought the religious traditions together in a common endeavour with the realization that they shared many common goals. Differences between religious traditions become illuminating rather than alienating.

Effectively the RE syllabus in a multi-faith context shared the same agenda as the religious traditions themselves, which is to cultivate the moral and spiritual development of individuals and society. As a result, the syllabus gained the strong approval of the Faith Leaders in the City. As a matter of policy, the Agreed Syllabus was developed on a basis of close consultation with faith leaders and their communities, with politicians, with teachers and schools so that it aimed to practise what it preached, namely to advocate a cooperative, reflective and responsible (in the sense of being accountable) society. After an agreement was reached, serious efforts were made to inform and engage parents and communities through the creation of DVDs to be shown in schools and in faith communities. The creation of a website in which everything was set out together with schemes of work and lesson plans, ensured that everything was accessible not only to teachers but also to parents and others. Only with this kind of openness could one gain the confidence of all the stakeholders in education.

Of course, such a radical rethink about the nature of RE, its future orientation and all that this entails was only achieved in Birmingham (UK) because of a number of factors that are not generally available elsewhere. First, the City's Councillors recognized the importance of religious communities to the life of the City in the past and believed these communities could continue to make such a contribution in the future. They saw the potential of faith communities cooperating on such a vital matter as the education of the young. Second, they were prepared to make substantial financial resources available to make the re-conception of RE and subsequent delivery possible. Third, the Faith Leaders of the City were prepared to participate in the exercise of reconfiguring RE and to be partners in the exercise. They wanted to own RE and were willing to represent its interest with politicians at all levels. They readily took part with teachers and the general public in open meetings on RE. Fourth, it required educational professionals who were prepared to rethink their subject and to enter into discussion with the other stakeholders about what might be possible. Most of all it required optimism about the future and what people might become with the help of faith traditions that look not only to the past and present but which have a clear focus on the future.

There are some easy criticisms to make of this approach to Religious Education. These may be of an educational, religious or organizational nature.

Organizationally, the whole system of agreeing syllabi for RE locally has been brought into question (Chater and Erricker 2013). Should we not be guided by a national or an implicitly international framework? If we are not, it is suggested, then we are in danger that the whole educational experience will be fractured. It will isolate RE from other subjects, and for both teachers and pupils, it will make movements around the country between local authorities difficult and discontinuous, inhibiting progression in learning. In response one can only observe that recent decisions in Britain by its Secretary of State have sought to localize responsibility for the curriculum even further on the assumption that there can be little scope for experimentation and improvement in education without such devolution and elements of 'competition'. If the assumptions of the Secretary of State are correct, then the local determination of RE is entirely appropriate and in line with current educational trends.

However, in the case of Birmingham (UK) it cannot be said that what is proposed to be taught there in RE is either idiosyncratic or disuniting. The organizational fracturing is countered by a substantive unity and harmonization in education under the aims and objectives of education set out in law which speaks of the 'spiritual, moral, social and cultural development of pupils and of society'. Much of what has been made explicit and consciously pursued in the City's RE curriculum is implicitly sought in other parts of the curriculum and in education across the country. Only by being made explicit and in being consciously pursued does the educational agenda become more effective. In many respects, the virtues and dispositions that are proposed in the Agreed Syllabus have united religious traditions as these virtues and dispositions are believed to have a universal appeal. If people resist them then it is up to them to argue their case honestly and openly with their peers and their pupils. The clear focus on virtues and dispositions in education provides the one sure and effective way of providing coherence and an 'alignment' with other subjects across the curriculum.

Religiously, there may be three obvious criticisms. First, there is the accusation of hypocrisy within schools. Teachers are role models and if they are to nurture these virtues and dispositions in others they must also embody them. If they do not then teaching these virtues will elicit the accusations of hypocrisy. The envisioned teaching task is a difficult assignment for all teachers because none of us are perfect and we shall all fall short. However, our moral and spiritual failures should not throw up obstacles to our aspirations for ourselves and for others. We might at least learn to be 'merciful and forgiving' with others and ourselves. Second, at the core of Christianity and other religious traditions lies the notion that 'we live by grace and not by works'. One might suppose that such a virtue curriculum directly counters this religious insight. However, the acknowledgement of grace is not an invitation to indifference on the part of the recipient. In the light of grace one sees the world differently and will seek to live differently. If St Augustine could invite us to 'love God and to do as we please', he was effectively saying that what pleases us when we love God is very different from the stage and time when we do not love God, that is, when we love God we will be pleased by truth, honesty, justice and the many other virtues here advocated. To be inspired by a religious vision, or person, is to seek to realize it or to emulate him or her. Third, the criticism has been made that this approach will not give pupils a comprehensive and systematic view of a religious tradition. It must be conceded that this way of teaching will not provide the pictures of a religious tradition offered by professors in the study of religion or by 'theologians'. But religions more than anything are ways of life and to engage young people with such ways of life is precisely to take them to the heart of the matter. For the rest, some will never have a comprehensive and systematic account, were they to study a religion full-time for their entire life. Our knowledge is always partial and incomplete so we must learn to live with that. And we can live with that provided we have the core of the matter in hand.

Educationally, we encounter the difficulties caused by the requirement to assess pupils and our own teaching. One can hardly assess moral and spiritual progress, not least because one needs access to motivations and intentions which in principle are only ever partially revealed if at all. (Do we always know our own?) So it is true: one cannot make any final or conclusive assessments but we will always be able to test the matters informally and tentatively, for 'by their fruits ye shall know them'. Dispositions and virtues are recognized in what people do. If pupils never demonstrate their creativity and are never engaged in acts of compassion, then one cannot claim success in teaching this syllabus but neither can one be accused of having totally failed. Final judgements in these matters lie elsewhere. However, the strictly tentative judgements of this world are made and encouraged in Birmingham (UK) according to set descriptions of what pupils are expected to do or be capable of doing at various ages. At a minimum, pupils can at least demonstrate what they know about what it means to live well according to the perceptions of the various religious traditions. More generally, we might observe that due to the critical role of freedom and responsibility, the failure to achieve in the spiritual and moral domain cannot always be attributed to the teaching received. On the other hand, 'a pilgrim's' progress in this sphere is achieved far less likely without pupils being introduced to what is inspiring and helpful and where they are not alerted to the obstacles.

Perhaps some will complain that this programme of teaching is not 'objective' or dispassionate enough. These issues have been addressed earlier. However, against the 'objectivity' of neutrality we offer the 'objectivity' of a passionate commitment to honesty and to a truthfulness that excludes partiality, self-deception and the deception of others. This is a willingness to go wherever the truth may lead us as distinct from being a bystander in life. Of course, this requires modesty, a willingness to listen to others, to think and act differently, and to observe with the purpose of living better.

Conclusions

It is possible to subvert religious life with RE if one uses the subject to depict religions as just so many 'worldviews' to be described and talked about. Treating religions 'objectively' misses the point of religious life. The objectivity aspires to leave the self out of the picture, whereas religious life in its very essence puts the self, or human subjectivity, 'in the dock'. There is no religious education which does not begin or end in treating the young as responsible agents, as named doers, with the task of living for what is good and true. To fulfil this task one needs to provide the young with more than information and descriptions of the so-called facts 'about religions'; one needs to move from a retrospective to a prospective RE. A properly prospective religious education has at its core a vision of the future, of what kind of persons the young are to become, together with a vision of society in which justice, compassion and mercy prevails. To make the future a reality the young will need to engage with the world. This requires that they develop their feelings and a determined will to act alongside their reflections and their emerging skills of reading their environment and reading the stranger. It is only in this context that religious sensibilities have their proper function and place.

In order to develop the judgements and the religious sensibilities of the young, one has to guard against 'impertinence'. It is the impertinent who believe that the ultimate authority lies within the self; they end by putting God in the dock (Job, chapter 1, verse 22). Religious sensibilities presuppose the authoritative nature of the good and the true and the beautiful; this authoritative voice cannot be reduced to declamations of the self. Religious traditions without exception seek to characterize this authority and to show where one might encounter it. It is the punitive outworking of a rampant secularism that nothing is experienced as sacred and that authority is located solely in the self or in the collective self.

A first step to being liberated as professional educationalists is to enter into serious dialogue with the other stakeholders in education to explore and agree what the future is that needs to be realized. In a democratic society, it is agreement that sets the limits of this educational exploration. A second step in the context of religious education is to identify the resources which are available from within religious traditions that may help us to define and shape that future. A third step is to realize that this future will always elude the young, and society generally, unless the whole person is addressed and engaged. In this matter, religious traditions have a long history of experience and from which educationalists might well learn some useful pedagogies.

Notes

1   For example, by regulating sexual activity, or by defining and encouraging the unconditional commitment of marriage for the benefit of children.
2   This is also a religious requirement if Martenson writing in the nineteenth century is to be believed (Martenson 1860).
3   This is how the scriptures see people, as 'doers' with feelings, that is, with a heart, see Ezekiel, chapter 36, verses 26–27.
4   A disturbing trend in modern Universities, due to its increasing bureaucratization, is to treat people 'equally' by dealing with them anonymously as numbers.

5 The faculty to do with willing.
6 Marianna Papastephanou complains that the emotional gains no recognition in the aims of Britain's 2000 national curriculum (Papastephanou 2009, p. 89).

References

Barrett, W. (1987) *Death of the soul: from Descartes to the computer*, Oxford: Oxford University Press.

Black, D. M. (2011) *Why Things Matter, the Place of Values in Science, Psychoanalysis and Religion*, Hove: Routledge.

Chater, M. and Erricker, C. (2013) *Does Religious Education have a future? Pedagogical and Policy Prospects*, David Fulton Books, London: Routledge.

Dunlop, F. (1984) *The Education of Feeling and Emotion*, London: George Allen and Unwin.

Goldie, P. (ed.), (2010) *The Oxford Handbook of Philosophy of Emotions*, Oxford: OUP.

Janik, A., and Toulmin, S. (1996) *Wittgenstein's Vienna*, 1st pub. 1973, Elephant Paperbacks, Chicago: Ivan R. Dee.

Kierkegaard, S. (1940) *The Present Age and two minor ethico-religious treatises*, trsl. A. Dru and W. Lowrie, London: Oxford University Press.

Martensen, H. (1866) *Christian Dogmatics, a compendium of the doctrines of Christianity*, trsl. W. Urwick, Edinburgh: T & T Clark.

Papastephanou, M. (2009) *Educated Fear and Educated Hope, dystopia, utopia and the plasticity of humanity*, Rotterdam: Sense publishers.

Qualifications and Curriculum Authority & the Department for Education and Skills, (2004) *Religious Education, the Non-Statutory National Framework*, London: QCA.

The 2007 Birmingham Agreed Syllabus and associated resources may be found at http://www.faithmakesadifference.co.uk/

CHAPTER TWO

The need for responsible Religious Education in the light of the 'Value Free' society

Brenda Watson

CHAPTER OUTLINE

This chapter discusses the contemporary proclivity to see the world in black and white, as either a matter of knowledge or as a matter of belief and mere opinion. It seeks to challenge this simplistic division particularly where it allocates values and religious faith to the realm of opinion. The implications for RE of positivism and the pervasive relativism in the fact/belief divide, their impact on education and the increasing secularization of the West are analysed. This is followed by developing a more constructive approach to religious education that follows a detailed examination of the meaning of 'God'; the nature of knowledge and the place of mystery; and the importance of overcoming the fact-belief divide in, for instance, valuing school worship and the affective domain. A new vision of RE is called for that abandons the naive embrace of a secular view of education together with its secular ways of studying religion.

T. S. Eliot, profoundly disturbed at the time of the Munich crisis 1938, asked: 'Was our society . . . assembled round anything more permanent than a congeries of banks, insurance companies and industries, and had it any beliefs more essential than a belief in compound interest and the maintenance of dividends?' Richard Harries (2008, p. 174) comments: 'The question posed by Eliot is even more pressing now. On what, if anything, is our civilisation based?' Jonathan Sacks (2011, p. 22) voices similar disquiet: 'Has Europe lost its soul to the markets? A moral revolution is needed when capitalism is no longer a system for the common good but an end in itself.' He sees a close connection between financial and moral failure. 'The market gives us choices; so morality itself becomes just a set of choices in which right or wrong have no meaning beyond the satisfaction or frustration of desire.' He ends with a rallying-cry 'to recover the Judeo-Christian ethic of human dignity in the image of God'.

Beliefs and values belong together. We value what we believe is important. Radical controversy regarding the basis of reality and therefore of society abounds. Thus according to many people, human dignity depends on throwing off the yoke of religion rather than attempting to rescue it. There was a striking reminder of the enormity of the task for which Sacks calls at the bottom of the very same page as his article. Matthew Syed reminds readers: 'Richard Dawkins condemns Christians for teaching youngsters to believe in an (according to him) fictitious deity. Bertrand Russell argued that religious education is evil because it teaches children to believe in something that is untrue.' Is this an indication that the West is confused about belief and therefore what is of value?

A value-free society?

How can any society be value-free? The term appears to be a misnomer. Values are being expressed and communicated constantly through everything spoken and not spoken, written and not written, done and not done, reported and not reported. Every aspect of life, whether politics, media, education, the law, sport or religion, is drenched in values. For at its simplest level values refer to what is valued – what is deemed important. So what can value-free mean?

'Value-free' is a term originally used in sociology and anthropology to describe a presumed non-judgemental approach to the study of data. Its purpose was to eliminate prejudice, whether cultural, political, religious or personal, so that objective facts could emerge. It had a moral component in that it was to ensure, so far as possible, that truth could be reached in describing the people studied fairly and accurately.

This approach to knowledge was first at home in the sciences. The term 'methodological naturalism' has been used to denote the paring down of factors affecting investigation of scientific subject matter. Where physical/empirical evidence is unavailable to resolve disputed judgements, factors displaying value-judgements must not interfere with research.

Applied to the study of human beings, this approach is, in one of its common manifestations, more widely known as 'phenomenological'. It seeks to avoid controversial consideration of the truth or otherwise of beliefs and behaviour studied, resting satisfied with a description of them. This apparently value-free methodology is not however as straightforward as it seems. Michael Poole (2010, p. 259) pertinently observes: 'Science too can be studied phenomenologically . . . while the bracketing out of truth-claims is unexceptionable as a methodological principle, once it involves denying that truth-claims in science are an important and a legitimate area of study, it has overstepped its remit.' So too in every other area of knowledge. The sociologist, Frank Furedi (2004, p. 4f.) considers that this has indeed happened on a wide scale. 'If the truth is relegated to the status of subjective outlook and interpretation, it ceases to be a subject of fundamental importance.'

The fact/belief divide promoting relativism

This rift between fact and opinion lies at the root of the value-free society, for it has consigned values to the status of mere opinion. The fact/belief divide is a convenient way of summarizing an attitude to the life of the mind which seeks absolute certainty which, since the Enlightenment, many regard scientific method as supplying. By comparison, intellectual activity appealing to experience, intuition, use of imagination, or acknowledgement of any insight from tradition, is held to be suspect and regarded as too vague to constitute knowledge properly speaking.

The fact/belief divide is a product of the academic illusion that an entirely accurate presentation of reality in conceptual terms is possible and, further, that that is the only legitimate purpose of the search for knowledge. The inadequacy of such an approach should be obvious by considering the difference between a map of a location and the actual multidimensional world thus reduced to a flat surface. Is not real life messy and in the round, not to be fully captured in two-dimensional terms?

This extreme puritan understanding of knowledge has been the temptation par excellence of the academic world since the Enlightenment's powerful love affair with science. The fault lies not with science but with its idolatry. The amazing achievements of science and technology can be fully appreciated without denying validity to other ways of knowing.

Values are never abandoned in real life even though their subjectivity constitutes an affront to attempts at tidy, clinical accuracy in portraying reality. It is easy therefore to slip into seeing values as simply what someone happens to think, consigning them to a vague area of 'live-and-let-live' necessary in practice to hold a community together. The marked globalization of the twentieth and twenty-first centuries in creating pluralist societies has brought this emphasis not on truth but on the right to hold an opinion to ever greater prominence.

This is a situation of moral relativism: 'a perspective that contends that conceptions of truth and moral values are not absolute but are relative to the persons or groups holding them' (Furedi 2004, p. 4). According to this view, no values exist per se irrespective of human wishes or needs. The concepts of right and wrong, good and evil, are purely human concepts useful in negotiating a path through life, enabling societies to thrive. They do not have any metaphysical substance; they cannot be true or false as such for they do not relate to anything beyond the physical or psychological world.

Berger and Zijderveld (2009, p. 67) note a major way in which such relativism is spread: 'not primarily through the propaganda of intellectuals, but by numerous conversations at places of work, across backyard fences, and even by children of different backgrounds meeting each other in kindergarten'. Thus, largely inadvertently, people come to assume that discounting questions of truth regarding what people believe and value is necessary for peaceful co-existence. It follows that even contradictory opinions must be accepted non-judgementally. The current liberal focus on freedom of speech, tolerance, openness, and celebration of diversity is a natural consequence of the attempted clear-cut division between fact and opinion.

Far from providing a firm intellectual basis for society, however, emphasis on these values has exacerbated confusion. Furedi's book, *On Tolerance*, (2011) has evoked much interest in his thesis that tolerance has become a refusal to make any judgement at all. Values and beliefs come to stand outside the province of rational scrutiny, reflecting only social and cultural identities. Madeleine Bunting begins her review of Furedi's book (*The Guardian*, 5 September 2011) with these words: 'For a secular godless age, there is one value we promulgate about ourselves at almost all opportunities: tolerance.' But she notes it is clear that the meaning of tolerance is far from clear! Can it indeed stand the weight placed on it? Accepting that a person's race provides no reason for hostility may be straightforward. The concept however runs into difficulties when faced with, for example, freedom of speech. Julian Baggini in his review of Furedi's book (*The Financial Times*, 16 September 2011) comments that Furedi 'is right to say that we shouldn't restrict freedom of speech to stop "mere offence", as Mill put it. But sexist talk in the boardroom can undermine or silence female colleagues.' There is indeed much confusion as to what tolerance really is and how it can operate in practice without violating other prominent liberal values.

Positivism and its hold on education

Such pragmatic relativism and the confusion it causes have been aided by specific intellectual enquiry which has endowed the fact/belief divide with prestigious intellectual status. The underlying philosophy which came to be known as Positivism was powerfully at work even in the nineteenth century; it emerged in its most self-conscious and clear-cut form in the Logical Positivism of the first half of the twentieth century, which dismissed to the category of 'meaningless' any statement not concerned with empirical reality. Andrew Wright (2010, p. 141) considers that the influence of positivism is now in academic circles 'virtually non-existent'. He may be right, but it will be a long time before the effects of that demise are filtered down through the rest of society, so effectively has a positivist view on life been conveyed to people over two centuries.

People in the most formative period of their lives have imbibed positivism through constant exposure in obligatory schooling which has privileged an attitude of stick-to-the-facts. This colossal emphasis in all education systems in the West has served virtually to condition people into the fact/belief divide. Very few actually use such a term or are aware of how influenced they have been, but we should remember that the presence of conditioning can most effectively be detected by other people, not by the recipients, as a failure to see certain possibilities. Conditioning is most apparent when recipients are completely unaware of what is influencing them.

Priorities in the curriculum of schools for time, staffing, funding, resources and status indicate clearly what has been happening. Mathematics, English Language proficiency, the Sciences and IT are easy winners over the Humanities, the Arts and Religion. As just one example, countless surveys have indicated the power of music in motivating students. The remarkable Venezuelan system of education – *el sistema* – through classical music has won acclaim throughout the world and receives verbal plaudits from politicians, but to write any serious commitment to such education into the curriculum alongside the teaching of core subjects would require a seismic change in thinking.

Again, assessment is regarded as hugely important defining the success or failure of schools, of teachers and of students. The search is for fair and efficient ways of reducing what is learnt to closeness to 'correct' answers, even boxes that can be ticked. This is presumed to guarantee objectivity regarded as automatically preferable to anything subjective. Increasing concern about the many inadequacies and pitfalls of assessment is being expressed. Yet this does little to dent the fundamental faith in examinations, in targets which are precise and checkable, and in procedures for teaching presumed definite, objective and certain. All such are thought to circumvent the unreliability of trusting teachers as capable of making their own judgements. Indeed in most people's minds education is to be equated with successful test results, even by those most eager for reform in education.

The reality of this alternative positivist faith at work in our society and in schools is well expressed by Trevor Cooling (2012, p. 88). After teaching science, his own experience at the chalkface as an RE teacher brought him up sharply against the prevailing dominant world view. 'It felt like being in charge of the school's curiosity cupboard. Science was the kitchen of the school curriculum.'

Values, secularism and religion

The fact/belief divide has outlawed not just values but also religion. The secularism of the West which is now becoming clear to almost everyone has had a long incubation period. According to the fact/belief divide religious beliefs can have no intellectual substance. Belief in God is like believing in fairies at the bottom of the garden as even a distinguished philosopher like A. C. Grayling (2007, p. 89) has put it.

Many argue that the secularization of society does not need to result in the value-free, morally relativist condition. In Britain, the Schools Council Working Paper 36 (1971, p. 70) assumed that 'Moral knowledge is autonomous.' A deep awareness of right and wrong is almost universal; there is indeed that awareness in basic humanity to which appeal can be made. Thus, for example, the evil of torturing young children is deeply perceived by almost everyone. Kant could speak of 'the moral law within'.

People who disbelieve in God may indeed be not only as moral, but perhaps even more moral, than those who do believe in God. This is because they can be free from certain tendencies within religions to infantilize some people into mere obedience of rules in the hope of future bliss or the avoidance of hell. By contrast, atheists/agnostics may appear to be wholly disinterested, pursuing goodness for its own sake.

The problem however lies in the vagueness of the source of those values. This is not an irrelevant matter as the temptation to selfishness is extraordinarily strong and needs help in resisting. When belief in God is taken for granted, as is the case in almost every society ever known except our own, the transcendence of values is never in doubt. Values are not relative because they originate in the character of God. Humans do not just create values: they discover them, for there is a moral universe which lays claims on all of us, to which we must relate.

So, what has secularism put in its place? Philip Barnes (2011, p. 133) notes that today 'philosophers are much less sanguine and much more divided about the intellectual plausibility of secular justifications of morality'. This is not just a matter for academic debate because its impact has wide repercussions in society as a whole. Living as if there were no God cuts people off from benefiting from all the accumulated insights of religion. Richard Harries (2007) uses the word 'enchantment' to describe the way in which religion puts the task of seeking truth and goodness within a vastly meaningful overall context.

It is interesting that currently many atheists and agnostics are aware of the lack of secularist enchantment. The popular philosopher Alain de Botton (2012a) advocates copying religion by building temples to atheism.

Stephen Cave (2012) ends his article 'The God Gap' arguing that 'Secular society should be unembarrassed about adopting what is best from the believers. It is time for a new Cult of Reason.' Like Janice Turner (2012) who writes that 'God may not be great, but religion can be,' they see that religion carries benefits for which they themselves yearn if only they can be disentangled from belief in a non-existent God. But, as Charles Moore (2012) points out, this enchantment depends on its being true.

The task for RE

Here is an obvious cue for RE. Responsible RE needs to offer a better way forward. It needs to help people raise the question of the existence of God instead of simply assuming that there is no God. The following three-fold focus could help.

1. Work on the concept of God

What is most essential for RE is to illuminate the concept of God at its highest. As Geoff Teece (2011, p. 169) says: 'The legitimate purpose of the study of religion in RE should reside in the centrality of the transcendent.' In the search for the identity of RE this is the central point. This is what distinguishes RE from every other subject on the curriculum. The title of an article by Penny Thompson (2011), 'She made me think about God,' makes a good summary of what RE should be.

There is no reason – and the term is used advisedly – why anyone should imagine that the question of the existence of God is closed. Such belief cannot have empirical evidence, but neither can belief in the non-existence of God. God, if God exists, is the creator of the empirical world, not to be discovered as such within it. The homely analogy of the cook and the pudding readily makes this point even for KS1 pupils!

Holding a naive concept of God has serious consequences. Alain de Botton, for example, was raised 'in a committed atheistic household, as the son of two secular Jews who placed religious belief somewhere on a par with an attachment to Santa Claus' (2012b, p. 25). It is unsurprising that he considers the question of the existence of God closed, being clearly contradicted by science and common sense. Nor is scientific investigation possible. As Elliott Sober (see Garvey 2012, p. 23), a leading philosopher of science and an atheist confirms: 'You cannot deduce the non-existence of God from the theory of evolution, or from quantum mechanics, or from plate tectonics, or from any scientific theory.'

Combating the naivety of the concept of God with which many people operate needs more than refuting the supposed science–religion opposition. It needs to pay attention to other serious objections to faith in God. Commenting on Darwin's distress at the death of his 10-year-old daughter,

Sober adds, 'I don't think the theory of evolution does anything to challenge theism beyond what the problem of evil does.' (p. 25)

Mostly treatment in RE of such problems is reserved for older students. Yet it is crucial to engage even young children with thinking about truth claims. They need to acquire a sophisticated concept of God. This can be done. Rowan Williams (See Myers 2010, p. 3), for example, has given a model in very simple language in his reply to a letter from a six-year-old girl. What he wrote did not foreclose the subject but opened it up for further questioning, impressing indeed her agnostic father. The teaching of the concept of God, from KS1 onwards, needs to tie in with this dimension of openness to what is infinitely beyond us. Children can appreciate the immensity of reality, and experience awe and wonder.

2. Enabling an enlarged understanding of knowledge

To tackle such questions concerning truth claims, indeed, something else of crucial importance needs to be in place: an enlarged concept of knowledge as literally beyond what we can in simplistic fashion presume to imprison within our own understanding and language. Such an attitude presents a radical challenge to positivism and narrow forms of religious adherence alike.

The word *mystery* is useful here, provided that its two quite distinct meanings are taught. Its common usage denotes a problem to be solved. Its second meaning refers to what necessarily lies beyond our cognitive and interpretative powers. To become religiously literate would involve encompassing both meanings. It involves more than a basic use of language; it involves appreciating the poetry of language and the way that language itself has constantly to be annihilated in order that it continues to point beyond itself to what is true. The mystic, Meister Eckhart, wrote that 'Only the hand that erases can write the true thing.' Rowan Williams (Myers 2012, pp. 32, 18) expresses the same kind of thought like this: 'When God's light breaks in on my darkness, the first thing I know is that I don't know, and never did.' He likens this renunciation of grasping possessive knowledge to how we get to know another person. 'Understanding another person is never a completed task but only a continuing labour.'

The real enemy RE needs to fight, as should the rest of education, is the desire for absolute certainty. This desire motivates artificial and misplaced dogmatism of all kinds, whether secularist or religious. It closes down the possibility of further insights as one progresses through life. It is in every respect a dead end, spiritually as well as intellectually and emotionally. It ceases to have a hold on people once they gain real awareness that we are limited beings in an extraordinarily complex world where modes of communication, including the meaning of words, are ever changing.

Paying attention to imaginative opening up of possibilities through the arts is signally important in RE. The arts transcend easy-going literalist understanding of reality; they clearly appeal to emotion as well as intellect, and point towards greater vision in which the everyday world is caught up and transformed.

Similarly, RE should be closely associated with assemblies giving opportunities for all to experience what worship is like. As Fergus Kerr (Myers 2012, p. 15) noted: 'If we cannot imagine what it is to observe rites, enjoy singing hymns and the like, the nature of religion is bound to remain opaque.' The case can be argued that without some such exposure to worship almost certainly religion will not be understood at all.

3. Overcoming the fact/belief divide

There is however a grave objection against assemblies for all pupils which include religious material, namely a presumed compromising of integrity for those who are not religious. To resolve this we need to look again at the impact of the fact/belief divide which artificially separates what needs to be simultaneously practised. Assemblies giving specific opportunity for worship should be couched in terms which enable all to participate at their own personal level. Provided the educational purpose of such assemblies is explicitly stated, atheists and agnostics, or members of other religions than the one focused on in a particular assembly, need not feel like outsiders nor feel that their conscience has been violated.

This is not some idealistic, purely cognitive solution. It works. An ex-pupil of mine once told me that the school assemblies were perhaps what she found most inspiring, yet she was and remains an atheist. All it needs is to introduce hymns with some such phrase as 'Sing this as a song or as a hymn' or prayers prefaced with 'Listen to this prayer, and if you wish silently say Amen.' (See, e.g. Watson and Thompson, Chapter 11, esp. p. 192)

The distinction drawn here is easily overlooked because of the fact/belief divide which separates activities into cognitive/objective and emotional/subjective domains. In Britain, the two commonly stated Attainment Targets in RE, (namely, learning about and learning from faith) indeed do this and need bringing together; otherwise vision will be myopic. Participation-with-integrity in assemblies containing religious material requires not compartmentalism but both/and thinking. The mind has to be active in distancing oneself from what is presented and reflecting on it, while the emotions must at the same time be engaged in a willingness to share with others who are different from oneself, open towards possible fresh understanding.

This is how participation in the arts in general works. Millions of people visit art galleries and look deeply at religious works of art without any sense that their integrity is being thus compromised. Similarly, millions of choral singers and listeners are deeply moved by Bach's *St Matthew's Passion* regardless of their religious views and commitments.

This double process of distancing and attempted closeness is also how we gain real knowledge of the world around us, especially of other people.

In sound relationships we are aware that our own thoughts and experiences are unique and distinct, but yet are willing to relate imaginatively to those of others. This provides the only basis on which to move forward beyond where we now happen to be.

What does this mean for the practice of RE today?

Can this threefold focus be aligned with the trend in RE in Britain since the 1970s? Michael Grimmitt supplies a convenient summary of this trend in the book he recently edited (2010, pp. 263, 266, 271). 'The most productive period of research and development in RE in the UK: . . . brought education and religion into a new relationship by combining *a secular view of education with secular ways of studying religion.*' (The italics are mine.) This created 'a proper method for conducting the public study of religion in an open, democratic, plural and increasingly secular society'. This 'newly acquired state of RE's educational maturity' would have come of age but for the rearguard action of conservative Christians who at the time of the 1988 Education Reform Act wished to retain unequal privileges for Christianity. He equates this view with 'uncritical confessional activity' by contrast with an RE which embraces 'description, interpretation, critical analysis and evaluation'.

He acknowledges that this creates some kind of a gap between what religions are and how they are seen in RE in which 'religious beliefs and practices fulfil an instrumental function which is distinct from the intrinsic worth and status which they enjoy within faith communities'. Failure to agree with this instrumentalist function is an 'obstacle which causes many to question whether religious faiths and the concept of religion itself can ever contribute to social and community cohesion but must always be seen as divisive'.

This embodies grave criticism of religion and requires answering. The approach, which can broadly be characterized as phenomenological, should not stand on its own. If it does, is it not likely to become dogmatic and exclusive, failing to renounce the very criticisms it makes of old-style religious confessionalism? It can be argued that the above summary illustrates this tendency in at least four ways:

1. The danger of a secularist understanding of religion being regarded as normative

Such an understanding loses touch with how religious people see religion. Does it not contradict RE's impeccable aim of teaching a genuine understanding of religion if an insider's view is presumed off-centre? It also embodies a highly negative attitude towards religious people in general. RE should be challenging secularism at this point, rather than going along with it. Otherwise it is likely by default to nurture students further into both secularism and what tends to accompany it, the moral relativism of the value-free society.

2. The danger of imprisoning religion within sociological/cultural boxes

Collapsing religion into religions needs questioning. The pluralist situation of the twenty-first century is alerting more and more religious people to the importance of transcending artificial boundaries between religions. Ought not RE to be aiding a fuller vision which outstrips such pigeon-holing? Should not RE be at least raising the question whether rigid boundaries between religions actually inhibit religious and spiritual insight? By focusing on the concept of God we can help students to see that religion is more than just a sociological/cultural category. This can also help RE relate to the very many, especially in a secularist-dominated society, who may believe in God but who, for a variety of reasons, do not practise religion outwardly.

3. The danger of RE's pursuing a particular political agenda

Defining religion as basically about religions makes it easy to prioritize the notion of equal treatment to all religions regardless of other factors and other values. To expect a country like Burma, for example, not to acknowledge its Buddhist inheritance would defy common sense. Similarly, in the West, talk of studied equal treatment for Christianity alongside all other religions and world views is hardly an intelligent response to its heritage. In a supposedly value-free society, to avoid controversy, the risk is that the equality on offer is one in which all religions are equally ignored. As discussed above, reliance on tolerance invites controversy. The politicization of the associated value of equality can be similarly critiqued. Anthony Browne (2006, p. xiii) has argued that political correctness, once so much needed, is capable of riding roughshod over the more fundamental values with which RE should be concerned.

4. The danger of assuming that a secularist approach is non-confessional

The secularist claim to neutrality is a mirage, for it is impossible to stand literally nowhere. (See, e.g. Watson 2011.) Grimmitt's 'instrumentalist function' is itself a form of confessionalism whereby the purpose of teaching becomes nurturing in specific values and beliefs. That this is so may readily be seen in how, as Liam Gearon (2010, p. 118) points out, RE risks state manipulation in the interests of what he defines as a newly emergent 'liberal autocracy'. 'Religion is politically sanitised. Serving to cohere rather than critique the state, religion is not seen as true but useful'. Without confessionalism of some kind, no policy is possible, nor any education whatever.

Dogmatism can be avoided in these four instances by the simple expedient of opening up for students' key questions such as:

1 What is religion? Why do we use the word?

2 Is it always appropriate to see religion in terms of religions?

3 Do values such as tolerance and equality deserve the absolute priority they are often given? What values are truly fundamental?

4 How can indoctrination of any kind be avoided in schools?

A major achievement of the secularist challenge to RE has been in drawing attention to the way that nurture/education into whatever religion or world view is held ought to open out into invitation instead of being indoctrination. We have now become aware of what was not clearly seen before in old-style religious confessionalism, namely, that it is easy to teach one's own view dogmatically instead of leaving space for recipients to think for themselves and disagree if they wish.

RE should be unafraid of taking on board radical controversy. Margaret Heffernan (2011, p. 329) remarked in her book *Willful Blindness* 'Yes I can hear a thousand teachers despairing at the prospect of more argument, but it's the silent classrooms that scare me'. In such genuinely open RE, the outworn confessional-versus-phenomenological confrontation can be banished. We can acknowledge that both emphases are needed in an ongoing polarity. For freedom of thought is an essential prerequisite either for faithful religious response or for informed atheist/agnostic refusal. Furthermore, debating such questions will help to cut at the root of the relativism behind the value-free society.

References

Barnes, L. P. (2011), 'What has morality to do with religious education?' *Journal of Beliefs and Values* 32, 2 August: 131–41.

—(ed.), (2012), *Debates in Religious Education*. London: Routledge.

Berger, P. and Zijderveld, A. (2009), *In Praise of Doubt: How to have Convictions without becoming a Fanatic*. New York: HarperOne.

Botton, A de (2012a), *Religion for Atheists: A Non-Believer's Guide to the Uses of Religion*. London: Hamish Hamilton.

—(2012b), interviewed by Sameer Rahim 'Sage puts his faith in temples for atheists', *Daily Telegraph*, 30 January 2012.

Browne, A. (2006), *The Retreat of Reason: Political Correctness and the Corruption of Public Debate in Modern Britain*. London: Civitas.

Cave, S. (2012), 'The God Gap', *Financial Times*, 21/22 January.

Cooling, T. F. (2012), 'Faith, religious education and whole school issues' in L. P. Barnes (ed.), *Debates in Religious Education*. London: Routledge.

Furedi, F. (2004), *Where Have All the Intellectuals Gone?* London: Continuum.

—(2011), *On Tolerance: A Defence of Moral Independence*. London: Continuum International Publishing Group.

Garvey, J. (2012), 'Did God have a hand in the origin of species? Elliott Sober tells James Garvey that only philosophy can settle the debate between creationists and evolutionists', *The Philosophers' Magazine*, Issue 56, 1st. quarter.

Gearon, L. (2010), 'Which community? Whose cohesion? Community cohesion? Citizenship and religious education' in M. Grimmitt (ed.), *Religious Education and Social and Community Cohesion, Explorations of Challenges and Opportunities*. Great Wakering, Essex, UK: McCrimmons.

Grayling, A. C. (2007), 'Philosophy and Public Understanding', in Baggini, J. and Stangroom, J. (eds), *What More Philosophers Think*. London: Continuum.

Grimmitt, M. (ed.), (2010), *Religious Education and Social and Community Cohesion An Exploration of Challenges and Opportunities*. Great Wakering, Essex: McCrimmons.

Harries, R. (2008), *The Re-Enchantment of Morality: Wisdom for a Troubled World*. London: SPCK.

Heffernan M. (2011), *Wilful Blindness: Why We Ignore the Obvious at our Peril*. London: Simon & Schuster.

Moore, C. (2012), 'Religion's usefulness is drawn from its truth', *Daily Telegraph*, 30 January.

Myers, B. (2012), *Christ the Stranger: The Theology of Rowan Williams*. London: T & T Clark.

Poole, M. (2010), 'Science and religion' in M. Grimmitt (ed.), *Religious Education and Social and Community Cohesion, Explorations of Challenges and Opportunities*. Great Wakering, Essex, UK: McCrimmons.

Sacks, J. (2011), 'Has Europe lost its soul to the markets?' *The Times*, 12 December.

Teece, G. (2011), 'Too many competing imperatives? Reflections on the public role of religion in a modern society'. *Journal of Beliefs and Values* 32, 2 August: 161–72.

Thompson, P. (2011), 'She made me think about God'. *Journal of Beliefs and Values* 32, 2 August: 195–205.

Turner, J. (2012), 'God may not be great, but religion can be', *The Times*, 28 January.

Watson, B. (2011), 'Democracy, religion and secularism: reflections on the public role of religion in a modern society. *Journal of Beliefs and Values* 32, 2 August: 173–83.

Watson, B. and Thompson P. (2007), *The Effective Teaching of Religious Education second edition*. Harlow: Pearson Longman.

Wright, A. (2010), 'Community, Diversity and Truth' in M. Grimmitt (ed.), *Religious Education and Social and Community Cohesion, Explorations of Challenges and Opportunities*. Great Wakering, Essex, UK: McCrimmons.

CHAPTER THREE

Virtue ethics – Background and current popularity

David Carr

CHAPTER OUTLINE

This chapter sets out a case for character development in schools, which draws on religious traditions without becoming another form of confessional education or religious instruction. In drawing up the case, it makes the necessary conceptual distinctions in understanding education and religion. It also makes an important distinction between personality and character traits. The chapter further draws on the history of virtue ethics, showing a distinct preference for the contribution of Aristotle with the suggestion that these are natural qualities acquired through practice and training.

It concludes with observations about the valuable contributions that religious and theological traditions have made without denying the potential of contributions from the non-religious world.

Persons, religion and education

This work is about the formation of persons as a legitimate educational enterprise and the potential or possible contribution that some appreciation of religion and religious life or experience might make to such formation.

This is a philosophically complex issue and it is rather hard to know where to begin with the conceptual questions that it raises. For one thing, it is far from clear what the formation of persons might mean. For example, this should not be confused with the formation or cultivation of *personality* as this is ordinarily understood: for it is not obviously the business of educationalists or teachers to make John extrovert or witty or to make Janet less shy and retiring – even though there might be some case for shy and retiring Janet becoming a bit more confident or assertive. Again, as will soon become clear, it is no easier to see exactly what 'some appreciation of religion or religious life or experience' might amount to. As it is made clear elsewhere in this work, while this might mean something rather stronger than merely acquainting pupils with 'propositional' knowledge concerning the beliefs of different religious cultures (though it should also include this), many (including the present writer) would want to insist that it must fall short of turning Ali into a committed Muslim or Anne-Marie into a lifelong practising Catholic.

In this light, we may be reasonably sure that the 'confessional' drift of the British 1944 Education Act – much referred to elsewhere in this work – is no longer defensible, if it ever actually was. Indeed, if it now no longer appears acceptable to engage pupils in a daily act of (implicitly Christian) worship in British schools that are nowadays predominantly populated by Sikhs or Muslims, it can hardly have been so even then – unless one takes the dubious view that education might properly involve the transmission of prevailing cultural norms and values simply because they happen to prevail (and one might doubt that Christian norms did so prevail even in the British post-war settlement). To be sure, one might now encounter the common (relativist) objection that one can only be here speaking of education as it has come to be understood in 'liberal' societies such as our own: surely, there are societies in which confessional induction of the young into religious beliefs and values is the very foundation of education. To this, however, one may equally – and no less plausibly – reply that societies in which schools engage in the confessional inculcation of religious values are simply not engaging in *education*. But is this to say that there can be no such thing as *confessional education*? Indeed, it is nowadays fashionable to hear it argued (by defenders of religious schooling) that whereas non-confessional (phenomenological and other) approaches to RE may be suitable for state secular contexts, 'confessional' approaches might be deemed more appropriate for faith schools. But this rather begs the question by failing to appreciate that there may be bad as well as good RE in both secular and faith school contexts. The key question now, however, is surely that of what good RE is? And there is surely something suspect about supposing that what is *educationally* appropriate for young people in one context should not be so for those in another.

Two dimensions of religious and other education

While it is not possible in this short chapter to describe in any great detail what such good religious education might be, we may suggest at least for now that it should have two key dimensions or functions: first, an 'academic' or theoretical function; secondly, a more practical or moral function.

To begin with, then, while religious education might not be limited to mere instruction in the past and present beliefs and practices of religious groups or cultures, such instruction or acquaintance is nevertheless important if not indispensable. Indeed, it is crucial from a broad educational viewpoint for atheists and agnostics no less than religious believers to be fully acquainted with the religious ideas and ideals that have shaped contemporary world cultures. Without such knowledge, one could scarcely understand modern political conditions and events or the motives of those implicated in such events from Israel to Ireland or Utah to Iran. But, from an educational viewpoint, it is crucial for such knowledge to be taught critically, so that as well as the faithful coming to admit the great human harm and suffering that religion has often caused in the world (to be, as C. S. Lewis once put it, 'ashamed of their history'), would-be atheists (unlike some of the foremost contemporary spokesmen of atheism) might come to appreciate how religious belief and practice has often been a force for great human good and benefit through the philanthropic work of great moral and social reformers. But, in addition to this critical dimension, religious education also needs – as has been increasingly recognized in latter day British RE – a *philosophical* dimension to assist appreciation of the crucial questions about human life and existence that the causal explanations of natural science do not seem quite equal to addressing. Indeed, major philosophers from Plato and Aristotle to Kant have offered powerful (and as yet un-refuted) arguments for supposing that notions of mind or soul (as opposed to brain), value and meaningful action are presently (if not in principle) beyond the scope of natural scientific explanation, and that the narratives and myths of religion (as such modern psychologists as Jung have recognized) may be seen as serious attempts to address the deepest questions of human concern.

However, secondly, religious education might have a more personally formative educational function – precisely in so far as that this is arguably a legitimate function of education anyway. As earlier indicated, however, it is necessary to distinguish those aspects of human personhood that might be of legitimate educational concern from those that should not be. Thus, although our criteria of human personhood would normally take fairly wide account of what people believe (including their religious beliefs) and of their personality traits, tastes, habits, character strengths and weaknesses, interpersonal relations and friendships and so forth, we have seen that not all of these could really be of proper educational concern. Just as it would be educationally improper (in the present view) to try to turn Ali into a devout Muslim or Anne-Marie into a faithful Catholic, it may be no less intrusive to try to make John more witty or Janet less melancholic. That said, we may here draw a useful distinction between personality and character: for whereas it may be no business of teachers to tinker with John's optimism or eccentricity, it should be of some concern to them that he is lazy, intemperate, impolite, spiteful, dishonest or unfair. Indeed, it would seem right not just to criticize John for such traits, but also to take steps to try to educate him in the contrary qualities. In short, one key difference between qualities of personality and such character traits as honesty, temperance and fairness is that whereas the former are to a considerable degree matters of private 'aesthetic' taste or concern, the latter are traits or dispositions that human agents have some *moral obligation* to acquire or cultivate.

Still, it may be said, is it not the very height of moral impropriety – the ultimate human intrusion – to try to persuade, coerce or manipulate others to some alternative moral viewpoint? Surely, as a free moral agent, John is entitled to be unfair, dishonest, bullying and backsliding if he so wants and there can be no justification for trying to make him otherwise? But one needs only to state this position to appreciate its manifest absurdity. To begin with, the argument clearly trades on a serious ambiguity in the idea of being morally *entitled* to certain beliefs or dispositions. On the one hand, to be sure, anyone is entitled as a free moral agent to believe or act as he or she pleases. On the other hand, however, this is not at all the same as saying that one has a moral right to be unfair, dishonest, bullying and backsliding – since such conduct is evidently not *morally correct*. In short, it does not follow from the fact that any and all moral agency must be freely chosen (in order to *be* moral agency) that there are no wrong moral choices, or that such wrong choices should be free from censure. Moreover, it also does not follow that such moral censure would have to take the form of manipulating or forcing others to behave better. On the contrary, it may be a much better way of getting agents to behave better to show them the hurtful consequences of their actions or to set them a good example to follow. Above all, however, encouraging John to be honest, self-controlled, fair or compassionate is not a matter of converting him to some other moral viewpoint – at least in any problematic indoctrinatory sense – since there really is *no* other moral viewpoint.

Ethics, virtue and moral reason

Such moral qualities of character as honesty, fairness, courage, self-control, patience, compassion and responsibility have been traditionally called 'virtues'. The term virtue derives directly from the Latin *virtus* and more indirectly from the ancient Greek term *arete* – which generally just meant 'excellence'. In this ancient sense, the term had broad application to any features of agents, objects or events that might be good or exemplary of their kind: thus, for example, the '*arete*' of a sword would lie in its effectiveness as a tool for killing. In this regard, the earliest philosophical attempts by ancient Greek thinkers to understand what 'excellence' might mean as applied to human affairs seem to have focused upon the characteristics that might make an (primarily male) agent effective, successful or worthy of honour among his fellows. In the society depicted by Homer, such high regard would have been accorded primarily to those who possessed the warrior virtues of courage, leadership and military skill or prowess. For a later generation of thinkers – known mainly from the works of Plato (Hamilton and Cairns 1961) as the 'sophists' – the question of human excellence seems to be conceived more in terms of the kind of qualities that might win an (again male) agent success, honour and wealth in the political assemblies of the emerging Athenian democracy: in this context, the art of rhetoric or persuasion assumed high priority. It should be noted, however, that none of these ideas of virtue had especially 'moral' connotations. In the dialogues of Plato, sophists are depicted as arguing that the qualities that ensure human success or flourishing are those of self-interested competition and manipulation of others more than anything that we would nowadays associate with the term 'virtue'.

From the dialogues of Plato, it would appear that the first philosopher to have construed human excellence or virtue in the distinctive moral sense that it has for us today was his own teacher and mentor Socrates. It is Socrates who Plato represents as arguing that the ruthless pursuit of success – invariably at the expense of others – cannot be regarded as the prime goal of human flourishing or the hallmark of virtue. It is certainly not sufficient for human flourishing or virtue, since there are many who have succeeded in gaining great power and wealth who would be widely regarded as wicked or despicable human beings; but it does not seem to be necessary either, for there are many who are regarded as good or saintly people who have lived lives of material renunciation and selfless service to others. Indeed, Socrates argues more strongly that those devoted to the selfish pursuit of power and wealth at the expense of others are invariably mere slaves to such vices as vanity, hubris, avarice, intemperance and insecurity that are far removed from the self-possession and self-knowledge of the good or virtuous agent. In the strikingly Socratic observation of a much later thinker – Jean-Jacques Rousseau (1973) – those who think themselves the masters or superiors of others are actually greater slaves than those they would dominate. Precisely, they lack power over themselves and the real human freedom that only such power can give. In New Testament (and also Socratic) terms, they seek to gain the world at the expense of their very souls. Much of Socrates' dialectical effort – as recorded in the most influential of Plato's dialogues – is devoted to showing how agents may promote the health of their souls through the development of the genuine human virtues of courage, temperance, justice and wisdom.

It turns out that for Socrates (and, to a great extent, Plato) the key virtue for the flourishing of the soul – that to which the other virtues are much reducible – is the virtue of *wisdom*, and the key to the development of wisdom is the pursuit of truth through the exercise of reason. For Socrates, the tyranny, injustice and cruelty of the wicked agent is the direct result of ignorance and self-delusion. Wicked agents are not really responsible for their actions since – as no-one who knew the difference between right and wrong could reasonably act wrongly – they cannot really know what they are doing. Above all, their self-centred or selfish actions should not be confused with 'self-interest' in so far as those who perpetrate cruelty and injustice clearly fail to appreciate what actually lies in their interest. Here, of course, the point is not just the commonplace of modern ethical contract theory that – as a social being – one's interests and welfare are clearly bound up with those of others, but the deeper claim that one's very moral nature stands to be corrupted by dishonesty, injustice and cruelty. To be sure, the fact that the wicked agent's actions stem from ignorance does not mean that they are to be excused or left unpunished; but Socrates' interest clearly lies more in the redemption of wickedness through the agent's appreciation or recognition of the truth through which the evil of his nature and conduct may be revealed for what it is. Plato's philosophical efforts are mainly directed towards the development of a method of moral enquiry – exemplified in his Socratic dialogues – through which such moral truth might be revealed.

Despite significant differences between ancient Greek and modern ethics, Socrates and Plato may nevertheless be seen as having set the agenda for subsequent 'analytical' ethics in conceiving such enquiry as concerned mainly with development of rational decision procedures for right moral action. Thus while some modern moral sentimentalists (such as, notably, Hume) seem to have taken the line of some ancient sophists that moral agency follows more from emotion than reason, the most influential of modern ethical theories have been broadly rationalist and concerned with clarifying the logic of moral inference and argument. It should also be familiar to anyone of the slightest acquaintance with philosophy that the two most influential modern theories of ethics have been those of Kant and utilitarianism. Briefly, whereas Kant's so-called deontological ethics construes moral agency in terms of obedience to duties conceived as formally universal commitments, utilitarians locate moral justification in the socially or other beneficial consequences of actions. Clearly, these accounts are far from consistent – what might count as a permissible or right action for utilitarians, such as a socially beneficial murder, would not be so for Kantians – and neither theory gives primacy or even prominence to the place of qualities of character or motive in determining what might actually count as appropriate moral judgement or conduct. For this, we need to turn now to ancient and modern developments of so-called virtue ethics.

Past and present virtue ethics

The first western philosopher to have understood moral life in general and virtue in particular in terms of character is Plato's great pupil Aristotle. According to Plato, Socrates regarded virtue as the cultivation of moral wisdom and construed such wisdom in terms of knowledge of the good. In turn, Plato tried to give a more developed account of the epistemic status of such knowledge: he regarded such knowledge – which he termed 'dialectic' – as a higher kind of theoretical enquiry through which agents of appropriate ability might grasp the meaning of abstract moral notions of justice and good. Aristotle crucially departs from Plato in distinguishing moral reason and deliberation as a distinctive kind of *practical* capacity. In short, as he makes clear in his *Nicomachean Ethics* (1941a), it is the task of practical reason – which Aristotle distinguishes from both theoretical and technical enquiry as the moral wisdom of *phronesis* – not to give us abstract knowledge of the good, but to help us become good people. To this end, *phronesis* is primarily concerned with the promotion or production of good *character* which he precisely understands in terms of the proper ordering – in the interests of a defensibly good or flourishing human life – of our natural instincts, desires and passions (see Carr 2009). However, although Aristotle does highly value the contemplative life, a flourishing or virtuous human life is not generally some Platonic denial of lower bodily appetites in favour of higher intellectual enquiry, but one of balanced appreciation of the appropriate place of such appetites. Thus, for Aristotle, virtuous character is not simply the suppression of importunate appetites and desires, but the achievement of an appropriate 'mean' state between inappropriate excess and defect of such appetite or desire.

Despite some unsympathetic philosophical treatment (Russell 2004), Aristotle's doctrine of the mean represents a deep insight into the nature of moral virtue. On the (probably Socratic) view that Aristotle rejects, the virtue of courage consists in the suppression of fear – which is regarded as a bad or negative emotion. The courageous agent is therefore the one who truly appreciates the harmful effects of fear and who is able to reason it away (or otherwise suppress it). For Aristotle, apart from the consideration that one who felt no fear could hardly be described as courageous, fear is a perfectly natural human emotion that is not necessarily negative. Indeed, morally suspect action may follow no less from too little fear than from too much: the warrior who rushes into a hopeless battle high on fear-inhibiting drugs is not wise or virtuous, but reckless and foolish. Thus, the virtue of courage is not just opposed to cowardice understood as too much fear, but lies in a mean between the excessive fear of the coward and the insufficient fear of the reckless. The virtuous trick is to feel the right degree of fear in the circumstances. Much the same applies to anger which, when experienced excessively can be one form of intemperance, may also be morally obligatory – in the right measure – in some circumstances. But what is the right measure? For Aristotle, there can here be no general rules for this, because the right measure is precisely determined by the particular moral circumstances. Thus, whereas it would be wrong not to feel anger in the face of large-scale injustice and cruelty, it would be inappropriate to get excessively angry because someone else has used one's favourite teacup. So generally, for Aristotle, virtuous conduct needs to be contextually appropriate to time, place, motive, the characters and responses of others, and so on.

What mainly needs to be recognized here, however, is that Aristotle shifts the ethical focus from right action to virtuous character. Unlike much later modern ethics that is inclined to define virtue in terms of the performance of independently determined right action, Aristotle is more inclined to define right action in terms of what a *virtuous agent* would do. So his *Nicomachean Ethics* is primarily concerned with identifying educational and other processes required for the cultivation of virtuous character – three of which may be briefly mentioned here. To begin with, since virtues are practical dispositions, Aristotle clearly believes that they need to be acquired through practice – in the first place through training in basic patterns of good conduct. Thus, just as one may not become a skilled performer on this or that musical instrument without practising the required instrumental techniques, so Aristotle holds that mature moral virtue needs to be grounded in early training in habits of honesty, self-control, courage, other-regard and so on. But it therefore follows that the good example of others – parents, guardians and teachers – must also play a large role in such training. However, such exemplification of good character may also be found in great art and literature – and Aristotle has much of importance to say in his *Poetics* (1941b) about the educational value of poetry for teaching good character. Last but not least, however, since a virtuous education cannot be reduced to mere training and imitation and involves all important cultivation of the critical judgement of *phronesis* or practical wisdom, it also seems to require a broad liberal education in which exposure to literature and arts may again strongly feature.

Before leaving this section, we should note the significant revival of Aristotelian and other virtue-focused ethics following the publication of a pioneering paper 'Modern moral philosophy' by the British philosopher Elizabeth Anscombe in 1958. In that paper, Anscombe launched a powerful attack on the Kantian and utilitarian moral philosophical orthodoxies of the day, advocating a return to an Aristotelian ethics of virtuous character. In the half century since the publication of Anscombe's paper, an enormous volume of literature has appeared devoted to the development of a wide variety of forms of virtue ethics – not all of which may be clearly (if at all) regarded as Aristotelian – to which we may here give only the briefest of attention. To begin with, there is the mainstream virtue ethics of Aristotle

(1941a) – revived by Anscombe (1958), Peter Geach (1977), and Philippa Foot (1978) and variously developed by such other philosophers as James Wallace (1978), Nicholas Dent (1984), Rosalind Hursthouse (1999), Martha Nussbaum (1988, 1995, 1996) – which seems broadly *naturalistic*: on this view, goodness or virtue is a beneficial natural property of human soul or agency. However, a somewhat different (though yet broadly Aristotelian) virtue ethics has been developed by John McDowell (1997) and others in the context of modern ethical realism, which defines virtue more in terms of correct perception of moral truth. But yet another development of Aristotle's ethics is also discernible in Nancy Sherman's (1989, 1997) attempt to reconcile an Aristotelian ethics of virtue with Kant's views on virtue, character and emotion.

However, other recently influential accounts of virtue have departed considerably, if not entirely, from Aristotle. Thus, although the highly influential virtue ethics of Alasdair MacIntyre (1981, 1988, 1992) certainly claims both Aristotle and Aquinas as key influences, this philosopher explicitly rejects the naturalistic approach of Aristotle (his so-called 'metaphysical biology') and proceeds on a more idealist or anti-realist basis – arguably owing as much to Hegel and Marx as to Aristotle. For MacIntyre, virtues are dispositions cultivated in the context of 'social practices' defined in terms of 'rival', if not incommensurable, moral traditions. Yet another recently influential account, evidently more related to care ethics – and probably owing much to the ethical 'sentimentalism' of Hume and others – has also been developed by Michael Slote (1983, 1992). Other distinctive perspectives on virtue have included the 'intrinsic consequentialism' of Thomas Hurka (2001) – which clearly relates, albeit critically, to the ethics of utility – and Catherine Swanton's (2003) 'pluralistic' virtue ethics which draws heavily (among others) on Nietzsche. This list is far from complete and other significant variants of virtue ethics have been developed that need not detain us here. That said, many of these virtue ethical alternatives have been criticized by the present author elsewhere (see Carr 2005) – largely in favour of more traditional Aristotelian naturalism. So, while it need not be denied that these diverse virtue ethical developments contain significant elements of ethical truth, the present view is that the best generally viable account of virtue is still to be found in some version of traditional Aristotelian naturalism.

Towards religious and other virtue education

At all events, the key present claim is that some form of (Aristotelian) virtue ethics gives us secure grounds for claiming that the promotion of moral character dispositions is a legitimate educational enterprise: to try to help children and young people to be more honest, self-controlled, fair or considerate persons is not a form of moral indoctrination (as teaching a specific set of moral beliefs might be) but a key task of schooling. However, in the present context, we need to look briefly at some remaining questions. One such question is that of what or which virtues should we aim to promote or cultivate. A second question is whether any such virtues have religious or spiritual dimensions – or, at least, whether some or all of these are of a character to which some acquaintance with religious views might significantly contribute. But a third question – one to which the rest of this work is more widely addressed – would precisely be the more practical one of how we might go about promoting or cultivating educationally significant virtues.

With regard to the first question, we can clearly make up lists of virtues until the cows come home and no two finite lists of virtues are likely to coincide completely. That said, as observed by philosophers from antiquity, it seems possible to regard more particular moral virtues as instances of broader general virtue types in recognition of certain common features of psychological structure or make-up. Thus, for one example, the sexual virtue of chastity has commonly been recognized as a form of temperance or self-control. For another example, more particular virtues of care and compassion might also be seen as instances of the more general social or other-regarding virtue of justice. For yet another example, the 'intellectual' virtue of practical wisdom – the virtue to which Socrates (and in a significant sense, Aristotle) saw all particular virtues as subservient – may be seen as exemplified in such more particular virtue traits as honesty, integrity and trustworthiness. From this viewpoint, it is arguable (see Carr 1988) that the four so-called 'cardinal' virtues of ancient Greek philosophy – namely wisdom, justice, courage and temperance – constitute the four main types of moral virtue to which all others might be in some sense or respect 'reduced'.

That said, it would seem that there is nothing especially religious – or even 'spiritual' – about wisdom, justice, courage and temperance, and certainly atheists may be as honest, fair, brave and self-controlled as any believers. Thus, if all particular virtues conform to these four types, it might seem to follow that virtues are in principle 'secular' and that considerations of spiritual or religious commitment are irrelevant to the formation of virtue. In this regard, however, it is of some interest that several key architects of modern virtue ethics – including, notably, Elizabeth Anscombe, Peter Geach and Alasdair MacIntyre – are Roman Catholics who have drawn on a virtue ethical tradition that specifically derives from Aristotle via St Thomas Aquinas (1984). One of the notable features of this 'Thomist' tradition is that it supplements the four cardinal virtues of the Greeks with three so-called 'theological' virtues first identified by St Paul in 1 Corinthians, chapter 13 as faith, hope and charity, or love. To be sure, there are particular problems about accommodating these candidate virtues within the mainstream Aristotelian tradition of virtue ethics. One is precisely that it is not clear whether one might give sufficiently broad interpretations of faith or hope that would render them relevant to those outside of particular faith communities (in which particular objects or goals of faith are specified). Another is that it is not clear how Aristotle's doctrine of the mean might apply to such virtues: can there, for example, be excesses or defects of faith or hope? On the other hand, the theological virtue of love (*agape* or *caritas*) would seem to be universalizable enough, as well as also – in so far as there are arguably excesses and defects of love – conformable to the doctrine of the mean. It is also at least an open question – as contributions to this volume try to demonstrate – whether there are not common or broader senses of faith and hope that might show these to be universally necessary human virtues.

In any case, it does not at all follow from the observation that there can be genuine virtue education outside of faith contexts – or which does not necessarily draw on religious inspiration – that the cultivation of virtues might not be considerably assisted by some acquaintance with the great spiritual traditions and narratives in which virtues of wisdom, courage, temperance, justice and love have been richly explored. From the fact that one might learn to be honest, fair or brave without having heard of Jesus or Buddha it does not follow that one's appreciation of honesty, justice or courage might not be greatly enhanced by study of such qualities in Christian and/or Buddhist narratives – as well as in more widely religiously influenced literature. Indeed, apart from the fact that it is well-nigh impossible to understand the provenance and development of (for example) western virtues and values without some knowledge of the specifically Christian tradition that has shaped them, it is all too readily overlooked in militant contemporary atheist haste to dismiss any and all things religious that while atheist creeds (such as social Darwinism, Fascism and communism) have often been responsible for much global moral corruption, evil and suffering, religious belief has often inspired the highest courage, selflessness and justice. Thus, while it cannot reasonably be part of our educational mission to convert pupils to Christianity, Islam or (for that matter) atheist Marxism, it should be appreciated that to deny young people access to some of the most powerful narratives of (religious) moral formation ever written is no less indoctrinatory than any uncritical confessional education. It is in recognition of this truth that this collection has been assembled.

References

Anscombe, G. E. M. (1958), 'Modern moral philosophy'. *Philosophy* 33: 1–19.
Aquinas, T. (1984), *Treatise on the Virtues*. Notre Dame: Notre Dame Press.
Aristotle (1941a), 'Nicomachean Ethics', in R. McKeon (ed.), *The Basic Works of Aristotle*. New York: Random House.
— (1941b), '*Poetics*', in R. McKeon (ed.), *The Basic Works of Aristotle*. New York: Random House.
Carr, D. (1988), 'The cardinal virtues and Plato's moral psychology'. *Philosophical Quarterly* 38: 186–200.
— (2005), 'On the contribution of literature to the educational cultivation of moral virtue, feeling and emotion'. *Journal of Moral Education* 34(2): 137–51.

— (2009), 'Virtue, mixed emotions and moral ambivalence'. *Philosophy* 84: 31–46.

Dent, N. J. H (1984), *The Moral Psychology of the Virtues*. Cambridge: Cambridge University Press.

Foot, P. (1978), *Virtues and Vices*. Oxford: Blackwell.

Geach, P. T. (1977), *The Virtues*. Cambridge: Cambridge University Press.

Hamilton, E. and Cairns, H. (eds) (1961), *Plato: The Collected Dialogues*. Princeton: Princeton University Press.

Hurka, T. (2001), *Virtue, Vice and Value*. Oxford: Oxford University Press.

Hursthouse, R. (1999), *On Virtue Ethics*. Oxford: Oxford University Press.

MacIntyre, A. C. (1981), *After Virtue*. Notre Dame: Notre Dame Press.

— (1988), *Whose Justice, Which Rationality?* Notre Dame: Notre Dame Press.

— (1992), *Three Rival Versions of Moral Enquiry*. Notre Dame: Notre Dame Press.

McDowell, J. (1997), 'Virtue and reason', in Crisp, R. and Slote, M. (eds), (1992) *Virtue Ethics*. Oxford: Oxford University Press.

Nussbaum, M. (1988), 'Non-relative virtues: An Aristotelian approach', in Nussbaum, M. C. and Sen, A. (eds), (1993), *The Quality of Life*. Oxford: Oxford University Press.

— (1995), 'Aristotle on human nature and the foundations of ethics', in J. E. J. Altham and R. Harrison (eds), *World, Mind and Ethics*. Cambridge: Cambridge University Press.

— (1996), 'Love and vision: Iris Murdoch on eros and the individual', in M. Antonaccio and W. Schweiker (eds), *Iris Murdoch and the Search for Human Goodness*. Chicago: University of Chicago Press.

Rousseau, J. -J. (1973), *The Social Contract and Other Discourses*. London: Dent.

Russell, B. (2004), *History of Western Philosophy*. London: Routledge.

Sherman, N. (1989), *The Fabric of Character: Aristotle's Theory of Virtue*. Oxford: Oxford University Press.

— (1997), *Making a Necessity of Virtue: Aristotle and Kant on Ethics*. Cambridge: Cambridge University Press.

Slote, M. (1983), *Goods and Virtues*. Oxford: Clarendon.

— (1992), *From Morality to Virtue*. New York: Oxford University Press.

Swanton, C. (2003), *Virtue Ethics: A Pluralistic View*. Oxford: Oxford University Press.

Wallace, J. D. (1978), *Virtues and Vices*. Ithaca, NY: Cornell University Press.

CHAPTER FOUR

The demise and rebirth of moral education in English Religious Education

L. Philip Barnes

CHAPTER OUTLINE

This chapter provides a genealogy of Religious Education in schools in Britain. In the process of adapting Religious Education in schools to an increasingly secular and multi-faith society, RE moved away from confessional RE and under the influence of *Working Paper 36* dissociated itself from the role of moral education. This was done on the supposition that morality was an autonomous area of study and independent of religion. The consequence was that RE was not only impoverished but became untrue to the religions themselves, which indisputably have moral and spiritual direction at their core. A form of secular RE has ultimately led to the reaction in one of Britain's major cities, Birmingham, to reconnect RE to this dimension of religious life as one of the means of uniting religious traditions in their common cause of enhancing personal and communal life.

In a recent study of curriculum development in English religious education, which adopts a case study approach, Stephen Parker and Rob Freathy (2011) traced the changing nature and content of religious education through a close analysis of successive Birmingham Agreed Syllabuses from the 1970s until the present, namely the 1975, 1995 and 2007 Syllabuses. In the context of their discussion they record how the 2007 Syllabus establishes a 'strong linkage between children's moral education and their RE', while noting that it is a linkage that has 'often been deliberately disassociated [by religious educators and others] from the 1960s onwards' (2011, p. 258). This is a perceptive observation by two highly respected historians of religious education in Britain. Unfortunately, the context militated against any expansion, justification or illustration of the way in which moral education first became detached from religious education in modern English education and now reaffirmed in its role and contribution to religious education by the most recent 2007 Birmingham Agreed Syllabus; it is this that the present chapter will attempt to do. My focus, however, is not chiefly historical, if by this is meant assembling the facts and identifying the historical steps whereby religious education and moral education, for the most part, went their separate ways and have now reconnected, rather it is genealogical, in Foucault's sense of that term – in this instance to uncover the beliefs and commitments that initiated and consolidated the separation of moral and religious education, albeit through their historical manifestation and sequence, and then their reconnection in the most recent Birmingham Agreed Syllabus.

How did the discourse of autonomous moral 'knowledge' come to displace and supplant religious interpretations of morality and religious morality in religious education? Our answer to this will naturally focus on intellectual and (to a lesser extent) social influences on English religious education, but it is also important to note that the secularization of morality within religious education is part of a wider process of secularization within both education and society generally. This wider narrative forms the backdrop and the inspiration for much that has happened historically in religious education from the late 1960s until the present: as, for example, in the work and writings of John Hull (e.g. 1992 and 2005), who pioneered a 'secular' approach to religious education, according to which all schools should 'reinterpret' confessional commitments on educational grounds and adopt secular norms on the basis of their inherently rational nature. Certainly, one of the reasons why moral education became disassociated from religious education is because a thoroughly secular form of discourse came to dominate discussion and debate in public institutions, including schools. This wider narrative of how, under the guise of rationality, 'the secular' has banished 'the religious' from English education, while relevant, unfortunately cannot receive the attention in this context that it deserves.

My argument is structured in the following way. First, attention is given to the 'modern' narrative of English religious education, whereby confessional religious education gave way to secular, non-confessional religious education; in this realignment, moral education eschewed a religious foundation and aspired to be fully rational, progressive and, of course, inclusive. Second, this narrative is complemented by a critical review of the different ways in which

the contribution of non-confessional religious education to moral education
has been conceptualized and practised. What this genealogical review reveals
is that the role of moral education in religious education, as envisaged by
educators from the 1970s until the present, has been largely procedural and
formal, and overlooks not only the moral content of the different religions
but much of the potential that religion brings to the enterprise of moral
education. In a third section, the negative thesis that religious education is
largely disassociated from moral education is further developed, qualified
and defended. Finally, attention is given to the 2007 Birmingham Agreed
Syllabus and its attempt to revive moral education, in the form of character
education, in English religious education.

The transition from confessional to non-confessional religious education

It is not necessary for our purposes to delve deeply into the institutional
history of confessional education, which dominated religious education in
British schools from the late nineteenth century (when the state committed
itself to public, 'elementary' schools) to the mid-1960s. At this point social
and political consensus on the educational appropriateness of confessional
religious education was beginning to break down (see Copley 2008, pp. 61–88),
against a backdrop of diminishing numerical support for institutional religion
(Bruce 1995; Brown 2001, pp. 170–92), widespread questioning of traditional
Christian beliefs and values, questioning often initiated by Christian theologians
themselves (e.g. Robinson 1963; Vidler 1966), and, chiefly as a result of post-
war immigration from former colonies, a growing awareness of the multi-faith
nature of modern Britain. Within the field of religious education critical voices
were also raised against the prevailing orthodoxy. Research seemed to indicate
that the staple diet of bible study and church history, so central to post-war
agreed syllabuses, was meeting with limited success in terms of capturing
pupils' interest in Christianity and in terms of advancing their understanding
and comprehension of basic Christian beliefs (Sheffield Institute of Education
1961; Goldman 1964).

Most religious educators accepted that change was necessary, but what
new direction should religious education take? A few, Brigid Brophy (1967)
and A. J. Ayer (1967, pp. 489–92), for example, argued for the abandonment
of the subject and its replacement with secular moral education (this is
somewhat ironic given the subsequent history and secular commitments of
post-confessional religious education, see below). Others argued for a more
'life-centred' (Hubery 1960) or 'experientially focused' form of religious
education (Loukes 1961). Loukes contended that religious education in
the secondary school should focus on moral issues that are relevant to
the life and experience of adolescents. The weakness in his proposals was

that they tacitly assumed the truth and normative value of Christianity, at a time when it was becoming increasingly difficult to maintain that publicly funded schools should commend and nurture Christian faith. As a consequence, Loukes's positive (and arguably educationally appropriate) call for religious education to focus on morality, while influential in the mid-1960s, was increasingly perceived as an interim solution. The 'solution', when it did appear, came in 1971, with the publication of *Working Paper 36: Religious Education in the Secondary School*, produced by the Schools Council, and written under the inspiration and direction of Professor Ninian Smart of Lancaster University (see Thompson 2003, pp. 35–46). *Working Paper 36* recommended a non-confessional, multi-faith approach to religious education that modelled itself on the academic discipline of the phenomenology of religion. Although much has subsequently been written on the strengths and weaknesses of a phenomenological approach to religious education, few commentators and interpreters have identified or explored its legacy or implications in relation to the contribution of religious education to moral education.

Working Paper 36 devotes just 4 pages to its discussion on 'religious education and moral education' (1971, pp. 67–71). The section begins with the comment that 'moral philosophers argue that the study of ethics and the study of religion are separate and distinct academic disciplines or areas of study' (WP 36, 1971, p. 67). Much that follows is appropriately described as footnotes to this assertion. The assertion, it may be granted, reflected the view of most moral philosophers at the time of writing. This is entirely to be expected. Moral philosophy is a sub-division within philosophy, and philosophy since the Enlightenment has asserted its independence of theology and religion. Philosophy traces its origins to the sixteenth century and the beginning of the process of the secularization of knowledge and of education (the writings of Hugo Grotius 1583–1645 may be cited as a convenient starting point for moral philosophy). In an important sense the *modus operandi* of moral philosophy is to describe and explain moral principles, beliefs and practices in non-religious terms; in other words, without recourse to religious beliefs and concepts. Moreover, in the 1960s and 1970s, particularly, many moral philosophers and philosophers of education worked under the assumption that ethical principles and rules can be stated (and derived) independently of metaphysical and ontological commitments. This was the heyday of conceptual and linguistic analysis, which following in the wake of Logical Positivism, still looked askance upon such commitments. By common philosophical consent it was accepted that morality is not derived from religion and religion does not (indeed cannot) provide a foundation for morality. Accordingly, moral education is an entirely secular undertaking, appealing (necessarily) to secular, non-religious norms of reason that govern behaviour.

Working Paper 36 simply reiterated (secular) philosophical orthodoxy about the relationship of religion to morality, though attention is given to explaining why religion and moral education have traditionally been linked: religions prescribe a code of behaviour; religion and morality have features in common, for each is concerned with attitudes and beliefs; Christian moral teaching is enshrined in the law in Britain (this of course is not the case now); and finally, 'the Christian Church has played a central role in the history and development of education in this country' (WP 36, 1971, p. 68). In other words, there are historical reasons why moral education and religious education have been linked in the imagination of the public and of politicians and educators. Nevertheless, according to *Working Paper 36*, there is no logical connection between religion and morality: 'Moral knowledge is autonomous' (p. 70) and 'morality is an autonomous area of study' (WP 36, 1971, p. 69).

Under the influence of *Working Paper 36* and its advocacy of a phenome-nological approach to religious education, English religious education began both to focus on explicitly religious phenomena (to the neglect the moral content of religion) and to conform what remained of the contribution of religious education to moral education to secular commitments and aspirations.

A genealogical account of the contribution of religious education to moral education

If religion cannot provide a foundation for morality, contrary to what most religious educators had formerly assumed, what contribution could religious education make to the moral and social aims of education? The answer (given the independence of morality from religion thesis) is that religious education may provide and encourage religious motivation for attitudes and actions that express values and beliefs that can claim an exclusively moral justification. On this understanding, religious education can support secular norms of behaviour in a variety of ways, say by reinforcing the point that the same norms of behaviour are demanded by God, or by noting that morally good behaviour is pleasing to God or that God will reward good behaviour, and so on. Within this framework the role of moral education within religious education is reconceived as endorsing those moral beliefs and values that are enjoined by secular approaches to moral education.

There are three basic models of the role of moral education in religious education that can be distinguished in the post-confessional history of religious education in Britain. Consistent with the commitments of phenomenological religious education and of secular moral philosophy all assign a diminished role to the moral content of religion and to the moral ambitions of religious education when compared with confessional religious education. Each in part represents a distinctive conception of morality and of the needs of society in relation to moral education in schools. The three models are historically successive in influence, though later models do not entirely eclipse the influence of earlier models.

The first form of moral education in religious education that succeeded confessional religious education can be characterized as the Multi-Cultural Model. While admitting greater internal diversity than the Christian-Cultural Model that it succeeded, it broadly viewed acquaintance with the diversity of religions as a means to develop tolerance, understanding and mutual respect among Britain's increasingly diverse cultural and religious population. One of the reasons given by *Working Paper 36* in favour of the adoption of a phenomenological approach by religious educators was the potential it was believed to hold for challenging discrimination and fostering positive relations between different individuals and communities. We are told that the phenomenological approach enables pupils to gain a 'sympathetic understanding of the inner life' of others (WP 36, p. 23), which in turn fosters an appreciation of religious difference. Accordingly, religious educators believed themselves to be contributing significantly to the creation of an inclusive society. In this form of moral education, religious education moved from prescribing specific forms of morality to commending acceptance of 'the religious Other'.

That the Multi-Cultural Model was less effective in combating religious intolerance than was anticipated, was beginning to be recognized by the late 1970s, and this, in part, along with increasing political and social awareness of the growing challenge of criminal and anti-social behaviour by young people, underlined the need for a more effective and significant role for religious education in the provision of moral education. Identified associations between spirituality and certain attitudes and dispositions that are regarded as conducive to positive conduct gave impetus to the emergence of (what can be called) a Spirituality Model of the contribution of religious education to moral education. The concept of spirituality was perceived as providing a number of advantages over the traditional emphasis upon the different world religions in religious education. First, the language of spirituality, with its inherent ambiguity, is more inclusive in range than the term religion and its cognates. This means both that non-religious forms of spirituality can be incorporated into religious education, and hence conceivably contribute to the moral education of non-religious pupils, and that religious education cannot be accused of favouring one religion over another, or indeed favouring religion over non-religious beliefs and values. Second, the concept and language of spirituality is thought by many religious educators to draw attention to non-dogmatic, experiential forms of religion (as in Hay with Nye 1998), which are viewed as inherently more tolerant and conducive to social harmony than doctrinal (dogmatic) forms of religion. Such an opinion reflects the liberal theological commitments that undergirds much post-confessional religious education in Britain; it also, unfortunately, in part, helps to perpetuate the tradition in modern English religious education of ignoring the controversial issue of competing religious truth claims in the classroom (see Barnes 2009); and raises the critical question whether such a strategy is appropriate in a cultural context where many people disagree fundamentally about religion: is ignoring this issue the best strategy? According to its supporters the Spirituality Model contributes to moral development by seeking to enhance the dispositions of love, sympathy and responsibility that (are believed to) provide the mainspring for moral action, while simultaneously refusing to elevate any particular morality or any particular moral stance over others. Critics, by contrast, point out that by favouring and perpetuating liberal forms of religion, spiritual development effectively overlooks the moral content of the different religions and concedes priority to secular morality in both the personal and public realms.

The third and final model of the relationship of moral education to religious education is the Civic Model. This emerged in the first decade of the early twenty-first century, subsequent to the introduction of citizenship as a school subject by the then Labour Government (the Citizenship Order of 2000). According to this model, public education should be concerned with the creation of good citizens and not with the private lives and behaviour of individuals. What matters is adherence to the law. The law, *per se*, is not concerned with personal morality (often disparagingly referred to as 'private' morality) but with social morality. A 'good' citizen obeys the laws of the land and respects the rights of others. A number of religious educators, Mark Chater (2000), for example, have claimed that religious education provides an ideal vehicle for furthering the citizenship agenda.

The Civic Model, however, has a number of serious weaknesses. (In this context, problems relating to the epistemological and ontological status of rights will be overlooked; see Warnock 1998, pp. 54–74.) The first weakness questions the assumption that a focus within religious education upon social responsibility and citizenship, without attention to issues of personal morality and 'private' virtue, is likely to yield the desired improvements in public morality (construed as obedience to the law) and political participation. A plausible empirical case can be made for the view that those who are socially responsible are precisely the same people who adhere to high standards of personal morality. Personal behaviour and social responsibility are related, for morality is of a piece. Furthermore, it is the personal aspects of morality that provide the foundation for social morality: it is the commitments, values, beliefs and positive emotions that are cultivated and educated in the immediate and wider family, and subsequently reinforced by social situations and institutions that for the most part determine the character and practice of social responsibility. To ask schools to attend to social responsibility and to overlook its foundation in personal morality is to misconceive the nature of morality; and consequently to risk disappointment when the focus in schools on social morality alone fails to translate into increasing levels of social responsibility.

The second weakness relates to the observation that a rights-based approach to moral education provides only a minimum level of moral commitment, and that this level of moral commitment falls short of what is required for a stable, cohesive and respectful society. There is a clear distinction between what is good for individuals and for society and the legal and moral rights that individuals enjoy. For example, a society in which both parents took long-term responsibility for the well-being of their children would be a better society (overall) than one in which many children are born into single-parent households or households where the mother has serial, short-term (personally irresponsible) partners, given that statistics show the devastating effects on children of being brought up in such contexts (see Social Justice Policy Group 2006). Furthermore, not all immoral acts and instances of bad or irresponsible behaviour are regarded as criminal offences (or matters of public morality in the strict sense of attracting formal disadvantage or punishment). As a society we choose to enshrine some 'goods' in legislation, say unfair dismissal from work or a right to education, and allow individuals to choose other goods for themselves, say the viewing of pornography or the right to smoke in one's own home. We criminalize some activities in (British) society, say prostitution (which some other societies legalize and regulate), but allow married individuals to divorce or to pursue extramarital sexual liaisons if they so choose. The simple point is that the existence of a right may not necessarily mean that the right ought (morally) to be exercised. The existence of a right does not guarantee the morality of its exercise. To have a right to divorce does not mean that divorce is a good thing or that it yields positive effects for children or for society at large, though on occasions it may be the lesser of two evils. The realm of rights is not identical with the realm of morality and moral goodness (though there is overlap). The rights you enjoy as a citizen should not all be exercised and some certainly may be exercised in pursuits of dubious moral worth that are detrimental to society at large. If this is the case, then citizenship education with its orientation to rights is necessarily inadequate as a vehicle for creating a good society for all. A society in which everyone is extended courtesy and respect by others will be a better society than the one in which this does not occur; yet the kind of courtesy and respect that most people would like to receive cannot be legally required. Basically, a good society where individuals and communities are valued and respected is a society that requires the practice of a much 'thicker' conception of morality (see Williams 1985, pp. 140–3) than that required by adherence to and observance of human rights. If religious education is to contribute to the creation of a good society, where communities live harmoniously with each other, it needs to contribute to the development of personal and social virtues in pupils that extend beyond the realm of legally mandated morality of the form consistent with the observance of human rights. In other words, if religious education is serious about its commitment to the development of toleration and respect for others, it must extend its moral and social aspirations beyond the (narrow) realm of rights and their observance. To recast the social aims of religious education in terms of 'respect' for human rights alone is effectively to overlook much of the potential religious education brings to moral education.

Refining and defending the argument

Part of the legacy of non-confessional religious education in England is ambiguity about the role of religion (and of course religious education) in moral education. On the one hand, under phenomenology, religious education was relieved of the 'burden' of moral education; whereas on the other hand, the focus on explicitly religious phenomena, to the exclusion of a consideration of moral issues and the moral content of religion, led to disinterest among pupils. Under phenomenology, religious educators gained confidence in the belief that their subject demarcated a distinctive area of content in the curriculum, yet this confidence was eroded by recognition that in an increasingly secular and multi-cultural society the worth of religious education in schools is often judged by its contribution to the wider moral and social aims of education and the needs of the community. As phenomenological religious education was refined and complemented by other methodologies, so principled (if mistaken, see below) distinctions that divorced religious education from moral education came to be qualified and blurred. Theoretically, religious education was distinct from moral education; practically, it committed itself to the shifting moral and social agenda of the liberal nation state in efforts to ensure its educational relevance and continuing compulsory status in the curriculum. This contradiction lies at the heart of English religious education in its relationship to moral education and explains why we have the 'anomalous' situation where religious education, despite its theoretical stance, purports to contribute to the moral aims of education, while overlooking the moral content and teachings of the different religions.

It is the contradictory nature of the commitment of religious education to moral education and the tension between theory and practice, rather than disagreement over its actual (empirical) contribution to moral education (though this issue does have to be factored in as well), that chiefly explains the existence of opposing and contrary interpretations of the relationship of religious education to moral education. Let me illustrate: David Hargreaves in *The Mosaic of Learning* (1994) recommended that religious education should not be compulsory in state-maintained schools because, *inter alia*, religious education no longer makes a contribution or views itself as intending to make a contribution to moral education. Interestingly, he also advocated the creation of new faith schools where moral education would be explicitly linked to the religious tradition of the school. This position is in direct opposition to the oft-repeated 'official' narrative of many RE organizations, the Religious Education Council of England and Wales, for example, which presents the view that post-confessional English religious education makes a uniquely positive contribution to the social and moral aims of education.

Any argument that identifies a schizophrenic attitude towards moral education at the heart of religious education in England will obviously attract criticism from religious educators. Objections will naturally focus on questioning the contention that post-confessional religious education largely abdicated its responsibility for the moral education and moral development of pupils. A number of objections along these lines will be considered, and in the process of responding, my argument (at this point) will be further clarified and refined.

Some critics of the view that the moral contribution of the different religions to moral education has largely been overlooked may point out that Ninian Smart combined his support of phenomenological religious education with a dimensional account of the nature of religion which identified an ethical (or moral) dimension alongside five other dimensions: the ritual, experiential, mythic, doctrinal, and social dimensions (in later writings he added the material dimension). Furthermore, in the curricular materials produced by the Schools Council Project on Religious Education in the Secondary School, which Smart directed, some attention is given to moral issues and the moral dimension of religion. These observations, however, are not particularly telling. The point is that the disassociation of religious education from moral education is consistent with the assumptions and commitments of the phenomenological approach to religious education, as it is also consistent with the teaching of the phenomenology of religion, which, in part, traces its origins to Liberal Protestant opposition to Kant's notion of religion as a postulate of pure practical (moral) reason (see Barnes, 2013). In keeping with this, as the phenomenological approach gained ascendancy in schools during the 1970s, so the focus of religious education increasingly came to be upon explicitly religious material, with little attention or seriousness attached to the moral teachings of the different religions. This judgement is confirmed by reference to the locally produced agreed syllabuses of religious education that were produced in the 1970s and 1980s, most of which adopted and commended a phenomenological methodology. If the contribution of religious education to moral education is defined in traditional terms of acquainting pupils with the moral teaching of the different religions and in exploring the moral beliefs and values of religion as they relate to contemporary moral and social issues, or in presenting to pupils a vision of the form a moral life might take when religiously sanctioned and inspired, then clearly judged in these terms religious education has disassociated itself from moral education. One further piece of evidence that supports the view that moral concerns and moral education became peripheral to religious education with the rise of the phenomenological approach is that by the 1980s some religious educators were already beginning to question its appropriateness on the grounds that it neglected the personal and moral dimensions of education, as well as ignoring the pupil's quest for meaning and significance (see Cox 1983, pp. 131–5; Slee 1989, pp. 130–1).

A more serious challenge to the contention that non-confessional religious education largely renounced its role in moral education is that it is not that religious education renounced its role but rather that it redefined and reconceptualized its role in moral education. Moreover, is this not the true position of Smart, for although he argued that moral education should be a separate school subject from religious education (because morality is independent of religion), he also believed that multi-faith phenomenological religious education challenged religious intolerance and fostered positive attitudes to religious diversity? According to this narrative, religious education has been in the forefront of championing moral issues in education. Is this not what our genealogical review of the relationship of religious education to moral education reveals? There are two issues here: one empirical, the other conceptual and interpretative.

Is there any evidence to show that religious education has been successful in achieving the moral and social aims of education? Unfortunately, we do not have any direct evidence, chiefly, because the relevant research has not been undertaken and because there are conceptual matters relating to such research that are not easily resolved. There is some evidence, however, that is relevant, though difficult to access. In 2004, Dr Penny Jennings conducted a large-scale questionnaire survey of pupils' attitudes towards RE across a range of spiritual and moral issues in state-maintained secondary schools in Cornwall. The questionnaires were completed by 3,826 pupils (1,962 from Year 9 and 1,861 from Year 10) from 24 schools (i.e. over three-quarters of the total number) that are representative of the different variables that obtain in Cornwall's secondary schools; thus making this one of the largest surveys conducted into pupil attitudes and values in Britain. Her findings with regard to pupils' attitudes towards the moral aspects of RE are not encouraging. In response to the statement 'RE helps me to find rules to live by', 14 per cent responded positively, 60 per cent responded negatively and 26 per cent of pupils were unsure; in response to the statement 'RE helps me to sort out my problems', 8 per cent responded positively, 73 per cent responded negatively and 19 per cent of pupils were unsure; and finally, to the statement 'RE helps me to lead a better life', 9 per cent only responded positively, 68 per cent responded negatively and 23 per cent of pupils were unsure. What is the most reasonable explanation of these findings? There are two possibilities, both of which can be regarded as lending support to the thesis that post-confessional religious education is disassociated from moral education and the moral development of pupils: either religious education aims to contribute significantly to the moral development of pupils, but for the most part fails, or religious education does not aim (or at least is not perceived by pupils) to contribute to their moral development. To this may be added statistics that show that there are high levels of drug and alcohol abuse and criminal and anti-social behaviour (at least high compared with statistics for the 1960s) among young adults (see Social Justice Policy Group 2006). We also know that mental health problem, depression and suicide among the young remain at stubbornly high levels (Scowcrof 2012). How such statistics can be related to education and the influence or otherwise of moral education in schools is another matter. What can be said with some degree of confidence is that the moral influence on pupils of religious education is not all that obvious and what evidence there is does not inspire confidence in the moral achievements of religious education. In one sense this should not surprise us, given our genealogical review of models of moral education in religious education and the range of weaknesses there identified. Non-confessional religious education, in all probability, contributes little to the moral development of pupils because it pursues largely ineffective and conceptually flawed policies.

Attention to our genealogical review of the different post-confessional models of moral education in religious education also reveals a further disquieting feature that reinforces our earlier point that religious education largely overlooks the moral teaching and traditions of the different religions. Attention to the aims of the different models of moral education in religious education shows that they are extrinsic to the actual content of religion. There is no intrinsic connection between the content of religious education and the moral aims religious educators seek to realize. The religion of Christianity may be used to illustrate this. The moral and spiritual aims of Christianity do not centre on producing good citizens or on encouraging reflection on spiritual matters; instead they focus on the need for Christians to emulate the character of Christ and to practise justice and righteousness. Christian spirituality begins with recognition that individuals become acceptable to God by virtue of his grace and that moral obedience without faith in God is, in religious terms, not efficacious. Christian spirituality and morality are concerned with inspiring and encouraging those who trust in Christ for their salvation to obey the moral precepts of the New Testament. It is not that Christians are unspiritual or make poor citizens; it is that Christian spirituality and morality centre on loyalty to God, not on loyalty to the nation state and its evolving legal norms. The wider point is that when religious education pursues moral aims and seeks to contribute to the moral development of pupils it fails to connect with the actual beliefs and values of the different religions that are the proper subject matter of religious education. More critically, when religious education pursues moral education, religion is reduced to a set of formal moral principles that mirror secular morality and the shifting social concerns of the nation state. Religious beliefs and values are instrumental to the aims of secular moral education. Basically, religious morality is not allowed to speak its own voice in education but is required to mirror the truncated 'moral' aims of the secular state.

Religious education can claim to pursue moral aims, but this terse way of putting things disguises the fact that the moral aims it aspires to realize are entirely secular and have little to do with religion. Moreover, the formal and procedural nature of the modern aims of moral education, has almost nothing to do with morality or moral development, as traditionally understood, but instead have to do with 'respecting' the autonomy of others and keeping the laws of society. This I believe is a truncated understanding of the aims appropriate to moral education, but it is not a judgement that can be adequately defended in this context; what can be done however, is to give an indication of the positive (and not simply procedural) contribution religious education can make to moral education.

The rebirth of moral education in English religious education

How can the schizophrenic stance towards moral education at the heart of religious education in England be overcome? The first step is to reconnect religious education with moral education in a fully principled and educationally justified way. Two possibilities suggest themselves. The first strategy is to take up the point that one of the central aims of religious education is to understand the nature of religion. What it is to understanding a religion is not uncontroversial, but whatever form a broad ranging account takes, it must include an appreciation of the way (or ways) that religious adherents interpret their respective traditions and beliefs; and clearly religious adherents connect their beliefs and values to practices and behaviour that embrace and express moral commitments. Each of the religions has a vision of the good both for the individual and for society; each of the religions has a historically evolving body of moral teachings; and each of the religions has made important responses to contemporary moral issues. The legacy of those who held to the independence of morality from religion and reduced religious education to 'explicitly religious content' must be challenged. Why should secularists have the right to conform representations of religion in religious education to their secular commitments? There may even be a case for concluding that because secular commitments enjoy unopposed dominance in all other aspects of the curriculum, in religious education the primacy of the believer's perspective in the study of religion should be privileged (though not in such a way to exclude critical engagement and evaluation of religious truth claims).

The second strategy is to note that the view that morality and religion are ontologically separate no longer commands the same degree of philosophical support as it once did. Over the last thirty years or so there has been a revival of a range of different divine command theories of ethics among analytical philosophers (Adams 1999; Quinn 1978). Theists need not necessarily accept (and can muster good philosophical reasons for rejecting) the secular thesis that religion and morality are independent. Where there are no clear uncontroversial philosophical arguments to show that morality and religion are separate, it would be contrary to the spirit of inclusion and equality to limit the contribution of religious education to moral education to what those who separate the two consider in keeping with their particular prejudices.

The next step in overcoming the schizophrenic stance of religious education towards moral education is to recognize the educational advantages that may result from a rediscovered focus on religious morality and religious responses to moral issues in religious education. It is widely appreciated that by neglecting moral issues, under the influence of the phenomenology of religion, the subject lost much of its relevance to young people; though subsequently, to some extent, some religious educators have made efforts to reinstate the moral content of religion in religious education. The weakness in much of this, as we have already noted, is that this content is viewed as instrumental to secular moral aims and thus there is often a failure to engage fully and constructively with the moral traditions and visions of the different religions. The problem is that there is no intellectual framework currently available that properly justifies the inclusion of moral education in religious education. The proposals that are developed here are intended to provide such a framework. The chief educational advantage, however, of reconnecting religious education with moral education, and fully engaging with the moral content of religion, is the potential that the subject brings to the moral development of pupils. This is why the 2007 Birmingham Agreed Syllabus of Religious Education holds so much promise for the future direction of religious education. The syllabus aims to contribute to the development of both pupils and communities, not in the abstract way favoured by the National Framework (2004),[1] but by specifying the dispositions in pupils that are to be developed and then showing how the attainment of these dispositions can be furthered by reference to the teachings of the different religions.

What is distinctive and innovative about the Birmingham syllabus is that it specifies twenty-four different qualities or 'dispositions' that pupils should develop in religious education: these dispositions include, among others, being thankful, being fair and just, sharing and being generous, and being open, honest and truthful, being courageous and confident. The real strength of this focus upon the precise dispositions that are to be developed is that each disposition is linked to religious content from different traditions, as appropriate to the four key school stages. Moreover, this emphasis upon dispositions heralds a move away from the narrow focus upon intellectual development in British religious education to a wider focus on developing the whole person – intellect, emotions and attitudes. The syllabus aims to contribute to the personal and social development of pupils through the use of explicitly religious material. This overcomes the objection that the content of religion is extrinsic to the moral aims of education. Furthermore, by focusing on the qualities and dispositions of character, that is, by showing how religions can contribute to the development of persons that are honest, truthful, charitable, and so on, pupils will have the opportunity to engage with the moral claims of religion and the challenge of becoming 'a religious person'.

The chief emphasis of this chapter has been on identifying and considering the beliefs and commitments that initiated the historical disassociation of English religious education from moral education, and on the continuing influence of these commitments in subsequent reinterpretations of the role of religious education in moral education. While much of what is said is critical, the overall aim has been positive, namely to make a plausible case for the continuing relevance of religious education to the moral development of pupils and to provide an outline of the kind of intellectual framework that religious education needs to espouse if it is to reaffirm its role and contribution to moral education. The 2007 Birmingham Agreed Syllabus of Religious Education provides one interesting and stimulating example of what religious education looks like when it explores and exploits the content of religion for moral purposes in a way that is educationally appropriate yet faithful to the nature of religion. The remaining chapters in this book illustrate in detail the potential that an approach based on the cultivation of dispositions can bring to religious education as a force for good, both for individuals and for communities.[2]

Notes

1   For a comparison of the Birmingham syllabus and the National Framework, see Penny Thompson's article, 'She made me think about God'. *Journal of Beliefs and Values* 32(2): 195–205.

2   A small number of paragraphs in this chapter are taken from my 'What has morality to do with religious education?' *Journal of Beliefs and Values* 32(2): 131–41.

References

Adams, R. M. (1999), *Finite and Infinite Goods*. Oxford: Oxford University Press.

Ayer, A. J. (1967), in Department of Education and Science, *Children and their Primary Schools*. London: HMSO.

Barnes, L. P. (2009), *Religious Education: Taking Religious Difference Seriously*. London: Philosophy of Education Society of Great Britain.

— (2013) 'Values and the Phenomenology of Religion', in J. Arthur and T. Lovat (eds), *International Handbook of Religion and Values*. London: Routledge.

Brophy, B. (1967), *Religious Education in State Schools*. London: Fabian Society.
Brown, C. (2001), *The Death of Christian Britain: Understanding Secularisation 1800–2000*. London: Routledge.
Bruce, S. (1995), *Religion in Modern Britain*. Oxford: Oxford University Press.
Chater, M. (2000), 'To teach is to set free: Liberation theology and the democratisation of the citizenship agenda'. *British Journal of Religious Education* 23(1): 5–14.
City of Birmingham Agreed Syllabus Conference (2007), The Birmingham Agreed Syllabus for Religious Education. Online. Available http: http://www.faithmakesadifference.co.uk (accessed 5 March 2012).
Cox, E (1983), *Problems and Possibilities for Religious Education*. London: Hodder and Stoughton.
Copley, T. (2008), *Teaching Religion: Sixty Years of Religious Education in England and Wales*. Exeter: University of Exeter Press.
Goldman, R. J. (1964), *Religious Thinking from Childhood to Adolescence*. London: Routledge and Kegan Paul.
Hargreaves, D. (1994), *The Mosaic of Learning*. London: Demos.
Hay, D. with Nye, R. (1998), *The Spirit of the Child*. London: Fount.
Hubery, D. (1960), *The Experiential Approach to Christian Education*. London: National Sunday School Union.
Hull, J. M. (1992), *Studies in Religion and Education*. Lewes: Falmer Press.
— (2005), 'Religious education in Germany and England: the recent work of Hans Georg Ziebertz'. *British Journal of Religious Education* 27(1): 5–17.
Jennings, P. (2004), Cornwall Religious Education Survey 2004: Final Report. Online. Available HTTP: http://www.cornwallhumanists.org.uk/survey04.htm (accessed 5 March 2012).
Loukes, H. (1961), *Teenage Religion*. London: SCM Press.
Parker, S. and Freathy, R. (2011), 'Context, complexity and contestation: Birmingham's Agreed Syllabuses for Religious Education since the 1970s'. *Journal of Beliefs & Values* 32(2): 247–63.
Qualifications and Curriculum Authority (2004), *Religious Education: Non-Statutory National Framework*. London: QCA.
Quinn, P. (1978), *Divine Commands and Moral Requirements*. Oxford: Clarendon Press.
Robinson, J. (1963), *Honest to God*. London: SCM Press.
Schools Council (1971), *Working Paper 36: Religious Education in the Secondary School*. London: Evans/Methuen Educational.
Scowcrof, E. (2012), Samaritans: Suicide Statistics Report. Online. Available http: http://www.samaritans.org/pdf/Suicide%20Statistics%20Report%202012.pdf (accessed 5 March 2012).
Sheffield Institute of Education (1961), *Religious Education in Secondary Schools: A Survey and a Syllabus*. London: Nelson.
Slee, N. (1989), 'Conflict and reconciliation between competing models of religious education: Some reflections on the British scene'. *British Journal of Religious Education* 11(3): 126–35.
Social Justice Policy Group (2006), Fractured Families. Online. Available http: http://www.centreforsocialjustice.org.uk/client/downloads/BB_family_breakdown.pdf (accessed 5 March 2012).

Thompson, P. (2003), *Whatever Happened to Religious Education?* Cambridge: Lutterworth Press.
Vidler, A. R. (1966), *Soundings: Essays concerning Christian Understanding*. Cambridge: Cambridge University Press.
Warnock, M. (1998), *An Intelligent Person's Guide to Ethics*. London: Duckworth.
Williams, B. (1985), *Ethics and the Limits of Philosophy*. London: Fontana.

PART TWO
Dispositions

CHAPTER FIVE

Being honest

foundational

Brenda Watson

CHAPTER OUTLINE

This chapter pursues the theme of honesty and related dispositions such as openness, truthfulness, being reflective, self-critical and modest. It examines these dispositions from the key perspective of search for truth in a plural society. It develops the argument that sound appreciation and application of these values depends on three more fundamental dispositions being in place. Critical affirmation in relation to the beliefs of others and awareness of human limitation should encourage reticence in relation to one's own beliefs about God, beliefs which can never fully comprehend the being of God. It concludes with reference to the role of religion in developing these dispositions.

The dispositions discussed in this chapter focus upon the importance of maintaining personal and intellectual integrity within a welcoming and generous-minded approach to others. The ability to do this within a pluralist environment is essential. As Michael Grimmitt (2010, p. 19) put it in the book he edited on *Religious Education (RE) and Social Cohesion*, 'The task of creating trust, mutual respect and cooperation between people holding many different viewpoints is an ambitious agenda for any society to contemplate but it is one to which RE can make a small but significant contribution.'

RE can indeed make quite a major contribution if it demonstrates what Andrew Wright (2010, p. 143) noted as crucial: 'to explore alternative faith traditions in a sympathetic and critical manner – especially by addressing questions of ultimate truth and truthful living in relation to the ultimate order-of-things'. Such an RE would be, as Matthew Thompson (2010, p. 145) expresses it, 'grounded in a spirit of humility, which facilitates the reflective honesty and heart-opening necessary to embrace the challenges of a multi-cultural and multi-faith society.'

Speaking from his experience in Northern Ireland, Norman Richardson (2010, p. 227) adds the importance of learning to live with uncertainty and differences that cannot be resolved. 'Religious learning must engage children both intellectually and affectively, helping them . . . to learn ways of living peacefully with life's many uncertainties and differences'. He notes that 'This process needs to start early in the school years if it is to become part of natural attitude development, informed by expanding knowledge and experience; it is too important to be left "until they are older."' Therefore the substance of this chapter is as relevant to teaching at Key Stage 1 as at Key Stage 4. Ways need to be found to engage even young children with this kind of approach.

> Do you agree that learning to accept uncertainty and differences needs to start at a very young age? If it does not, what problems are likely to emerge?

Difficulty with words

This chapter brings together an interesting cluster of words that can have very different resonances for people. *Openness*, for example, is very definitely today a hurrah-word, while *modesty* is in many quarters almost a boo word; yet here they are in the same group of desirable dispositions. Such words can easily be misinterpreted. On the surface they may even look like a recipe for vulnerability, self-doubt, even spinelessness.

Open: Having no convictions, being susceptible to any influence that happens to be around.
Honest: Simplistic, naive like a child.
Truthful: Saying what one really thinks whatever the likely impact on others.
Reflective: Putting off actually doing anything, time-wasting.
Self-critical: Implying self-doubt, apologizing for oneself.
Modest: Low profile, allowing others to write the agenda.

Listening to others: Assuming that one has nothing to contribute in conversation, thinking others much better than oneself.

Why are these not appropriate interpretations? It may be helpful to consider them in relation to their opposites. Words gain their significance within concrete situations in reaction to what is happening. The importance of *openness* has arisen within the context of many different beliefs being in close proximity in such a way that none can take dominance for granted. As a Muslim, Abdullah Sahin speaks of the necessity in such a situation for *taaruf* 'knowing and learning from one another'. What this means is well expressed by him: 'living in the face of each other requires reconsidering one's world view and recognizing, with humility, the limits of one's identity and the presence of the other in one's self-understanding. This challenging contextual reality could also facilitate a positive outcome: the gift of openness to one another.'

This gift of openness is far from easy. Being truly open and holding strong commitment requires both honest engagement with others in really relating to them, and much reflection and capacity for self-criticism combined with a willingness to change. All listening involves a widening of experience and the need to review one's own convictions and how they are expressed so as to be part of a wider picture. The sociologists, Peter Berger and Anton Zijderveld (2009, p. 31) point out: 'It's a given that, if we want to avoid change, we'd better be very careful as to the people we talk with.' Change can be uncomfortable and the real temptation is not to do this but go for the easy option of rigid adherence to what one already thinks; then, whoever thinks differently can be regarded as simply wrong.

For Sahin (2010, p. 166f) commitment and openness, so far from being opposed, belong together. 'Openness does not mean an unconditional subscription to a different life style for that would mean assimilation; openness means, rather, a critical awareness about one's core values and the felt need to be in continuous dialogue with the other. The alternatives to critical openness are either the emergence of minority ghettos or the dominant group's expectation of assimilation.' Thus openness properly stands for the opposite of closed-mindedness, obsession, dogmatism or arrogance.

What the other words properly signify becomes clearer by listing their opposites.

Honest: NOT self-deception or pretence.
Truthful: NOT duplicity, conveying half-truths, deceiving others.
Reflectiveness: NOT impulsive, unthinking, conditioned.
Self-critical: NOT bumptious, self-important, massaging a large ego.
Modest: NOT pushy, throwing ones weight around.
Listening to others: NOT holding the hog, uninterested in what others can contribute, shutting people up.

This understanding of the dispositions is aided by acknowledging that they all need each other; they are inter-dependent. The way to *openness* is via *honesty* to oneself, trying not to pretend or live by second-hand opinions. It is also via *listening to others* which requires both the capacity for *self-criticism* and *modesty*. Above all, openness requires us to be *reflective* and concerned with *truthfulness* in the sense of passionately caring about truth.

Yet are there not times when these values should not be practised? Honesty or transparency in what we communicate to others is hugely important in developing trust between people. Yet should we not sometimes refrain from simply telling the truth if it could be damaging for others to hear it? 'Better a lie that heals than a truth that wounds', as the proverb puts it. Naivety should not be part of the game. Complete honesty is impossible anyway because there is so much that could be said! Moreover, honesty depends on a great deal of self-understanding, as Virginia Woolf (1848) noted: 'If you cannot tell the truth about yourself you cannot tell it about other people'. John Ruskin's comment (1867) is thought provoking: 'To make your children *capable of honesty* is the beginning of education'.

> 'Honesty is a vice if it interferes with proper compassion or humility or respect.' Christopher Bennett, *Ethics*. Routledge, (2010, p. 101) Do you agree?

Similar points can be made regarding the other dispositions. Little is said about modesty, for example, in what the Qualification and Curriculum Authority (QCA) in Britain (2007) advises as the purpose of education to create 'successful learners, confident individuals, and responsible citizens'. Assertiveness training can be hugely important for some people who might otherwise be in danger of becoming doormats to others. Sex-grooming cases offer a horrific but obvious example of the virtue of standing up for oneself and refusing to be compliant with other people's agendas unless those agendas are sound and supportive. There is nothing that bullies like better than over-modest people who doubt they have much to offer in their own right.

Modesty is also unhelpful when it results in inaction, failing to say what would be helpful. For each person to play a proper role in society, using their gifts, it is important that they should not be shrinking lilies! Self-assertiveness needs balancing with modesty according to circumstances.

Discernment is called for, but on what basis can this develop? These values do not in themselves offer a firm-enough foundation in that they are not absolute, fundamental or universally applicable. They are pointers only as to how we should behave if circumstances permit; they depend upon many other factors being considered and held in balance. We need to consider what really is absolute, fundamental and universally applicable.

Fundamental dispositions upon which secondary dispositions depend for sound application

1. Concern for truth

Andrew Wright (2007) has noted that 'The quest for truthful living is bound up with the pursuit of truth'. But the very word *truth* has become a problem. Many people have learnt to be wary of truth claims because of the ease with which they can become an excuse for intransigence, hostility, even violence. In the name of tolerance people have been encouraged to fight shy of the notion, as discussed in Chapter 2.

Furthermore, post-modernist thinking has virtually abolished the concept of truth as hopelessly unattainable. It sees especially institutional truth-claiming as little more than power politics – a way for people to maintain their ownership, status and sense of being right. Mostly such dogmatism creeps up on people unaware. Caught up in the excitement of what they believe, and the infectious sense of belonging to a dedicated group, they do not learn much self-knowledge. Many others again are simply the products of fundamentalist-style traditions in which it is much the easiest thing not to challenge what they have been brought up to believe.

Post-modernism is nevertheless highly challengeable in seeking to dismiss the possibility of truth. It is both contradictory and hypocritical, for there is no way that the claim that there is no truth can escape from itself being a truth-claim. Nor will the truth about reality simply go away; mistakes and false beliefs can only be perceived as such on the basis of what appears more truthful. In practice, denouncing one meta-narrative as false is based on trusting another meta-narrative as true. Thus dismissing all religious truth-claims is based on confessional belief in the truth of another explanation for reality, for example, secularist humanism.

> Why do you suppose it is easier to be critical than to recognize what may be beneficial and positive in other people's commitments in life?

A fear of taking the search for truth seriously impinges on the meaning to be given to the values of *honest* and *truthful*. The all-pervasiveness of the fact/belief divide discussed in Chapter 2 discourages concern for the truth or otherwise of what is said in favour of the importance only of the speaker's authenticity. This has tended to happen particularly in the arts where the truthful moral content of a work of art is frequently not considered at all but only the creative originality of the artist. This is illustrated in the controversial appointment in 2011 of Tracey Emin as Professor of Drawing at the Royal Academy, London.

It has, however, even afflicted the sciences. The Climategate hacked e-mail scandal at the University of East Anglia (UEA) in England brought to light in 2009 offers an instructive example. These e-mails revealed attempts to prevent scientific data questioning the reality of man-made global warming from being released. All agree that keeping back data suggesting a contrary opinion to the official line was not being open, honest or truthful, but what this meant regarding the reliability of the truth claims being thus defended by such devious tactics by professional scientists was notably absent in the public response. On the contrary, great pains were taken to ensure that the fundamental question of the truth or otherwise of humanly induced climate change was not raised.

The official public enquiry clearing the UEA scientists was far from independent, being chaired by someone with financial interests in low-carbon energy production. Moreover, the questionable behaviour of politicized scientists to which Christopher Booker (2009) has drawn attention has received no serious public debate. The latest Climategate (2011) concerning e-mails between the BBC and the UEA indeed reveals the media becoming, in the name of science, partisan.

Mike Hulme (2009), UEA Professor of Climate Change, had already provided an argument in defence of such collusion. He claimed that we must move beyond 'normal' science to post-modernist science which 'must trade truth for influence'. Thus lying becomes justified if in a good cause – or what the person doing the lying thinks is a good cause. This is a truly dangerous path to take. Goebbels's declaration, 'Truth is what serves the German people', is a chilling example of dishonesty in a supposedly good cause, enabling malign manipulation of others and almost certainly also, in the end, self-deception. The fascinating point about Goebbels' assertion is that in one sense it is profoundly true. It is the truth that can set everyone, not just the German people, free. As the dissident Havel so often quoted Huss: 'Truth will prevail.' All depends, however, on integrity in seeking truth in the first place.

> If a controversial view is expressed to which someone says 'that's just your opinion' or 'I know where you are coming from', why is this avoiding the truth? Think of other ways in which people avoid truth and consider the serious consequences.

Regarding fear of dogmatism, the crucial point to realize is that it is not concern for truth that is dangerous, but the notion that I/we have the truth. A simple desire to find out and live by what in fact is true, real or actual is crucially to be distinguished from either the possessive, disguised lust for power on the one hand or the desire for an easy life untroubled by doubt of any kind on the other hand. The ability to make this distinction is vital. Those who say they 'have' the truth are possessive towards it, treating it as their property. In the end it is perhaps not truth that such people care about, but being right.

RE should help people avoid dogmatism. The secularist route of doing so by not bothering about truth claims is not an option, for we cannot avoid making truth claims; it matters very much in every area of life that, so far as possible, we move nearer to truth rather than further away from it.

2. Respect for all other people

The word 'all' is crucial here. Respect for all other people, not just those who happen to be congenial or share one's way of life, forces us to recognize the reality of difference. As Wright notes (2010, p. 137f) 'Genuine respect demands both honesty about fundamental and potentially irreconcilable differences, and a willingness to explore them in an educative manner'. As such 'differences are not detrimental to the learning process, but rather a necessary part of it: effective education requires pupils to listen to the voices of those from faith traditions other than their own, and to begin to discern and respond intelligently to similarities and differences between them'.

It is important to note that the fact of difference hides much in common. Much difference is due to factors over which the individual has no control; no one chooses to be born, nor into what culture or circumstances. Everyone is profoundly influenced by how they are nurtured and to what experiences they are exposed. Language, values and beliefs are part of the inherited tradition from whose influence no-one escapes, even if in later years people renounce them. This is as true of secularists as of religious traditions. These are facts which apply to all human-beings.

Reciprocal acknowledgement of unavoidable differences can encourage a less frightened and more welcoming view of what is strange. Celebration of diversity is indeed appropriate. Yet it is important that this does not mask out the need also for criticism. Emphasis on tolerance alone can obscure this need, which is why tolerance is a secondary not fundamental value, as discussed in Chapter 2.

Respect for all people by virtue of their humanity does not mean never disagreeing with them. On the contrary, real respect treats people seriously enough to challenge them on important matters, assuming that there is in them something to which appeal can be made. Thus it would be withholding respect to fail to confront with argument and disagreement a Nazi sympathizer who's anti-semitism fails to show basic respect for all people.

Differences, some serious, are unavoidable, but only those which offend against the fundamental dispositions are what require debate. Discernment is required to distinguish between what should or should not be tolerated. All depends, however, on how such argument is conducted. Lat Blaylock's frequent advocacy of the skill of 'disagreeing respectfully' is important. What this adds up to is the need for a respectful, benevolent, truth-seeking and peaceful-seeking style of disputation. Elsewhere I have spoken of *critical affirmation* as the kind of approach needed (2007, pp. 63–5). This seeks to affirm the other person as a person even as one disagrees.

Critical affirmation has another advantage. By trying first to understand and appreciate empathetically where the other person comes from, false confrontation can be avoided. So often arguments attack what is not being defended; all they do is create resentment, misunderstanding and hatred, the opposite of what is needed. So, critical affirmation approaches disagreement gently and in a kindly spirit. This does not mean that it is a strategy of weakness. On the contrary, because it does not argue over what is not the case anyway and is glad to accept difference that is not destructive, it can make progress on the real issues.

> Do you agree that hiding one's disagreements with another might be a symptom of a lack of respect?

Such an attitude of mind depends on the third crucial disposition, humility, for what often does damage in disputation is the self-righteous, insensitive and often bellicose tone of the person disputing.

3. Humility

There is an especially close connection between the virtue of humility and that of concern for truth. A humble person does not suffer from the delusion that they own the truth which only they can access and dispense with an absolute certainty that they are right. Humility enables a proper openness, that is, not having to pretend we have all the answers; it respects the experience of others and it acknowledges we live in a world of probabilities not of absolute certainties.

Nevertheless there is a particular conundrum. Commitment is essential for action and for meaningful living, and this psychologically needs a sense of certainty. To be habitually entertaining doubt would inhibit meaningful living. How therefore is it possible to feel sure yet, at the same time, be open to fresh insights and free from arrogant dogmatic certainty? Edward Hulmes (1979) used a helpful phrase to express what is needed. Realizing that certainties are but *partial and provisional* saves them from becoming damagingly closed. This indicates awareness of human limitations and the impossibility of attaining absolute certainty. It acknowledges that, even though we may wish to be on *terra firma* yet we have to live, as Kierkegaard in a memorable phrase put it, 'over 70,000 fathoms of water'. Another analogy might be that of a swift that is air-borne all the time except just briefly when raising its young.

Such an understanding of the partial and provisional nature of our certainties helps us towards a creative understanding of doubt: instead of seeing it as an enemy of truth it becomes an ally towards seeking truth. Engaging with what is different is a sign of maturity as we accept what is necessarily part and parcel of the human condition. Berger and Zijderveld's book *In Praise of Doubt* was well-named, provided that doubt does not become a new idol!

The crucial key to avoiding dogmatism yet being passionate for truth and committed to pursuing is awareness of our human limitations. The vastness and complexity and constantly changing nature of the world preclude any fixed understanding. The cognitive and affective capacities of even the most gifted impose further constraints. In addition, the unavoidably problematic misinterpretation of words can lead to grave problems concerning the 'bewitchment of language' to use Wittgenstein's powerful phrase. It is exceptionally difficult to communicate meaning satisfactorily.

Such a common sense awareness of limitations has received interesting academic underpinning in Michael Slote's book *The Impossibility of Perfection: Aristotle, Feminism and the Complexities of Ethics* (2011). He argues, following Isaiah Berlin, that perfection is impossible in principle. The possibility of being misled by ignorance, prejudice, conditioning or personal weaknesses applies to everything said, done or thought. *Absolute* certainty is a mirage. This does nothing to mitigate the necessity for decision-making in everyday as in academic life. An unanswered letter is, after all, answered. Berger and Zijderveld note (p. 122): 'In a sense, not choosing is actually a choice – and usually a tragic one.' So the situation is quite literally unavoidable. The harm comes from failing to acknowledge the impossibility of perfection and imagining that we are invincible and absolutely right all the time.

An important corollary to acknowledging the impossibility of absolute certainty lies in not expecting definitive answers where such are inappropriate. Aristotle (*Nicomachean Ethics,* 1.3) observed that the reasonable person looks for only as much exactness as the subject matter admits. Richard Smith (1997, p. 109) has commented: 'It is not a weakness of moral principles that they apply "for the most part" and cannot be used in the form of rigid algorithms, any more that it is a weakness of the principles of literary criticism that George Eliot cannot be conclusively proved to be a finer novelist than Barbara Cartland.'

Unfortunately, the great trust placed in testing and examining in schools sends out the opposite message. As discussed in Chapter 2, the positivist thinking behind reliance on assessment needs incisive critique. It is an uphill but essential task therefore to try to disabuse students of what has been so assiduously though unconsciously dinned into them through all their years of schooling.

Why do you think people find it difficult to think that they may be mistaken in what they believe? Does Hulmes' description of being certain in a partial and provisional way make sense to you?

The role of religion

Belief in God should temper the temptation for imagining we have absolute certainty. Desmond Tutu (2011, p. 6) has written: 'We should in humility and joyfulness acknowledge that the supernatural and divine reality we all worship in some form or other transcends all our particular categories of thought and imagining, and that because the divine – however named, however apprehended or conceived – is infinite and we are forever finite, we shall never comprehend the divine completely. So we should seek to share all insights we can and be ready to learn . . . .'

Nevertheless, an especially dangerous form of temptation is open to religious people. The sense of self-importance can be exacerbated through presuming to know the will of God who can thus become an aide and accomplice to what may be purely human pretensions. Voltaire famously quipped; 'God made man in his own image; man has returned the compliment'! A properly religious response sees things in an entirely different light: seeking to do the will of God indeed, but realizing how diabolically easy it is to interpret that will wrongly. For God is infinitely beyond human comprehension. All that has just been said about the necessarily imperfect state of human knowledge is underlined many times over by contemplation of God. All the saints and scholars of the world religions have acknowledged the extraordinary distance between themselves and the God they seek to worship. St Francis at the very end of a life which most people, whether religious or not, can acknowledge as saintly, used to say 'Brethren, *let us begin* to love our Lord Jesus'.

The importance of this point cannot be over-stated, for failure to see this lies behind recourse by some religious people to violence. They imagine that they have absolute knowledge of God that can be put into precise formulas, ritual and behaviour to be enforced upon other people. This constitutes the opposite of what true religion seeks – the humble worship of God as God is, not as people choose to imagine God. The subjective element in claims to knowledge needs to be acknowledged as sometimes unreliable, as well as the problems of communicating truth to others.

In learning the art of honest, truth-seeking engagement with people in a spirit of critical affirmation, much can be learnt from the example of Nelson Mandela. He was nurtured within a deeply religious tradition which he never disowned. Yet he became exceedingly careful of referring to his beliefs with other people because of the misunderstandings which would be likely to be conveyed. This was not a case of 'trading truth for influence' (see above) but rather of thinking out what was necessary or not for other people to know. In the struggle against apartheid he needed the support of people of many different persuasions – of other religions and of Communism. He did not deceive but simply withheld from saying what so many people would not understand anyway or would misinterpret as narrow-minded imperialist Christian aggressiveness on his part. He did something more important: he lived those Christian convictions such as the immense virtue of forgiveness and love for enemies. He did this without attaching a label to them, thus giving everyone the opportunity to discover those virtues within their own traditions.

In a letter Mandela (2011) wrote from prison to his granddaughter Maki Mandela on 27 March 1977, he opined: 'I have my own beliefs as to the existence of a Supreme Being and it is possible that one could easily explain why mankind has from time immemorial believed in the existence of a god. . . . From my experience, it is far better, darling, to keep religious beliefs to yourself. You may unconsciously offend a lot of people by trying to sell them ideas they regard as unscientific and pure fiction.'

Reticence today concerning what one believes is called for because of the misunderstandings liable to be triggered off by religious talk in a heavily secularized world. This is a difficult point for many religious people to appreciate, especially those who are most seriously convinced about their religious beliefs and call to mission and conversion. Yet is it not better not to say anything than unwittingly to increase distortion as happens when what is said is misinterpreted? Genuine conversation about religion in everyday life should of course be welcomed provided it is conversation and not monologue. If, however, as Mandela notes, other people are likely to hear what a religious person says as 'unscientific and pure fiction', and if they are in no mood to be challenged on that, then reticence is perhaps the wisest course. It is supremely important, however, that what cannot perhaps often be tackled in everyday situations is nevertheless addressed very fully in RE as indicated in Chapter 2.

RE should especially help students to see that religious belief can enable people to advance in the dispositions discussed in this chapter. Richard Harries (2008, p. 152f.) in a powerful passage speaks of the way that religion can help people to be humble without loss of self-esteem: 'Making decisions before God should encourage a greater degree of self-knowledge and honesty than is usually the case. For our decisions are driven by many factors that we are either unaware of or do not care to acknowledge. We are all prone to illusion and self-deception in varying degrees. The Holy Spirit probes us and brings hidden things to light. This is not to make us feel guilty or bad about ourselves, but to help us to be realistic about the inevitable degree of mixed motivation in nearly all that we do. For the God before whom we stand knows us through and through, much better than we know ourselves. But he is also a supremely gracious God who holds us close to himself through all growth in self-knowledge, however painful some of it may be. For God is on our side, totally for us.'

Harries writes as a Christian but is not the picture of God which he draws not to be found also at the heart of all genuinely-held worship of the Transcendent, whatever the precise spiritual tradition? At the very least this is what RE should explore, shunning the distraction of paying attention only to the externals of religion.

Honesty therefore stands for truth-seeking and truthful living, open to the insights of others, capable of self-correction, modest in the sense of not imagining oneself to be all-knowing, able truly to listen to others without any loss of personal integrity. This may be asking a lot, but ideals are like stars by which to plot a course. All children and all students deserve to have such high ideals put before them, and, even more importantly, demonstrated. The invitation is to intellectual and emotional pilgrimage, going forward with others confidently into the unknown.

D o you agree on the need for reticence about expressing religious commitment in today's secularist environment?

References

Berger, P. and Zijderveld, A. (2009), *In Praise of Doubt: How to Have Convictions without becoming a Fanatic*. New York: HarperOne.

Booker, C. (2009), *The Real Global Warming Disaster: Is the Obsession with Climate Change Turning Out to Be the Most Costly Scientific Blunder in History?* London: Continuum.

Grimmitt, M. (ed.) (2010). *Religious Education and Social and Community Cohesion An Exploration of Challenges and Opportunities*. Great Wakering, Essex: McCrimmons.

Harries, R. (2008), *The Re-Enchantment of Morality: Wisdom for a Troubled World*. London: SPCK.

Hulme, M. (2009), *Why We Disagree About Climate Change*. Cambridge: Cambridge University Press.

Hulmes, E. (1979), *Commitment and Neutrality*. London: Cassell.

Mandela, N. (2011), *Conversations with Myself*. London: MacMillan.

QCA (2007). *Secondary Curriculum Review*. London: QCA.

Thompson, M. (2010), 'Reflecting Honestly: Ideological conflict, religious education and community cohesion' in M. Grimmitt (ed.), *Religious Education and Social and Community Cohesion Exploration of challenges and opportunities*. Great Wakering, Essex: McCrimmons.

Tutu, D. (2011), *God is Not a Christian: Speaking Truth in Times of Crisis*. London: Rider.

Richardson, N. (2010), 'Division, Diversity and Vision: Religious education and community cohesion in Northern Ireland', in M. Grimmitt (ed.), *Religious Education and Social and Community Cohesion, Exploration of challenges and opportunities*. Great Wakering, Essex: McCrimmons.

Ruskin, J. (1867), Time and Tide letter VIII. London: Smith, Elder & Co.

Sahin, A. (2010), 'The Contribution of Religious Education to Social and Community Cohesion: an Islamic educational perspective', in M. Grimmitt (ed.), *Religious Education and Social and Community Cohesion, Exploration of challenges and opportunities*. Great Wakering, Essex: McCrimmons.

Slote, M. (2011), *The Impossibility of Perfection: Aristotle, Feminism and the Complexities of Ethics*. Oxford: Oxford University Press.

Smith, R. (1997), *Teaching Right and Wrong: Moral Education in the Balance*, eds. Smith, R. and P. Standish. London: Trentham Books.

Watson, B. and Thompson, P. (2007), *The Effective Teacher of Religious Education*, 2nd edn. Harlow: Pearson Education.

Woolf, V. (ed.) (1848), Leonard Woolf *The Moment and other Essays*. San Diego, California: Harcourt Brace.

Wright, A. (2007), *Critical Religious Education, Multiculturalism and the Pursuit of Truth*. Cardiff: University of Wales Press.

—(2010), 'Community, Diversity and Truth', in M. Grimmitt (ed.), *Religious Education and Social and Community Cohesion, Exploration of challenges and opportunities*. Great Wakering, Essex: McCrimmons.

CHAPTER SIX

Being compassionate

looking to others

Rod Garner

CHAPTER OUTLINE

This chapter sets out the meaning of compassion as found in diverse religious traditions and refers to the Charter for Compassion signed by major world religions. Literally the word means 'suffering with' thus relating love to suffering. For the Christian, it is grounded in the suffering God, whose love leads him to undergo suffering. This love evokes a thoughtful, affective and imaginative response in human beings. For leading mystics this response ultimately extends beyond human beings to nature and to animals. The nature of compassion is such that it is not easy to draw a line that sets boundaries to include some parts of creation while excluding other parts. The final corollary is that this compassion also includes self-compassion.

The duty of compassion is a unifying theme of all the great world religions. All major faiths view compassion as the fruit of authentic spirituality that has its source in the transcendent reality we call God, *Brahman* or *Nirvana*. Each has devised its own form of a fundamental ethical principle that is known as the Golden Rule: 'Do not treat others as you would not like them to treat you'. In its positive form this maxim translates into: 'Always treat others as you would wish to be treated yourself'. Compassion requires us to remember the poor and the defenceless and to see the world with a clear eye. It asks us to reject the comforts of illusion or denial in order to recognize that the world is shot through with suffering and pain as well as beauty and delight. Compassion, we might say, is both an adjunct of conscience and the outworking of tutored moral sense. We just know that duty to others forms part of faith and our common humanity. More will be said about this later.

> B efore reading on, think about a compassionate person you know and ask what it is about that person that models compassion.

But What Does It Mean?

A working definition will be helpful here. Compassion is a rather slippery virtue frequently confused with pity, unreflective benevolence or the spasmodic kindness we associate with international disasters or the Festive Season. The Oxford English Dictionary defines compassion as 'piteous' or 'pitiable'. A rather attenuated and meagre definition in some ways that could lead the casual browser to conclude that it means little more than feeling sorry for people. Compassion derives in part from the Latin *pati* and the Greek *pathein* meaning to suffer, undergo or experience. It means enduring or sharing something with another person as though their pain was our own and doing what we can to alleviate it. Compassion is principled, consistent and clear-sighted. It breathes the same air as altruism and recognizes in all forms of otherness fertile ground for service. The world rather than our narrow self-interest sets the moral agenda. Compassion will always fail without self-restraint. In a timely book concerned with how we should live in this new millennium the Dalai Lama (1999, p. 24) made clear that 'we cannot be loving and compassionate unless at the same time we curb our own harmful impulses and desires.' Here he is very close to the wisdom of St Paul:

> Love is always patient and kind; it is never jealous; love is never boastful or conceited; it is never rude or selfish; it does not take offence and is not resentful. Love takes no pleasure in other people's wrong doing but delights in truth; it is always ready to excuse, to trust, to hope, and to endure whatever comes. (1 Corinthians, chapter 13, verses 4–7)

In this passage, Paul desires that his readers should follow the better way of love and, by implication, refrain from the backbiting, bitterness, and intolerance that can blight the public face of religion. Both aspirations have recently been translated into a global manifesto following the launch of the Charter for Compassion on 12 November 2009 in 60 different locations throughout the world. Many thousands of people contributed to its formulation via a multilingual website in Hebrew, Urdu, Spanish and English. Their contributions were refined by representatives of six faith traditions (Judaism, Christianity, Islam, Hinduism, Buddhism and Confucianism) that met earlier in 2009 to agree a final text. Here is an extract:

> Compassion impels us to work tirelessly to alleviate the suffering of our fellow creatures, to dethrone ourselves from the centre of our world and put another there, and to honour the inviolable sanctity of every single human being, treating everybody, without exception, with absolute justice, equity and respect.
>
> It is also necessary in both public and private life to refrain consistently and empathically from inflicting pain. To act or speak violently out of spite, chauvinism or self-interest, to impoverish, exploit or deny basic rights to anybody, and to incite hatred by denigrating others – even our enemies – is a denial of our common humanity.
>
> We therefore call upon all men and women

- To restore compassion to the centre of morality and religion.
- To return to the ancient principle that any interpretation of scripture that breeds violence, hatred, or disdain is illegitimate
- To ensure that youth are given accurate and respectful information about other traditions, religions and cultures
- To encourage a positive appreciation of cultural and religious diversity
- To cultivate an informed empathy with the suffering of all human beings – even those regarded as enemies.

Since its launch, the Charter has been incorporated into faith communities and secular institutions with more than 150 global partners now working together to translate the Charter into practical action.

The roots of compassion

Pause now for a moment in order to rewind. Earlier we linked compassion with conscience and our capacity for moral reasoning. We need to understand the link a little better. Often we say that compassion springs from our conscience, that evident and compelling inner voice which serves as guide and moral compass. But what is conscience? The most famous philosophical definition belongs to the eighteenth-century Anglican Bishop Joseph Butler cited in D. D. Raphael's (1969) collection of Butler's sermons:

> There is a superior principle of reflection or conscience in everyone which distinguishes between the internal principles of our heart, as well as our external actions: which passes judgement upon ourselves and them; pronounces determinately some actions to be in themselves just, right and good; others to be in themselves evil, wrong, unjust.

How would you define conscience today?

On this account conscience appears absolute, intuitive and authoritative. Without any need of further argument, it demarcates right from wrong and directs us to one and away from the other. It is the 'moral sense' acknowledged by all but the morally maladjusted that functions as a torch might light up some objects. An inconvenient truth for this argument however is that conscience is not wholly reliable and can result in mistaken conclusions and bad ends. Thomas Aquinas (1224–74), one of the most important Christian theologians and one of the greatest Western philosophers believed in conscience but did not view it as either infallible or innate. For him it represents the judgement we come to on our behaviour or actions in the light of various rational considerations. On this interpretation conscience comes down to a process of reasoning, reflecting and judging based upon what Aquinas calls *synderesis* – the disposition of the human mind to grasp the basic principles of behaviour. Does this mean that Aquinas believes that the use of reason alone is sufficient to ensure that we always behave well and live a truly compassionate life? Actually, no. He insists that something more is required. We need virtues – the abilities, tendencies or capacities which dispose us to do certain things or to behave in certain ways. We are not referring here to any old sort of dispositions – bad ones will invariably lead to our decline as moral persons and regrettable outcomes, for ourselves and others. Good ones, by contrast, contribute to our flourishing and our acting well. Virtues are the means whereby as voluntary and rational agents we can with freedom participate in God's will for us and share, so to speak, in his ordering of things in the natural world. A huge claim we might think by any standards – nothing less than an invitation for mortals to become sharers in the divine nature.

Which virtues make us good?

Aquinas is very clear on this matter. Following St Paul, he asserts that the theological virtues of faith, hope and love are the means by which we come to God. They represent for him the heart of the life of grace which conforms us to God's image and without them we will not be as good as we can be in this life. As faith and hope are given extensive treatment in other chapters the intention in what follows is to highlight the relationship between compassion and faith and to say a little about love.

Compassion and faith

Unlike other theologians both medieval and modern who maintain that faith comes to us through experiential encounter rather than any intellectual assent to doctrines, Aquinas takes faith to be something which is bound up with the teaching of Christian creeds. He refers to them as 'the articles of faith' set down by the Church Fathers at the Council of Nicaea (AD. 325), which refer respectively to the majesty of the Godhead, the mystery of Christ's humanity and the mystery of godliness. There would seem to be a logical difficulty here – on the one hand we are encouraged to have faith in Christ as a result of a personal encounter that we experience as a relational truth and, on the other, faith in propositions. Both positions are tenable however once we realize that conscience and compassion alike can flow from the *truth of Jesus* mediated through experience and *the truth about Jesus* enshrined in preaching, creeds and scripture. An interesting and important distinction is being made here that enables us to say, without contradiction, that religious experience, sometimes sudden or overwhelming, can evoke a more compassionate or committed life but so too can a commitment to the teachings of the Church that set forth unequivocally the life, suffering, death and resurrection of Christ. Two examples make the point well. As she meditated on the poem 'Love' by the seventeenth-century English priest and poet George Herbert, Simone Weil became conscious that Christ was present – 'a presence more personal, more certain and more real than that of a human being' she wrote to one correspondent. This experience changed her life, enabled her to continue her struggle for a new and more humane order in the face of oppressive structures and ideologies and impressed upon her the presence of One who, like herself, learnt obedience in affliction and was perfected 'through what he suffered' (Hebrews, chapter 5, verse 8). Hold this image of a woman of rare intellectual gifts being possessed by Christ and then consider the remarkable poem *Seven Stanzas at Easter* by the American writer, John Updike (1995). On first reading it is about the propositional truth declared in the Nicene Creed that Jesus rose again from the dead. It is much more than that. The measured insistence of its lines demands to be seen as a compelling testimony predicated on what God has actively done in history and the difference this makes to the life of faith. Its refusal to reduce the resurrection to the level of parable or metaphor – here the emphatic requirement is *not* to see the resurrection 'as the flowers each soft Spring recurrent' or the risen Jesus 'as the Spirit in the mouths and fuddled eyes of the apostles' – points us instead to a stunning and mysterious transformation of the crucified body of Christ. It also suggests an 'awakening' of extraordinary power on the part of Updike, no less real than that experienced by Weil. Its striking emphasis on the sheer reality of it all declares that the doctrine of the resurrection, as it comes to us so mysteriously in the gospels, is not fully grasped if it is reduced to mere myth or symbol. It is a miracle – in scriptural terms, a mighty act of God – that leads to gratitude for the legacy of the lasting hope it confers upon humanity. Faith and thankfulness combine here and, as Updike (2007) notes elsewhere, both can lead to a redeemed and compassionate form of existence 'that through the millennia has manifested itself in art and altruism, idealism and *joie de vivre*'.

How important is it in your view that the material facts described here are actually true?

How could the factual truth of the resurrection described here inspire compassion in believers?

Love

The virtue of love (or charity as Aquinas expresses it) is held to be the greatest of the dispositions because it is a matter of possessing God. Love makes us more like God than anything else. It directs the acts of all the other virtues, brings truth and integrity to our aims and hopes and, as Brian Davies (1993) notes in a comprehensive survey of Aquinas's thought, includes compassion for our neighbour:

> The light in which we must love our neighbours is God, for what we ought to love in them is that they be in God. Hence it is clear that it is specifically the same act which loves God and loves neighbour. And on this account charity extends not only to the love of God but also to the love of neighbour.

Charity is the mother of all virtues because it reflects both our desire for God and what he essentially is. It should never be confused with or reduced to a matter of kindness between people or giving money out of a charitable impulse. But as we have seen in the previous quotation from Aquinas, doing good to others is part of what charity involves. It is bound up with what he describes as *amicitia* or friendship between human beings and God. In the gospel of John, Jesus declares 'No longer will I call you servants but friends' (chapter 15, verse 15) and Aquinas takes this as a way of defining what the Christian life, infused by grace, is all about. To the extent that we truly participate in the divine goodness and wisdom, we truly do love's work and this spills over into a deep and serious bonding with others that appropriates their hurts and needs as our own. For this to happen there has to be a theological 'go between' and this necessity introduces the work of the Holy Spirit. In his letter to the Romans, St Paul declares that 'God's love has been poured into our hearts through the Holy Spirit which has been given to us (chapter 5, verse 5). Contemplating this text, Aquinas comes to what he interprets as the only possible conclusion: the Christian virtue of love or charity is nothing less than the effect in us of the Holy Spirit 'who thereby produces in us what love is in God.' This exalted vision embraces both the joys and sorrows of the world and a preparedness on our part to discharge the obligation that is summoned by the sufferings of others. The twentieth-century Anglican theologian Austin Farrer (1966, p. 188) has written movingly of those who have grasped this vision:

> An overmastering sense of human ills can be taken as the world's invitation to deny her Maker, or it may be taken as God's invitation to succour his world. Which is it to be? Those who take the practical alternative become more closely and more widely acquainted with misery than the onlookers; but they feel the grain of existence and the movement of the purposes of God. They do not argue, they love; and what is loved is always known as good.

Is the problem of evil a failure of love?
    Why might 'taking the practical alternative' be dependent on a vision of the good?

The crucified God

Farrer's willing servants of the world are moved to works of charity by more than conscience or the prompting of the Holy Spirit. They carry with them a narrative and an image of a marginal Jew in first-century Palestine who, in a relatively short time, came to be understood, followed and worshipped 'as the image of the invisible God' (Colossians, chapter 1, verse 15). In Jesus Christ they see the Son of God who had compassion on the multitude and commanded his followers to do likewise (Luke, chapter 10, verses 30–37). They heed his words to feed the hungry, give water to the thirsty, clothe the naked, tend the sick and visit those in prison. (Matthew, chapter 25, verses 35–36) Furthermore, as they render such service in the name of Christ they also believe that in a fundamentally mysterious way they are also serving Christ in others (Matthew, chapter 25, verse 40). For them compassion is not just a matter of responding to a divine mandate set down in a holy book. It is also bound up with an image of great moral force and the unconditional response they make to the cross of Golgotha on which Jesus died.

The experience of being moved in this way has consequences. At the foot of the cross, disciples in every age become aware of their desire and need to become truly decent human beings and to share more fully in the suffering of God in the life of the world. They recognize in the crucifixion of Jesus more than a specific act of redemption for individual souls. It is nothing less than the disclosure of a divine love, the self-expression of God in the suffering and death of his Son. The symbol of the cross – too frequently misunderstood as only and ever a payment to the Father for the price of sin – is now seen in a different or deeper light. It opens the eyes of believers to the mystery of God's being as One who is spent and drained in a costly act of self-giving. Such an act of redeeming love elicits the obedience of faith, expressed in unending gestures of compassion on the part of those, who in the words of the famous hymn, come to know that 'love so amazing, so divine, demands my soul, my life, my all'.

It is not too much to claim that the crucified God revealed in Christ precipitates not only the desire to heal and redeem a broken world. The cross can also bring about the crucial existential decision whereby we determine for ourselves how we should live and what we ought to do in an ambiguous world of competing narratives and truth claims concerning the meaning and purpose of existence. (Farrer 1973, p. 157) Again:

> After all the defection of shams, the clarification of argument and the sifting of evidence – after all criticism, all analysis – a man must make up his mind what there is most worthy of love, and most binding on conduct in the world of real existence. It is this decision, or this discovery, that is the supreme exercise of a truth-seeking intelligence.

Compassion is the outcome of a decision, an encounter with the crucified and a life of faith informed by conscience, moral reasoning and divine grace infusing our moral dispositions. It is the continuing work of a faith journey where, necessarily, there will be light and darkness. The truth-seeking heart, fed by the intelligence, the emotions and the imagination embraces compassion as the proper way to live. It recognizes that life and discipleship alike have a cruciform shape. Both reflect the upward struggle of all living things – a struggle as Garner notes (2011, p. 33) that is set within the 'saving act of One who gives himself to the creation through love and asks us to do likewise'.

> What argument for living compassionately do you personally find compelling?

The scope of compassion

Because compassion recognizes no boundaries in relation to its practical concerns it can be seen, to paraphrase a recent book by John Berger (2007), as the human vocation to 'hold everything dear'. This section identifies four areas that fall within its compass. They do not exhaust the possibilities of what it means to be compassionate; rather they point us in the direction (sometimes unexpected) of the world's wounds and how they might be healed.

Suffering

For all those who think and feel, an observable feature of existence is the prevalence of tragedies, disease and undeserved sorrows. There are three hundred types of cancer and all of us are caught up in the flux of time and susceptible to an array of viruses, microbes and infections. Life, for many, remains nasty, brutish and short and the misuse of our human freedoms in acts of cruelty, lies, theft and wickedness serves only to compound the extent and depth of the misery in the world. Nature though beautiful is also indifferent. Natural disasters if not common place are by no means unusual and bring forth famine, earthquakes and floods.

Suffering in all its forms is the natural habitat of compassion because the agents of the latter are mandated to 'hold everything dear' – to repair what is broken – and to bring healing and hope where there is darkness or despair. Invoking Jewish wisdom, Mark L. Winer (2008, p. 439) describes this arduous process as *tikkun olam*, the means whereby we seek to fix the world, often in the aftermath of setbacks and disillusionment, but always drawing strength from a love of the world and the recognition of its beauty and fragility as the handiwork of God (Exodus, chapter 19, verse 5). Every righteous and compassionate person is able to add to the world's lustre by the conscious desire to eradicate the stains of human sinfulness and natural evil.

To what extent do the invitations to 'hold everything dear' and 'repair the world' help us to see suffering in a more purposeful light?

A more than human world

We can be forgiven for presuming that to speak of the world in relation to compassion is to have in mind only the human species and the observable hardships we encounter every day. Jesus had to withdraw from the pastoral needs of the crowds (Mark, chapter 6, verses 45–46) and all carers know how costly it is to care in personal terms for those who have been broken by the corrosiveness of time or circumstance. But there is a wider sphere beyond human needs and relationships that also has a moral claim on us – the natural world of plants, flowers, seeds, spores, ferns and great oceans. Scripture requires that we should not 'damage the earth, or the sea or the trees' (Revelation, chapter 7, verse 3) and to act on this imperative is to recognize that existence under God is not a matter of separation and competition but unity and reverence. Seen in this way, the whole creation assumes a power of meaning that calls for our allegiance, respect and commitment. A tree for example is no longer merely 'a green thing' but a discreet convergence of diffuse energies – sun, soil, star and seasons – and an affirmation of the interconnectedness of everything. Nothing exists independently of anything else. A tree has no autonomous life: it requires rain to fall on the soil, sunlight to nourish and sustain it, eyes to perceive it and compassion to preserve it against disaster. In return, a tree living for more than 50 years will provide oxygen, regulate humidity, control air pollution, provide shelter and fertilize the soil. The great religious Reformer, Martin Luther, recognized that every tree is precious, 'far more glorious than if it were made of gold and silver'. Three centuries later, the American mystic and Transcendentalist, Henry David Thoreau (2008) spent 2 years near the woods of Walden Pond, Massachusetts, where he frequently tramped through the deepest snow to keep an appointment with a beech tree, or a yellow birch. Thoreau was no sentimentalist and saw plenty of evidence of a natural order where teeming forms of life suffered and preyed on one another. But he approached trees in a spirit of profound respect – in the awareness of a shared interconnectedness 'am I not partly leaves and vegetable mould myself?' – and a conviction that they contained a key or clue to his own inner life. In the woods he found a whole universe: there he desired to foster his 'intelligence with the earth' for he knew himself to be part of a singular whole. The breath of life infuses every living thing, the entire and elaborate web of creation loved by God (Genesis, chapter 1, verse 31).

All creatures great and small

Whether we draw on Scripture, the life of Jesus or the examples of holy lives dedicated to Christ, there is much to persuade us that a compassionate concern for other creatures is a proper article of Christian faith. Notwithstanding the special status given to humankind in the book of Genesis, it still places men and women in striking proximity to furry and feathered species. Both are created on the same day with the provision of fruit and plants as their means of sustenance (chapter 1, verses 29–30). As the hugely influential theologian Karl Barth once expressed it, 'both are referred to the same table for their bodily needs.' The moral and theological implications are interesting: killing and slaughtering did not come into the world by divine command. We are slowly waking up to this truth along with its corollary – that the scriptural promise that mankind should have a dominion over every living thing (Genesis, chapter 1, verse 26) is not a licence to hurt or destroy but a requirement to reverence all living things and to defend creatures who have no power to speak for themselves and are often defenceless. This remit extends beyond the domestic world of pets and has a claim on our compassion which is often neither recognized nor honoured. A story concerning a Mass held on a glorious summer's day has some relevance here. As the service proceeded a wasp was buzzing furiously up and down the inside of a window trying to escape. A stout, middle-aged lady, one of the pillars of the church, became increasingly annoyed. Eventually, she took hold of *The Universe*, a Catholic newspaper, rolled it up and made for the window, the wasp locked on to her radar. As the priest uttered the words 'Blessed art thou, Lord God of all creation' she struck the wasp dead with a single swipe of her religious paper. At the precise moment when the gathering was blessing God for the inherent goodness of all things, she eliminated one of his creatures.

> Are there boundaries to compassion and if there are, where would you draw the line?

Quite possibly, many Christians would have done the same. In a recent book defending compassion for animals, Laura Hobgood-Oster (2010, p. 4) refers to Kay Warren, wife of the famous American pastor Rick Warren of Saddleback Church, who wrote on her blog that she was 'emotionally duped, then angered, by a heart-tugging television ad about suffering animals' Why? She believed that animals are not worthy of such compassion and continued: 'Jesus didn't die for animals; he gave his all for human beings' – a predictable claim that nevertheless fails to recognize a number of salient points which suggest a different conclusion. To say that Jesus died for humanity does not exclude the possibility of his and, by extension, Christianity's compassion for other animals as well. Consider this: Jesus spends forty days in the wilderness with wild beasts at the onset of his public ministry. He tells parables concerning God's care for the birds of the air and his followers are instructed to break the rules of the Sabbath in order to pull a sheep from a pit. In his final days, he enters Jerusalem on an ass, a poignant reminder of the ox and ass who adored him at his nativity. Many Christians and notable saints and scholars have been inspired by such stories and images and are venerated for their close connection to animals and their well-being. Francis of Assisi comes naturally to mind but we also have fascinating accounts of Jerome and the lion and Brigit of Kildar, a fifth-century Celtic saint revered for her hospitality to animals.

Despite the fact that earlier thinkers of the status of Aquinas and Kant have drawn a sharp difference between humans and animals (on the grounds of the rationality that demarcates the former from the latter) a different kind of conversation about animals is now emerging involving theologians, scientists and philosophers concerning how and why animals matter and how humans should relate to them. Collected essays under the editorship of Deane-Drummond and Clough (2009) stress the essential 'creatureliness' of humanity that connects us to other animals rather than separating us from them. Elsewhere, Kimberley C. Patton (2000) has enlightened readers with her survey of historical Christian mystical affirmations of the theological worth and special witness of animals. From the world of science, Lori Marino of Emory University in Atlanta, Georgia has argued on the basis of research, that dolphins, whales and their kind have brains as anatomically complex as those of humans and that these brains contain a particular type of nerve cell, known as a spindle cell, that in humans is associated with higher cognitive functions such as abstract reasoning. Discussing the ethical implications of Marino's argument, Thomas White, (2012, p. 80) a philosopher of Loyola Marymount University in Los Angeles, has sought to establish the idea that a person need not be human.

In philosophy, he contends, a person is a being with special characteristics, who deserves special treatment as a result of those characteristics. In principle, other species can qualify. From new thinking in theology comes the insight that as the Word was made flesh (John, chapter 1, verse 14) then all creatures (not just humans) that fall under the category of 'flesh' might also bear the image of God (imago dei) traditionally confined to humankind. Given this radical thought, the redemptive work of Christ, wrought by his living and dying, assumes a new significance. Jesus does 'give his all to human beings' but his self-giving, as scripture reminds us, is for the sake of the world (John, chapter 3, verse 16) – a world where 'kangaroos and chimpanzees, kookaburras and dolphins' by virtue of a 'creatureliness' so similar to our own are seen to matter to God because they too bear his image. All creatures call forth our compassion and empathy. Such a stance reflects not only the profoundest respect for the created order but also a radical incarnational theology that in this instance assumes the form of a question: If God is incarnated in Jesus does this not suggest the incarnation of the divine in all bodies and all creatures?

What has been your reaction to this section on animals? Did the argument change the way you think about the presence of the divine in the natural world?

And, finally, ourselves

This short concluding section takes the form of a postscript – a reminder that in the life-long practice of compassion we shall fail unless we apply the Golden Rule to ourselves. Unless we can feel genuine compassion for ourselves we shall not be able to extend it to others. This calls for a measure of self-knowledge that acknowledges our strengths and weaknesses and a spirit of humility. We all have a dark side – what the psycho-analyst Jung referred to as our 'shadow' – the disturbing motives, desires and inclinations that influence our thoughts, behaviour and ambitions. Similarly, we all know of the disappointments, rejections, betrayals and failures that still impede our growth as persons. Unacknowledged drives and past hurts invariably result in personal misery or hostility, suspicion and unkindness towards others, unless we can recognize and accept them as part of what it means to be human. Others experience similar pangs of frustration, jealousy, resentment and fear and when they attack us, they are probably experiencing the anxiety and frustration we identify in ourselves.

Directed to ourselves, compassion allows us to live with the knowledge that we are a complex amalgam of insecurities and a longing for control. We are not uniquely awful or bad, just human like everyone else. Commenting on this tangle of human complexities, Karen Armstrong (2011, pp. 76–7) one of the world's leading writers on religion and spirituality offers the following words:

> Before you can embrace the whole world you must focus on yourself . . . notice how much peace, happiness and benevolence you possess already. . . . Next, become conscious of your anger, fear and anxiety. Look deeply into the seeds of rage within yourself. Bring to mind some of your past suffering and the pleasure in things we all tend to take for granted. Finally, look at yourself with even-mindedness. You are not unique . . . you have failings but you also have talents.

Compassion is the means whereby we learn to accept ourselves in order to be more genuinely available to others without illusions, self-loathing or excessive self-centredness. From a Christian perspective it is also a gateway to divine grace and the trust that despite our limitations and imperfections God nevertheless loves us. Learning to accept ourselves is the key to the liberating discovery that we are also accepted by that infinitely greater love which 'moves the sun and the other stars' and finds its fullest human expression in the face of Jesus Christ.

> To what extent is learning to accept ourselves the key to a deeper and more compassionate way of life?

References

Armstrong, K. (2011), *Twelve Steps to a Compassionate Life*. London: The Bodley Head.

Berger, J. (2007), *Hold Everything Dear: Dispatches on Survival and Resistance*. London: Verso.

H. H. The Dalai Lama (1999), *Ethics for the New Millennium*. New York: Riverhead Books.

Davies, B. (1992), *The Thought of Thomas Aquinas*. Oxford: Clarendon Press.

Deane-Drummond, C. and Clough, D. (eds) (2009), *Creaturely Theology: On God, Humans and Other Animals*. London: SCM Press.

Farrer, A. (1966), *Love Almighty and Ills Unlimited*. London: Collins-Fontana.

— (1973), *The End of Man*. London: SPCK.

Garner, R. (2011), *On Being Saved: The Roots of Redemption*. London: Darton, Longman & Todd.

Hobgood-Oster, L. (2010), *The Friends We Keep: Unleashing Christianity's Compassion for Animals*. London: Darton, Longman & Todd.

Patton, K. C. (2000), 'He Who Sits in the Heavens Laughs': 'Recovering Theology in the Abrahamic Traditions', 401–34 *Harvard Theological Review* 93(4).

Raphael, D. D. (ed.) (1969), *British Moralists 1650–1800*. Oxford: The Clarendon Press.

Thoreau, H. D. (2008), *Walden*. New York: Fall River Press.

Updike, J. (1995), 'Seven Stanzas at Easter', in M. Batchelor (ed.), *The Lion Christian Poetry Collection*. London: Lion.

— (2007), *Due Considerations: Essays and Criticism*. London: Hamish Hamilton.

White, T. (2012), 'Whales are People Too' cited in *The Economist*. 25 February – 2 March.

Winer, M. L. (November-December 2008), 'Tikun Olam: A Jewish Theology of Repairing the World'. 433–41 *Theology* CX1 (864).

CHAPTER SEVEN

Being just

relationships with others

William K. Kay

CHAPTER OUTLINE

This chapter considers the role and learning of rules and the developmental stages through which human beings pass. This rule learning is the foundation that leads to the formation and recognition of moral rules and religious obligations. The changing cognitive abilities of children (first identified by Piaget) influence their grasp of morality as it does of religious obligations. The differences between moral and religious law are explored. According to Kohlberg, one's moral judgement may develop through the process of resolving the cognitive dissonance embodied in moral dilemmas. The religious learning takes place somewhat differently through concrete examples showing that religious obligations always admit exceptions. The more recent development of postmodern thinking complicates the picture somewhat often leading people to embrace a moral relativity and to talk of acquiring skills instead of focusing on content.

Beginnings

Children learn about rules in babyhood, even if they have no idea that the regularities they come to be aware of are 'rules'. Within the first 6 months or so the baby begins to recognize faces and react with a gurgle or smile.

Random sounds become word-like and are eventually applied to situations or objects, usually in an overgeneralized way. All men are, for a while, called 'Dada'. Later words are put together into mini sentences and soon after this words are made to conform to unconsciously held grammatical rules. Words are invented to conform to these rules. 'I saw two mouses' (not mice); 'I kicked the ball straightwards' (not forwards), and so on. It is the presence of these new but incorrect words that show how the child generates language rather than simply copying it. Generative rules are at work and they smooth out the irregularities of actual speech.

In those amazing early years, the child also learns about the physical world. The food is hot and might hurt, the knife is sharp and might cut, the dog is big and might bark. So he or she learns not to touch steaming food, not to pick up a knife by the blade and to be wary of the dog. The things that must not be done can turn into rules. 'Don't touch; it's hot', and even say 'please' when you want more chocolate. Here are the beginnings of rules of behaviour which, once solitary play gives way to play with other children, become the rules of sharing and taking turns. 'Let Johnny have a go on the swing now' is the start of a moral rule, a rule governing the treatment of others and implying fairness.

Of course, the description given above is one which presumes a stable and supportive home where parents hover over the child with love and concern. In all circumstances the child will need to interact with someone who speaks and shows care: no child can survive those early years without an older human being. It may be that the child receives very little verbal instruction or warning about the physical world and that most learning takes place by painful experience, perhaps in the company of other children or in an institutional setting. Even so, it is the regularities of the world that demonstrate the rule-based nature of the environment. If you drop something, it will fall; if you wait long enough, the night will end and daybreak will arrive.

Jean Piaget (1896–1980) and others

The pioneering work of Piaget started in the 1920s and continued for 40 years. In 1932 he published *The Moral Judgment of the Child* based on a study of children and starting with their playing of marbles, a game for children themselves without adult supervision. He asked children of ascending age questions about the origin of the rules, the changeability of the rules and the reasons for the rules. Younger children understood the rules to be immutable and to have been handed down since time immemorial. Older children understood the rules to be variable and to originate in the need for fairness where fairness means treating all players in the same way. What applies to one person, applies to all – and if rules are broken, there are rules about what penalties should be imposed. Older children came to appreciate that rules are what makes the game since they could understand how variants of the game arise as the rules are adjusted.

The ability to understand rules is in Piaget's work connected with the ongoing mental development of the child. He saw children constructing their view of the world by moving through a series of stages where at first everything is magically caused. Reality is hardly distinguishable from fairyland. The sun may rise and set because 'it wants to' or because it is blown about by the wind. Kings and queens exercise power and magicians cast spells. There is little or no mechanical understanding so that, even if a child is asked to draw a bicycle, the picture is vague about what the pedals actually do.

Piaget also asked children about moral dilemmas or situations. He asked children why lying is wrong (for young children this is because the words are 'naughty' or 'bad' but for older children the breach of trust implicit in lying is appreciated). The point is that children give different accounts of the wrongfulness of lying and these accounts stem not only from intellectual differences between children of different ages but also from the kind of world these differences entail. The younger children, according to Piaget, are typically egocentric: they can only see things from their own point of view. They fail to appreciate, even in the physical realm, someone standing at a distance from where they are will have a different perspective. Piaget showed this using a big model of a mountain and asked what they or others in different positions could see of the scene. This imaginative limitation on children is connected with a failure to appreciate reciprocal relations. For instance, if one person lends money to another, the other owes money back. If a boy has a brother and a sister, he may not appreciate that his sister has two brothers: he may think that his sister also has a brother and a sister. These intellectual limitations go to the heart of moral understanding since the sense of moral obligations depends on the capacity of seeing situations from the point of view of other people and, also, of appreciating their motives.

Piaget put an imaginary situation to children and asked them about blame. In one story he used, a child went to a party and accidentally dropped a tray of jellies on the carpet. Later another child deliberately threw one jelly at another child. When asked who was naughtiest, the younger children usually thought that the person who had dropped the most jellies was worse than the one who threw a single jelly. This 'moral realism' depended on seeing only the result of actions and not the inner dispositions that instigate them. Older children, of course, appreciate the weight of reasons for actions so that, if asked whether it is acceptable to tell a small lie to save a life, they are likely to agree that it is.

In keeping with his staged model of intellectual development, Piaget argued that children move from an egotistical heteronomous stage where moral rules are handed down from on high (in the case of young children from adults) to an autonomous stage where moral rules are reached by agreement and arise from an understanding of cooperation and personal interaction or, as it is termed, by 'reciprocity'. And cooperation is possible because older children can appreciate the viewpoint of others as their egotism diminishes. Rules are seen as having the purpose of enabling fairness.

This entire research programme was not without its critics, especially those who argued that children at a young age can make inferences about the feelings of others or who, like the sociologist Durkheim, considered moral rules simply to be group norms. Yet, the Piagetian account has withstood criticism and is still cited widely (as Google Scholar will show). One of the underlying features of the criticism has centred on the rational nature of rules. If they are rational, they are implicitly universal; if they are culturally defined, they are localized.

Even so, Lawrence Kohlberg (1927–87) took Piaget's account and applied it systematically to moral development. On the basis of empirical enquiry he concluded that moral reasoning and behaviour can be classified according to three levels each with two sub-stages. The youngest level is that of 'pre-conventional' reasoning where children simply obey rules to avoid punishment or, at the next sub-stage up, out of self-interest to gain a reward. Here rules are kept by egotistical young children without an understanding of their purpose or variability.

At the 'conventional' level children, and young adults, look for interpersonal accord and so internalize rules by seeking to be 'good', that is, by obeying rules willingly and not because of coercion. This moral level is autonomous in the sense that it is not imposed by authority. At the fourth stage, which is thought to be the one at which most adults function, rules are observed for the purpose of maintaining social order. At this point rules are kept not merely to gain individual approval but to help create a harmonious society. Although there is an understanding of the purpose of rules, there is little ability to deal with exceptions or new situations.

At the 'post-conventional' level, adults operate on the basis of principles. The fifth sub-stage stresses rights and values and is politically translated into a belief in a social contract. The final stage, which is thought to be rare, occurs where individuals act on the basis of universal ethical principles regardless of social norms as, for instance, Mother Teresa did.

Kohlberg's account of moral development was taken in unexpected directions. For instance, youth clubs and correctional institutes experimented by comparing authoritarian and democratic styles of leadership to assist young people appreciate the function of rules and to learn how to take responsibility for their actions. Democratic styles of leadership helped troubled young people understand why infractions of rules might be punished and showed that a whole range of sanctions might be applied rather than those based on physical pain. Even so, the scheme was criticized from a feminist perspective by Carol Gilligan (1982) who argued that the overarching theme of justice to which the whole stage developmental model aimed was itself flawed. Women, she maintained, preferred an ethic of care to an ethic of justice. When confronted by ethical dilemmas women preferred decisions that maintained relationships and expressed care for others rather than decisions which might appear to be equitable but which ignored personal feelings. In other words, the criteria for determining which level of thought someone operated at were mistaken.

> Must an ethic of justice conflict with an ethic of care? How would you explain the need for rules to a class of KS1 pupils? How would your explanation differ if pupils were KS3? Would your explanation concentrate on fairness or care for others?

Religious rules and religious principles

Nearly every religious system expresses itself through a multiplicity of rules. Famously Judaism is said to record 613 commandments given to Moses (Neusner 2008). Written texts were complemented and paralleled by a rich oral interpretative tradition in the Talmud. Christianity similarly, though its original mainspring rejected legalism in favour of simple faith, has at various points in its history expressed itself through canon law. Islam, also after an initial oral period, collected sayings about or attributed to Muhammad, the Hadith, which, together with jurisprudential deductions and precedents, were assembled into written guidelines that acquired legal force (e.g. in Hanafi, Hanbali and Maliki schools of law). There appears to be a sociological tendency for religions to develop from charismatic beginnings to bureaucratic conclusions (Weber 1930), and this tendency may be nothing to do with the nature of religion but rather stem from the nature of bureaucracy. The entire mindset that engenders bureaucracy is applicable to any and every self-perpetuating institution or agency. It is found in governments of all kinds and is most clearly exemplified in recent years, some would say, in the ever increasing bureaucratic scope and cost of the European Union.

Religious obligations are broadly speaking of two kinds: there are obligations to carry out certain practices (mass for Catholics, *Bar Mitzvah* for Jews, going on pilgrimage to Mecca for Muslims, etc.) and there are obligations of non-specific and general kinds (like honouring your parents). The binding requirement to carry out specific practices have little to do with justice, apart from the fact that societies which forbid religious practices of this kind deny basic freedoms and can therefore be classified as unjust.

The broader non-specific obligations are almost invariably ethical. Given that religions typically envisage a worshipping community, almost all contain strictures about community harmony, respect for tradition and older people, observance of the legal basis for marriage and inheritance and a vision of the future (e.g. Isaiah, chapter 11, verse 9). It is in the encouragement of these obligations, which may be expressed in the form of general principles, that an ideal of justice is to be found.

In short the minutiae of religious rules, whether these be connected with clothing, food, ritual or physical appearance have nothing to do with justice, where justice is defined, for example, as the equitable distribution of global resources. By contrast, generalized religious principles almost always enjoin equity on a large scale and love and kindness to strangers and neighbours on a smaller scale. It is these religious principles, which may become dispositions, that drive the human quest for national and social justice.

It will be noticed that the religious principles that concern justice are entirely compatible with Kohlberg's account of an ascending scale of moral reasoning from a conventional social level to a post-conventional and abstract level. Even if we accept Carol Gilligan's argument that levels of moral reasoning should prioritize an ethic of care, we can still see compatibility between religious principles and this ethic. For, after all, how could an ethic of care be more precisely expressed than by the words 'love your neighbour as yourself'?

Justice

Earlier, this chapter has defined justice as concerned with the equitable distribution of resources on a global scale. This is only one aspect of the concept. There are others. The character of distributive justice requires that resources be made available equally either in families or nations or, ultimately, between nations. Parents seek to love their children to the same degree and make equal resources available to them. Distributive justice demands equality of opportunity in the workplace so that the rewards for work are equally accessible to all. Distributive justice, it is true, is based on the notion that equal things must be treated equally and unequal things unequally. In families siblings are equal and in the workplace employees are, or should be, equal. In these cases, the distribution of resources is not according to need but according to unit of population – that is, unless needs or disabilities are thought to change categorizations. Thus parents might treat their children with absolute equality unless one of them was, for instance, disabled in a way that required additional resources.

Distributive justice is much harder to calculate when nations or countries are involved. This is because it is not practical to argue that global resources should suddenly be equalized. Indeed wealthy countries are likely to claim that they have become wealthy by merit – they have worked harder or been smarter and this is why they are now richer. Thus distributive justice at a national level tends to be concerned to mitigate the worst inequalities by breaking the cycle of debt brought about by the borrowing of international finance for the purpose of economic development.

Apart from distributive justice there is also procedural justice. Procedural justice is concerned with seeing that the same procedure is followed impartially irrespective of person or group. A referee in a football game should treat players on both sides in exactly the same way and penalize breaches of the rules without regard to celebrity or home team advantage. Planning applications for new buildings should be treated identically whether the applicant is rich or poor, well known or unknown.

Then there is retributive justice. Retributive justice is concerned with law-breaking. Here punishment may be seen as being administered for its own sake, i.e, as an expression of moral life, or as a deterrent (to warn other people from committing the same crime and to deter the law-breaker from re-offending). This sort of justice may also contain an element of restoration, where the person who stole or vandalized has to return or repair what was stolen or damaged.

Lastly, we might consider the notion of 'natural justice'. This is a corollary of 'natural law', a concept central to the thought of St Thomas Aquinas. In recent years, both in jurisprudence and in ordinary culture, the idea that justice was natural, or derived from nature, has been eclipsed by an evolutionary explanation of life on earth. At a time when the world, and all life on it, was seen as originating with a Creator, it was possible to look at nature itself and to say that certain things (e.g. the care of children by parents) expressed an intended order and were natural. In Shakespeare's *Hamlet* there is reference to 'carnal, bloody and unnatural acts' (5.2), a statement that shows how the idea persisted into the seventeenth century. Today natural justice amounts to little more than the belief that legal hearings should be judged openly and without bias.

Is distributive justice an impossible ideal? If so, can justice ever be said to be done?

Do you agree that restorative justice is part of retributive justice?

Does evolutionary theory mean that morality can no longer be located in nature?

Think of moral principles that might derive from evolutionary theory and examples in history of their application.

Postmodernity and relativity

Western thought has been characterized as passing through a period of postmodernity. In this phase, (which has connections with the globalization of knowledge), all kinds of knowledge are considered to be provisional and relative to other kinds of knowledge. The voices of many cultures compete for attention and claim to be speaking with truth. Another way of summarizing this situation is to say that there is now no longer a metanarrative or single defining story by which human beings understand each other. In the period after the western Enlightenment, say from 1780s onwards when Kant gave his lecture (1784), it was plausible to argue that the advance of human reason was taking civilization on an upward trajectory of steady improvement.[1] Diseases were being conquered, the natural world was being subdued, understanding was increasing and every problem was regarded in theory as being solvable. History was about the triumph of western thought and the spread of liberal values.

This story began to be challenged after the Great War (1914–18), for example, in the sphere of art when a multiplicity of styles emerged. After 1945, the challenge accelerated and instead of seeking truth, Existentialist philosophies encouraged us to seek authenticity (Camus 1948). Instead of prioritizing one viewpoint, we should listen to many. The canon of western literature was replaced by many canons – feminine, gay, black, post-colonial and others – and knowledge was now said to be 'constructed' rather than acquired. Opinions multiplied, especially as blogging and social media enabled thousands of like-minded people to find each other and form virtual communities, each of which had a different perspective on the world. In the lives and minds of young people in the West this phenomenon led to an acceptance of belief that truth was personal, right-for-me, and often based on nothing more than intuitive preference. A primary head teacher put it this way: just as you might have a favourite colour, so you might have a favourite religion.

This account of the world is too simple because it is clear that there are twenty-first-century metanarratives to be found in green philosophy or in atheistic evolution or both in combination. Yet, so far as religious truth is concerned, this is often treated as if it is a purely historical phenomenon, belonging to the past. What was thought to be true once is now no longer thought to be true anymore. Against this, it is evident that religious traditions are continuous and living. Nevertheless, many young people, whose beliefs are instinctively postmodern, will find it difficult to hold moral positions derived from religious beliefs. And where they do hold religious beliefs, they may find it difficult to apply these consistently. 'If you believe in the sanctity of life and therefore oppose abortion, why do you think it is right to kill in war?' is the kind of question the thoughtful young person may ask.

How would you explain the need for rules to a postmodernist? Consider how rules apply in some situations but not in others, for example, what is allowable in war is not allowable in peace, what is allowable in one country is not allowable in another. Why should this be? Does this mean that such rules are unimportant?

Skills and analysis

Disagreement over content in the curriculum is partly responsible for the reconceptualization of syllabuses in terms of skills. If knowledge is uncertain, let us instead learn to think in certain ways (e.g. reflectively, critically, mathematically) and then learn to develop certain attitudes (e.g. tolerance, respect for others, respect for the environment). Or, to put this another way, let us learn about religions so that we are familiar with beliefs and practices which have remained consistent over time and then let us learn from religion. In this way, we do not have to ask whether a specific religion is true because what matters is that followers of each faith believe that it is. Non-believers, it is thought, can still learn from believers and, as it were, use them as they would use the characters in novels and plays. The issue is not truth or falsity but usefulness or uselessness.

When we consider the moral rather than the doctrinal dimension of religion, issues of truth fade into the background. A full understanding of the moral dimension is impossible without an appreciation of the doctrinal dimension since we cannot, for instance, understand why Buddhists respect all life forms unless we understand the doctrine of reincarnation or why Christians value humility without appreciating Christian teaching about the incarnation of Christ. Yet, for classroom purposes, the moral teachings of the great religions are usually internally consistent and there is, as we shall see, some overlap between them. Moral teachings can certainly be made accessible to young people and moral ideals put before them.

There have been various attempts to launch moral education as a curriculum subject in its own right rather than as a dimension shared by several curriculum areas. An early attempt was made by John Wilson et al. (1967) to build moral education out of analytic components that pupils could learn. He sought to equip them with the tools to think about morality, where morality is characterized by its prescriptive or obligatory nature and its sense that obligations may be extended universally beyond specific situations. He listed four components appropriate for moral training: the notion of empathy (to identify other people's emotions), compassion (benevolence, love), the ability to work out and source relevant facts, and the ability to act after thought. These components he named *Emp, Phil, Gig* and *Krat* from shortened forms of the relevant Greek words.

Others like Peter McPhail based their approach to moral education on dilemmas young people were asked to discuss. For instance:

Tony was going out to meet friends on the other side of town and drove there in his car. He promised his mother he would be back to babysit his sister because his mother had to go out to work. He forgot to look at his watch and his mobile phone was not working. Should he break the speed limit to get home in time or should he keep to the speed limit and be late?

Such dilemmas were similar to the Heinz story used by Kohlberg:

> A woman was near death from illness. One drug might save her, a medicine that a pharmacy in the same town had recently discovered. The pharmacist was charging £2,000, ten times what the drug cost him to make. The sick woman's husband, Heinz, went to everyone he knew to borrow the money, but he could only get together about half of what it cost. He told the pharmacist that his wife was dying and asked him to sell it cheaper or let him pay later. But the pharmacist said 'no'. The husband got desperate and broke into the man's store to steal the drug for his wife. Should the husband have done that?. . . . Why do you think so?

Here learning is expected to take place by classroom discussion rather than instruction. The stories are intended to raise moral questions by putting moral duties or feelings in opposition to each other. In the Heinz story, the feeling of care and love for a wife is opposed to the duty to keep the law.

What do you think is the right thing to do in these situations? Is your answer based on instinct, reason, your own experience or a personal belief?

Is the second story an example of an ethic of care conflicting with an ethic of justice?

Dispositions in the classroom

Consider the following statements, each of which is taken from a religious text. The first, in the words of Jesus, is often called the Golden Rule and the others are similar. The rule concerns rejecting childish egotism and tells us to put others on a level with ourselves. Its fullest and most precise expression in the Gospels is also its widest. 'Do unto others . . .' without exception or qualification what 'you would have them do to you'. Ask yourself what you would want, and then do this for others. In the other formulations the scope is a limited to aliens, friends or brothers.

In everything do to others as you would have them do to you; for this is the law and the prophets. (Jesus, Matthew, chapter 7, verse 12)

And you are to love those who are aliens, for you yourselves were aliens in Egypt. (Deuteronomy, chapter 10, verse 19)

Friends love each other reciprocally from choice and their choice springs from a habit. (Aristotle, Ethics 8.5)

None of you believes until he loves for his brother what he loves for himself! (Muhammad, Hadith 13)

When we look more closely at the words of Jesus, we can see that he is telling us that other moral rules, or commands, are wrapped up in the Golden Rule. So the Ten Commandments which forbid stealing, lying, killing and so on are all covered by the command to treat others as we would be treated: if we do this, we will not steal, lie, kill and so on. Each of the other commands is an expression of failing to treat others as we would want them to treat us.

This tells us that moral rules can imply each other or be contained by higher, more general rules. If we accept the Piagetian account of mental development during which children move from a concrete operational stage (dealing with things they can touch and see) to an abstract stage (dealing with things that are conceptual), the most general rules will need to be addressed through the simpler more specific ones. So young children might be taught not to steal from each other ('don't take his pencil, Johnny') and move from here to reciprocity which depends on imagining a new hypothetical situation in which roles are reversed ('don't do that . . . how would you feel if Tommy took your pencil?').

As we know from the New Testament, moral rules are best conveyed by stories or parables, and these often evoke emotion. A man goes from Jerusalem to Jericho and is robbed, stripped and beaten (Luke, chapter 10, verses 25–37). He is left unconscious and badly injured. The situation cries out for an emotional and compassionate response. The priest and the Levite ignore the injured man but the Samaritan goes to the rescue, and all this in the context of loving your neighbour as yourself. So the rule needs to be illustrated and brought to life and not buried in a book of regulations. Moreover, we might also controversially say that the Golden Rule shows how moral action is more important than religious obligation. The two people who pass by on the other side and fail to come to the aid of the injured man are both steeped in religious obligation. The priest must carry out temple rituals and the Levite must sing or function as an assistant. Their focus on ritual duties blinds them to the emergency in front of their eyes.

All this suggests how the material might be ordered:

1   Teach a moral rule.
2   Teach a story illustrating the rule.
3   Teach another moral rule.
4   Teach another story illustrating the rule.
5   Teach about moral rules and their interconnection without a story.

Or,

1 Teach about religious duties and obligations (e.g. Pillars of Islam).
2 Teach stories illustrating these obligations.
3 Teach a moral rule.
4 Teach stories illustrating this rule.
5 Discuss what happens when obligations and moral rules appear to conflict.
6 Tell a story which illustrates a dilemma (drawing on Kohlberg or McPhail's example).
7 Discuss how the dilemma is to be resolved.

In using this approach, it should be noted that religious obligations nearly always admit exceptions. For instance, a Muslim going on pilgrimage, Hajj, has exemptions if he or she becomes ill; an Orthodox Jew, if in a situation where there is no kosher food, may in the last resort eat fish since fish were not judged at the time of Noah's flood. Sometimes, the dilemma can be resolved by invoking these well-known exceptions.

None of this is intended to minimize the value of religious obligation but it is intended to show how religious obligations function within a religious community to create identity, to serve as markers at the point of admission or in other ways make religious tradition explicit. For a Catholic to attend Mass or for a Jew to be circumcised is a matter of religious obligation that is not strictly moral because it has no universal application; thus, Catholics could not think it right for Buddhists to attend Mass. We may say that religious obligations are carried only by those who freely enter into them. For the Jewish believer, there is a precise moment when he or she takes on these obligations and that is at the point of *Bar Mitzvah* (*Bat Mitzwah* for girls) to become a 'son or daughter of the law'.

It would be helpful if schools could make it clear to pupils the nature of religious obligation either in RE lessons or in Citizenship lessons. Equally, it would be helpful if older pupils are enabled to understand the distinction between religious obligation and moral obligation. Moral obligation may be felt by irreligious people and felt in the same way by people of all religions and none. Thus, moral obligation (e.g. not to kill or steal) can be universally carried. The difference for a religious person is that such moral obligations are supported by religious authority. The young religious person may not steal because he or she has been told that Jesus or Moses or Muhammad would not approve. The older religious person will understand that stealing is also wrong because it undermines social cohesion or creates injustice or is irrational. Gradually, just as the child learns to speak by adopting the rules of language, the religious person learns to live by adopting the moral rules of their faith.

We might all believe that stealing is wrong but what in practice prevents us from stealing when it seems no-one will ever find out?

Is it possible that a religious person might resist temptation more readily than someone without a religious allegiance?

What change to your life would adopting the 'Golden Rule' require?

Note

1 I. Kant, Konigsberg in Prussia, 30 September 1784, 'An answer to the question: what is enlightenment?'. See http://www.english.upenn.edu/~mgamer/Etexts/kant.html [accessed 14/1/12]

References

Camus, A. (1948), *The Plague*. New York: Doubleday. First published in French in 1947.

Gilligan, C. (1982), *In a Different Voice*. Cambridge, MA: Harvard University Press.

Kohlberg, Lawrence (1976) 'Moral stages and moralization: The cognitive-developmental approach', in T. Lickona, (ed.), *Moral Development and Behavior: Theory, Research and Social Issues*. Holt, NY: Rinehart and Winston.

McPhail, P., Ungoed-Thomas, J. R. and Chapman, H. (1972), *Moral Education in the Secondary School*. London: Longman.

Neusner, J. (2008), 'The Golden Rule in Classical Judaism'. *Review of Rabbinic Judaism* 11(2): 292–315. Brill.

Weber, Max (1930), *The Protestant Ethic and the Spirit of Capitalism*. London: Routledge. First published in German in 1905.

Wilson, J., Williams, N. and Sugarman, B. (1967), *An Introduction to Moral Education*. Harmondsworth: Penguin.

CHAPTER EIGHT

Being courageous

required by the pursuit of justice

D. Ieuan Lloyd

CHAPTER OUTLINE

This chapter is concerned with defining courage and how it can be taught. The variety of examples used illustrate that there is no simple definition of courage though many of the characteristics manifested in the different settings overlap. It is noted that courageous acts may be valued differently and would normally presuppose approval. But how is courage learnt? Is it transferable from one situation to another? Does it imply human flourishing? Is it reasonable? Does luck play a role? What is the role of discipline? Is there such a thing as feminine courage? These and a number of other considerations are evaluated. The chapter also explores obstacles to being courageous; weakness of will, the difficulty of teaching courage and the importance of role models. Finally, the chapter concludes that a love of a person or object is central to being courageous.

When one is faced with the task of writing about a single word, the temptation is to define it. Soon one finds that what appear to be legitimate examples of that word do not fit the definition and so one has to think again because of the significant differences between them. This is true of the idea of courage. Take the following two examples:

Example 1

A young German officer recovers a British soldier while under heavy enemy fire at Ypres, in order that the soldier was given an honourable burial.

Example 2

On 1 December 1955 in Montgomery Alabama, Rosa Parks refused to obey the bus driver's instructions to give up her seat to a white passenger. She was arrested, charged with violation of the segregation law. She also lost her job in a department store as a result. She abhorred the way black people were treated and did not fear the consequences of what she did.

It does not seem that these two examples have a great deal in common, yet they are clear examples of courageous acts. But consider the differences: first, one occurs in war, the other in peacetime. Second, the German officer was trained in a military code to do what he did. Mrs Parks had no such training. It was sufficient that she had a strong sense of justice and injustice. Third, the German Officer probably experienced fear under those circumstances, but Mrs Parks was fearless in her resolve. Fourth, the officer faced possible death, but not so Mrs Parks. Fifth, risk is present in both, though the nature of the risk is different. Even if we widen the definition to include the differences as well as the similarities in these cases, we may still mistakenly leave out some other acts of courage. For example, feats of endurance may qualify as courageous. That is when a person has to meet hardship and temptation. Here fears of life and limb are not present but endurance requires grit, a will to keep on going despite setbacks which may not be life threatening.

Are there times in your life when you have shown courage? What motivated you?

The above considerations suggest that an attempt to produce a clear definition of courage that will suit all cases may not be possible. We should not be surprised by this, for human qualities and their manifestations occur in a whole variety of situations. J. O. Urmson (1958), in a much discussed article 'Saints and Heroes', makes a similar point, and concludes that 'on the whole the best philosophy is little affected by theory'. There must of course be some connection within the variety of cases but it would be a mistake to rule out instances theoretically which normally we would include in our non-philosophical conversation about courage. (Urmson, himself was decorated for his courage and skill in World War II). What is common to the two examples cited above is that the persons concerned act in a way of which not everyone would be capable, and do so without a concern for their own welfare.

Two further points need to be borne in mind here

First, not all courageous acts are of equal value, because the causes that are defended may differ in their value or importance. A person who risks his life in rescuing his child may be described as courageous but not be considered so courageous if he risks his life for an animal where he may be thought to be foolish. If the object of the 'courageous' act is a factor, then further complexities arise. Is there a difference if the child is his own or someone else's?

Is it more courageous to rescue a dog or a hamster?

Second, when one describes an action as courageous it must mean that we approve of the action. For example, we might say of the Great Train Robbers (in Britain) that they were bold and daring but because of the brutality shown in the robbery we cannot sensibly describe what they did as courageous. The reason for this is that we cannot square courage with violence and ruthlessness, even though the action may still be incompatible with cowardice.

So far, it appears that:

1 Courage can be manifest in different situations, in wartime and peacetime.
2 Courage may be preceded by training but not necessarily so.
3 Fear may or may not be felt.
4 An action must be approved of for it to be courageous.
5 The causes can be of different values and so courage may receive different levels of approval.

Now we turn to a number of other issues which relate to courage and which have a bearing to some extent on the other virtues too.

Transference of abilities

A common theme in recent education literature has been the transference of abilities and skills. The value of an ability or skill, it is claimed, has the advantage of being capable of being employed in an area different from that in which it was first acquired, and is therefore economical in its nature educationally. Could this be true of courage?

In the case of Mrs Parks, it does not seem that the courage she showed was the result of any training. In fact, she may not have been aware of what she was capable until the event itself. She showed a determination that might have surprised her. She might have reflected 'I did not know I had it in me.' The explanation of her action is that she felt so strongly about the issue of civil rights for black people that nothing could have made her budge or refrain from what she did. But it is also true that it would be a mistake to infer from this one instance that she has a general character trait of courage that would be evident in other parts of her life. Take the recent example of a teacher who rescued some of his class from a burning building. It would not be difficult to imagine that he had a fear of fire and concern for his own safety yet he overcame those fears. But again one would not want to infer from that one event that courage was even a general feature of his character. In both these cases we do not have to learn more about their history to decide whether they were courageous on those singular occasions. The courage shown by Mrs Parks or the schoolteacher was neither a general skill nor a talent.

Despite the singular nature of courageous actions in the two examples just given we do in other situations frequently attribute certain character traits. Thus, the soldier was possibly put in particular positions of leadership because his superiors may have witnessed his courage on a number of occasions. It is not unusual to write a testimonial or reference for a person, where it seems we are able to generalize about a person's qualities and state that these qualities are firm character traits. So of a boy or girl, whom we might recommend for a senior position, we might say that they are mature in their judgement, that they relate well with pupils, and have a good deal of common sense. Or else we might recommend adults to serve on a committee on account of their shrewdness, their ability to handle people well, and capable of presenting their views convincingly.

So the conclusion that must be drawn is that a person may display a quality such as courage in a particular situation without it being justified to claim that it is his or her character trait which is transferable to a variety of situations. Yet of another person it appears we can and do attribute such traits of character. The subject worthy of consideration in this context is the idea of 'uncharacteristic actions', and how they arise.

> Are 'uncharacteristic actions' worthy of more praise than habitual ones?

Human flourishing

An increasingly popular view in ethics is that of human flourishing. The idea here may be that we educate for the qualities of character rather than for particular acts, such as the ones which acknowledge the call of duty or the ones which lead to human happiness. Yet, one can easily understand how the idea of human flourishing can be misleading. The idea has a botanical image, where something blossoms into its full potential and enjoys that maturity. Put like this the goal of human flourishing appears rather egocentric, especially if 'flourishing' is seen from a psychological point of view. We might regard or think of a happy person as flourishing. But what would we say in the case of Emily Davison, a suffragette who threw herself in front of a horse at the Derby Races in 1913? Was she 'flourishing' when it was the end of her life? And what of the martyrs in the past and in the present who suffer torture and even death because of their faith? Jesus who suffered and was crucified for his belief and actions is the most revered example. So the confusion that arises when speaking of human flourishing is between 'flourishing' as a psychological description and as a judgement of value. This is brought out in Plato's dialogue, the *Gorgias*. Socrates describes the tyrant, Archelaus, much to the astonishment of his opponents, as the most miserable of men (471a). But this seems to go against common sense. The tyrant has all he wants, wealth and power. Surely, psychologically, he is the happiest of all men. But Socrates is not speaking about his state of mind but about the state of his soul. It is a description of the moral worth of his life. So the idea of flourishing, if we want to use it at all, must be compatible with a psychologically unhappy life, that is, where something may have been sacrificed and where the consequence of what one has had to do has been deepening rather than satisfying.

If the expression 'flourishing' has both of these two senses, the ambiguity may suggest the word is more of a hindrance than a help. In Chapter 3, David Carr refers to the need for further reading on the subject; this is yet another case.

You may be familiar with the story behind Albrecht Durer's painting *The Praying Hands*. Durer was able to pursue his dream of going to the art school in Nuremburg because his brother Albert worked down a mine to finance his studies. By the time Durer had become famous and offered to send his brother to Nuremburg, his hands were too badly damaged. So Durer produced the famous painting, modelled on his brother hands. Which brother could be said to have flourished or fulfilled his potential?

There is a further point worth considering which is related to an earlier point. A naming of a character quality cannot be described independently of what we think of the values to which a person is committed. Take the example of loyalty which on the face of it is a quality in a person that one should normally respect. But consider the case of Himmler. He was not a very intelligent man, so those he chose to work under him were even less intelligent, but the one character trait on which Himmler depended was their 'loyalty'. It was their sense of 'loyalty' that enabled them to overcome their revulsion in the execution of his orders to murder hundreds of thousands Jews. Clearly even the character trait of 'loyalty' is subject to moral assessment before we applaud someone for it. We simply cannot describe Himmler's men as truly courageous or genuinely praise their loyalty because their acts were evil.

Discipline

The German soldier had been effectively 'disciplined' to carry out certain instructions during his military training, so that he is not overcome by what could be a deflecting temptation likely to weaken his resolve in carrying out his duties even when faced with the possibility of a threat to life and limb. Captain Sullenberger who landed his stricken plane (both engines having failed) in the Hudson River had gone through the discipline of dealing with crises in the air through many simulations. That is not to say that his reactions were automatic, or even that that was the most important part of the success in landing the plane, but the rehearsals of how to land were nevertheless indispensable. Discipline at a more mundane level is to ensure the machinery of an organization or institution runs smoothly, such as ensuring one should walk down school corridors on the left hand side. However, discipline requires a habit to be formed so that there will be a predisposition to follow the rules no matter what personal inclinations one may have. It is to some extent, an antidote to moral weakness.

Weakness of the will

The other side of the coin of discipline is weakness of the will. This human frailty has puzzled philosophers down the centuries, even though it is so common. We are all familiar with promising ourselves on New Year's Day that we will take up more exercise, reply to letters and emails received more promptly, and so on. Yet it is only a matter of weeks or even days that we fail to do what it seemed we wanted to do. Some philosophers have deemed this to be a bogus problem. They take the view that if we failed to do something it is because we did not truly desire it in the first place. Weakness of the will for them is an illusion. But the problem is not so easily dismissed, for we may still have real regrets about what we have not done. Other solutions have been offered, such as that we have been distracted at the moment of action or that we have been forgetful. But none of these explanations are truly satisfactory. Yet another solution offered is that the weakness has a physical or psychological cause. One example of this is the difficulty that smokers have in giving up their habit. Or, a person may really want to go to work but suffers from agoraphobia that stops him or her. In war, shellshock was often the effect of overwhelming fear. But when we are thinking of weakness of will it is usually not one of these cases with a physical or psychological obstacle but of someone of whom we want to say they are both free to do what they want, but fail to do it. Perhaps the explanation lies in our mistake in thinking that the mind is like a committee which meets and takes a vote when there are competing views, and that the majority vote will be carried.

The problem of the weakness of will has sometimes been put in the form of the battle between a better judgement and a superior judgement, superior meaning the more powerful and the better judgement being the more sensible. We can then contrast the weakness of the will in some people with those we have already mentioned who have overcome competing forces of self-interest or self-preservation. The strength of their religious, moral or political beliefs has been so strong that even under conditions of torture they have not recanted; such is their single-mindedness. An interesting example of the strength of a belief overcoming physical factors is that of an island where the eating of a particular fish was held to be the cause of promiscuity. For some inhabitants it then became a virtue to eat the fish and yet remain celibate. J. M. Barrie in his St Andrews Rectorial address goes even further in highlighting an overriding single-mindedness by suggesting that we 'greet the unseen with a cheer'(1922, p. 47). He, in turn, had been inspired by his close friend Captain Scott who in his final letter to Barrie wrote, 'We are in a desperate state-frozen, etc. no fuel and a long way from food, but it would do your heart good to be in our tent, to hear our songs and our cheery conversation.' (1922, p. 32)

Can you think of other examples where an individual's strength of religious, moral or political beliefs has enabled that individual to overcome self-interest and preservation?

In summary, perhaps it is a confusion to think of the will as some unseen mechanism of the brain. Instead, one should consider more closely what constitutes the strength of a person's beliefs. There is no shortage of literature on the subject.

Moral luck

Kant thought that the intention to carry out an action was a sufficient ground on which to judge a person. One modern philosopher, Nagel has a similar idea in that he sees that the consequences of someone's actions are strictly irrelevant in judging the merit of what one has done. For him there is no moral difference between an attempted murder and a successful murder, the intention of the perpetrator is the same. So accordingly, the degree of culpability is the same. This appears to be an attractive idea. Why should something not under one's control, like a jammed mechanism in a handgun, make a person less blameworthy if he intended to shoot someone? One way of seeing that this view is mistaken, is to consider the case of a positive act. Compare an attempted rescue with a successful rescue. The hero is generally one who has been successful. We do not applaud one who attempts to win a race as much as one that has. Should we award plaudits or medals to all people who have courageous intentions but who do not succeed in their attempts? This would seem to follow from Nagel saying that the consequences of one's actions do not enter into our moral judgement of what a person has done. It has other implications, for example, for the nature of regret. President Reagan was pushed aside by one of his aides when an assassination attempt was made on his life. If the assassin later considers what he has done, and regrets it, his regret cannot be the same as if he had actually killed the President. He may well be grateful for the fact that he failed in his attempt. The moral picture is different for him depending on the success or failure of his action. Thus in contrast, he might reproach himself for having failed. That too, would be a different moral attitude than if he had succeeded.

In our discussion of courage, success or failure in performing an action must enter into our judgement of whether a person has performed a courageous act. That is not to say that we should not praise someone for a courageous attempt, but a courageous attempt is not the same as a successful courageous act.

Risk

Courage is often spoken of as if it can only be present where there is a risk and where the risk concerns one's own welfare. The risk can be to one's health and safety in food, in sports and in living. Larger risks have to do with certain kinds of technology, terrorism, and global warming. The concept of risk is much discussed nowadays, not least because our life is constantly changing where often we do not know how serious the risks are. Even so, it is clear in times past and in the present, people have been prepared to take risks and show courage when confronting them. But not all risks are equal in their severity. Whether the actions are wise or reckless will depend on the value of what is at stake. Consider the difference between risks taken in free climbing or bungee jumping for the pleasure they give to the participants. In contrast, other risks are taken for the benefit to other people. Equally we may disagree on the importance these ends have as well as differ in the accurate calculation of those risks. There is the case of the Dutch teenager, Laura Dekker, who sailed around the world alone. Her plan was regarded as so risky the matter came before the courts on the grounds that her sail around the world might harm her emotional and social development, let alone the possibility of any physical harm and risk of drowning. If she had not succeeded, many would have said they knew the whole enterprise was foolish from the start, but because those unpredictable and hazardous events did not occur, (which were not in her control), she was regarded as a teenage heroine.

Fear

Fear is often present when a person has to be courageous. Some are fearful and do not show it, others are fearful and show it, but are still courageous, and others are fearful, show it, and run. Fear is perhaps the emotion most associated with courage. To be without fear in some situations is dangerous. In fact, it has been said that the person to fear is the person who has no fear. The person can be incautious and reckless. Fear can help to ensure one has a realistic view of a situation. It is a brake on impetuousness. Children who do not have a sense of fear, such as some who are autistic, make themselves vulnerable to people and events. However common it is for fear to be present in some stories of a courageous act, it is not always present as was evident in an earlier example.

Men and women

In Greek times, it was considered that courage occurred almost exclusively in the area of warfare in which only men took part. This is evident from the

Greek word *andreia* which means 'manliness'. Thucydides did concede that whenever women were described as courageous it would be unusual but more generally he considered it 'beyond their nature' (Hobbs 2000, p. 71). Aristotle was more generous. Yet even 'for Aristotle good men and good women are not good in the same way' (Hobbs, p. 71). This is a point worthy of discussion. Are the virtues in general and courage in particular, available to both men and women? If not, is that because they have different roles in life, or that their natures are different? Aristotle, in spite of his concession to women that they too can be courageous, believed that courage in battle was the noblest. It follows that whatever courage women show; it cannot be equal to that of which men are capable. We now recognize that this is clearly false. Women have shown themselves equally courageous in a variety of situations. Numerically, it may still be true that the opportunities for men to show courage in conflict are greater than for women, mainly because more men serve in the military forces than women, but this is a numerical difference not a qualitative one.

A complex picture of courage has emerged from the above considerations. The transference of abilities, the notion of flourishing, the development of discipline, the sense of weakness of will, the actual consequences of our actions, the risks taken, the presence or absence of fear, gender differences, all appear to have some bearing on the attribution of courage.

We now turn to the matter of teaching the virtue of courage.

Education and courage

Some moral qualities, such as kindness and honesty, can be taught and acquired from quite an early age. Courage is more difficult. It is not easy to think of situations, whether artificial or real, that can be created for children to develop this virtue. But there is one thing that teachers can do. Plato in The *Republic* recommends recounting stories of courageous people. Angela Hobbs in her scholarly work, *Plato and the Hero* (2000), believes that this opportunity of narration has been neglected over the years. Stories of heroism can inspire the young and convey to them what is important and what is unimportant. The narratives can extend and deepen the understanding of what is possible. They can be stories about courageous acts in various walks of life, in medicine, in exploration and in ordinary life. Mrs Edna Oakeshott, the wife of Professor Michael Oakeshott, published a booklet, *Childhood in Autobiography* (1960), which she intended to supplement the more technical subject of educational psychology. The book provides a list of biographies in which the early upbringing of the authors is fully described. Perhaps what is needed today in teaching is something similar for the virtues; stories both of fact and of fiction that portray courage in the flesh rather than by the skeleton of theoretical analysis.

In Britain, another relevant source are the true stories told in the television programme, 'Children of courage', stories of the lives of real young people. Some of these accounts are of children who have experienced serious illness and who have coped courageously and even cheerfully with painful treatment. Other examples are of children who have carried out courageous acts well beyond those expected of their age or of their maturity.

Does discipline have a place in the acquisition of courage at least at a preliminary stage? Some organizations for children have discipline as one of their core aims. They include organizations such as the Scouts and the Guides Movements and ones more directly connected with religious institutions (e.g. the Boys' Brigade). The Duke of Edinburgh's Award Scheme has since 1956 encouraged personal discipline. In the current education climate, there have been objections to these institutions in that some see them as authoritarian and of that they disapprove. That is prejudice. Even a school choir or sports clubs require rules to be obeyed. A distinction must be made between the institutions and particular expressions of them. There is nothing wrong with the novices in an institution having to conform to its rules. The same can be said of schools as a whole. They all have rules to be obeyed, though the form that the rules take can vary from the regimes of Boot Camps to the somewhat more relaxed school of A. S. Neil's Summerhill. Discipline is not essentially punitive.

> Do you agree that discipline has a place in the acquisition of courage? If so, why?

If discipline can be an ancillary to becoming courageous, wherein lies the main source of courage? I believe it is given in the renowned chapter of 1 Corinthians, chapter 13 of the New Testament, which is summed up in the final verse where we are told that of the three important things, faith, hope and love, the greatest is love. In those cases described earlier of those who have been trained to be courageous or where there is no history of training, what elicits an act of courage from them *in extremis* is the love of the object, which they may want to defend or preserve. The object of love may be a person, a place, or a belief. The religious martyrs embraced death willingly because of the love for their faith. The soldier faces death courageously because of the love he has for his country. The teacher runs into the school that is on fire to rescue his children because of the love he has for them. So within the classroom what the teacher has to cultivate, to use an older phrase, is a desire (Eros) for the good. It is only this love that can change self-interested inclinations to a selfless desire for the good. What can the teacher do about this? Sometimes what is called from a teacher in some areas of teaching is to exercise a greater effort, that is, more of the same. But where courage is being taught, it has to do with who the teacher is than with any effort he or she can make. For this is a qualitative difference. The teacher must be seen to be caught up in something larger than himself or herself. It is only in this way that the child comes to see things differently and to have a deeper regard for things.

> Is there a relationship between being courageous and having religious faith?
> What would inspire you to be courageous?

Teaching virtues, like courage, is not like teaching a skill or teaching mere information. This is why Plato states that virtue is knowledge, that is, the knowledge from encounter and acquaintance. What therefore is demanded of the teacher is that the virtue of courage must mean something to the teacher. One learns from the teacher, because of whom the teacher is. In short, the character of the teacher affects what the child learns. If the teacher is shallow or proud, the child will learn little. In such a situation, the pupil may learn about what is called courage, but that is to learn it at a distance, as one might learn the classification of plants.

Here is another way of looking at the difference between learning a skill and acquiring a virtue. Suppose a child wants to learn how to play a game, say basketball or netball. But after a while the child decides to give it up, and says of the game, 'It's not for me'. The teacher may shrug his or her shoulders, and regard the change of interest as just one of those things. But when one is taught about courage one is not being taught how to be good at courage. And the teacher would have failed if the child said of courage, 'It's not for me'. For when one is taught to be courageous, that teaching changes one, such that if one fails to be courageous, it will be something that one will regret and regret because in an event of cowardice one has learnt something about oneself.

> Do you agree that a teacher has failed if she does not convince pupils of the value of courage?

Frequently in the educational literature on moral education and in Plato, reason is an important element in performing a courageous act. This emphasis

I suppose is to contrast it with actions that are impetuous and reckless. Yet, one should feel uncomfortable when speaking of acts of courage as if they are always the most reasonable thing to do. One can imagine that the priest in the story of the Good Samaritan saying, 'I did what reason told me'. I think it was a great naval commander who once said, 'Leap before you look.' This does appear to be a recipe for disaster. Certainly, there are occasions when the outcome should be 'reasoned' but other times not. In the Children of Courage accounts a phrase that keeps cropping up is 'without any thought for their own safety'. There was MCayla Johnston whose life was changed in a moment after being hit by a car. Doctors predicted she would never walk or talk again, but she battled against the odds, began a campaign to prevent further accidents in the dangerous place where she met her accident. It seems odd to speak of her courage as springing from reason. This is true also for Tom Phillips, an 11 year old boy who saved his father from certain death on a farm by driving a tractor – he had been instructed never to drive – at a bull that was goring his father. An adjective such as sensible, or rational, does not fully capture the quality of what he did. In Hardy's epic drama of the war with Napoleon, *The Dynasts* (1908), the French commandant says, 'More life may trickle out of men through thought than through a gaping wound'. Thought and beliefs can be more potent than physical threats.

D o you agree that love or concern for the object is the key to being courageous?

I quoted earlier from 1 Corinthians, chapter 13 about the overarching virtue of love and its importance. This idea is anticipated in Plato's dialogue, *Symposium*. Agathon in his speech says, 'For the principle which ought to be the guide of men who would nobly live-that principle, I say, neither kindred, nor honour, nor wealth, nor any other motive is able to implant so well as love. . . . I say of Love that he is the fairest and best in all other things.'

The presence of love, I want to say, ensures courage to be at its strongest. (*Symposium*, paras. 178, 197).

References

Barrie, J. M. (1922), *Courage*. London: Hodder and Stoughton.
Hardy, T. (1908), *The Dynasts*. (Penguin Classics). Harmondsworth: Penguin Books.
Hobbs, A. (2000), *Plato and the Hero*. Cambridge: Cambridge University Press.
Oakeshott, E. (1960), *Childhood in Autobiography*. Cambridge: Cambridge University Press.

Plato (1971), *Gorgias* (Penguin Classics). Harmondsworth: Penguin Books.
—(1970), *Symposium* (Penguin Classics). Harmondsworth: Penguin Books.
Urmson, J. O. (1958), 'Saints and Heroes', in A. Melden (ed.), *Essays in Moral Philosophy*. Seattle: University of Washington Press, 1958.

For a remarkable example of courage, see the story of Hubert (Bert) Lovegrove in Chapters 8 and 9 of No Citation by James Allan, Angus and Robertson 1955.

I would like to acknowledge a helpful discussion with Huw Lloyd in the preparation of this chapter.

CHAPTER NINE

Being hopeful

looking to positive outcomes of actions

Penny Thompson

CHAPTER OUTLINE

This chapter explores what it means to be hopeful. It refers to the work of the educational philosopher David Halpin and the theologians Jurgen Moltmann and Tom Wright. Hope provokes discontent with the present and inspires positive action based on the belief that endless creative possibilities are open to human beings. The practice of hope is an important part of the teacher's armoury. Hope looks to a future good and trusts that such a goal can be reached. It offers sustenance in times of difficulty, in particular through trust in God. The argument that hope is a distraction from serious engagement with the present is considered along with theological replies. The future of God and the Utopian imagination are considered.

Introduction

Scholars have increasingly paid attention to the virtue of hope in recent years.[1] A remarkable fact is the choice of the title 'Hope' for a university created in Liverpool, UK, in 2005. Liverpool Hope University has a joint Catholic/Anglican foundation and the choice of the word 'hope' is a conscious attempt to reflect its Christian foundation. It may also reflect the partnership between Archbishop Worlock and Bishop David Sheppard whose public work together did much to overcome traditional suspicions in the city. A recent paper by David Halpin, entitled 'Hope, Utopianism and Educational Renewal', cites a large number of articles in which the word hope or a word closely related to hope appears (Halpin 2003). Mary Warnock (quoted in Halpin) has stated that of all the attributes she would like to see in her children or pupils, 'the attribute of hope would come high, even top of my list. To lose hope is to lose the capacity to want or desire anything; to lose, in fact, the wish to live.' (Halpin 2003) This may reflect a sense that the world and education in particular is in need of an injection of hope. Certainly this is the view of David Halpin in the aforementioned article. Global recession, and, at the time of writing, the crisis in the eurozone, certainly serve to increase this sense. The decision of Birmingham City Council in the United Kingdom to adopt a syllabus which deliberately fosters the virtues and dispositions related to them can also be seen as a response to a culture perceived to be lacking in faith, hope and love along with other traditional moral virtues. This chapter builds on the work of the educational philosopher David Halpin, incorporating theological material from theologians Jurgen Moltmann and Tom Wright to suggest how hope can inform the teaching of religious education.

Hope – a theological virtue

Hope features strongly within Christian thinking and also within its liturgical tradition and hymnody. Its place among the cardinal virtues developed by St Thomas Aquinas may be due to the well-known words of St Paul:

> 'So faith, hope, love abide, these three; but the greatest of these is love',
> 1 Corinthians, chapter 13, verse 13

At first sight this famous verse may seem to downgrade the place of faith and hope. These words come in a section in the letter where Paul is (gently) berating the church at Corinth for a variety of shortcomings, but in particular a lack of unity and a lack of care for one another. Hence, from a practical point of view, the emphasis is on love. That Paul placed great emphasis on faith is not in question. His views on hope are perhaps less well known but nonetheless of importance and will be referred to later.

Halpin takes hope to be directed to a future good that one desires. It consists in having faith that one may, through what one does in the present (and through help received), attain to such a good. For Aquinas the future good is eternal life, the enjoyment of God. And hope attains God by leaning on his help in order to obtain the hoped for good.

What is it that you hope for in life?

For Halpin the message for the educator is that hopefulness entails both anticipating future happiness and trusting in present help to attain that happiness. Being a hopeful teacher entails having both high expectations of learners' potential and faith that the educational process will help them to realize this potential. Faith, hope and love are combined inextricably here whether one talks in theological terms or more secular ones. Faith believes that the future good is attainable, hope in the potential of the pupils spurs the teacher on and love is both the attitude of the teacher towards the pupil and the ultimate goal.

What one hopes for is critical in character development since one is likely to develop in ways that reflect the hope that one aspires to. The philosopher Grayling (quoted in Halpin) writes: 'you discover more about people when you learn about their hopes than when you count their achievements, for the best of what we are lies in what we hope to be.' 1 John, chapter 3, verses 1–7: 'Beloved, we are God's children now; what we will be has not yet been revealed. What we do know is this: when he is revealed, we will be like him, for we will see him as he is. And all who have this hope in him purify themselves, just as he is pure.' Anticipating or dwelling on the hope of becoming like God acts in some way to bring about or at least reflect something of the future transformation that is hoped for. The principle of faith that what one is doing will bring about progress is clearly vitally important as is having a vision of what one is aiming for.

What hopes do you have for your pupils?

Hope provokes discontent

Interestingly, Halpin begins his exposition with the insistence that hopefulness 'entails . . . a critically reflective attitude towards prevailing circumstances.' Hope can provoke discontent with things as they are since the present situation may not only fall far short of what one hopes for but also actually work against improvement. He writes of 'frustrations that frequently occasion the practice of education which often entails working against the grain of conditions that are antithetical to effective learning'. (Halpin 2003) Tales of hopelessness within education can be read as an appeal for things to get better, indicating a submerged vision of what things could be like.

Where faith develops into hope, the theologian Jurgen Moltmann argues, '[it] does not calm the unquiet heart, but is itself this unquiet heart in man'. (Moltmann, p. 21) Discontent with the present situation is driven by the vision of what the future holds out for God's world, the possibilities that at present we see through a glass darkly: 'He promises a new world of all-embracing life, of righteousness and truth, and with this promise he constantly calls this world into question – not because to the eye of hope it is as nothing, but because to the eye of hope it is not yet what it has the prospect of being'. (Moltmann, p. 64)

In this context, the Biblical record of prophetic outrage against injustice of every kind and, in the case of Israel, the constant call not to fall back into ease and forgetfulness of the demands of Yahweh also reflects this theme. Moltmann argues that the Christian can never be reconciled to things as they are: 'in beginning to hope for the triumph of life and to wait for resurrection, he perceives the deadliness of death and can no longer put up with it.' And, 'as long as 'every thing' is not 'very good' the difference between hope and reality remains, and faith remains irreconciled and must press towards the future in hope and suffering.' (Moltmann, pp. 214 and 215)

The nature of the Christian hope and how life in the present relates to it is taken up later in this chapter.

How useful do you think discontent with such things as salary, conditions, resources and opportunities for children might be in bringing about improvement? Would you be prepared for the frustration and aggravation that such discontent could bring?

New possibilities

Hope provokes discontent with present wrongs on the basis that the future holds out ever-greater possibilities, possibilities that cannot always be conceived or even imagined. Halpin writes of the hopeful person being one who develops imaginative solutions to seemingly intractable difficulties. In addition 'it (hope) can visualise a state of affairs not yet existing; and, more than this, it can both anticipate as well as prepare the ground for something new.' Perhaps this is what Jesus meant when he told his followers, when carrying out merely what was expected of them, to think of themselves as unprofitable/unworthy servants. (Luke, chapter 17, verse 10)[2] Moltmann writes: 'hopes and anticipations of the future are not a transfiguring glow superimposed upon a darkened existence, but are realistic ways of perceiving the scope of our real possibilities'. (Moltmann, p. 25) In a Christian perspective one's real possibilities lie in what it means to be a child of God. I quoted earlier from 1 John: 'we are God's children now . . . what we will be has not yet been revealed'. Our possibilities are only limited by what limits God. And God is without limits, literally, infinite. Our possibilities are to be measured by our status as children of a God for whom only endless possibilities exist. This magnitude, this sense of 'beyond everything' is found in another well-known passage from the apostle Paul: 'what no eye has seen, nor ear heard, nor the heart of man conceived, what God has prepared for those who love him' (1 Corinthians, chapter 2, verse 9).

This may seem somewhat remote for the hard-pressed teacher coping week by week with a group or groups of reluctant pupils. It may be that just making the effort is worthwhile, even if not much seems to be achieved. I remember one pupil commending my efforts with a particularly recalcitrant group of Y11s (aged 15–16), saying that I never gave up despite the difficulties!

What would it mean, in practice, to be a hopeful teacher? Is it realistic to look for limitless possibilities in teaching?

Hope presupposes 'the Good'

Halpin argues that hopefulness is oriented to the good and yearns for it. 'Something good could still materialise' he puts it. It is a disposition that results in a person being positive about both his or her own life and the lives of others. It is particularly relevant, he argues, in education. Without hope there could be no planning: 'the resonance with the education project hardly requires elaboration other than to remark that the wish to succeed as a classroom teacher or school leader is likely to be accompanied by a yearning hope to do well in one's work, allied to a propensity to innovate in order to achieve the best results.' It is easy for pupils to give up hope, particularly when they stand, yet again, in the office of the head teacher and not for praiseworthy reasons. I remember one Head saying how his aim was always to hold out a glimmer of hope to even the most recalcitrant of pupils.

Being hopeful then involves a 'taken-for-granted belief in the ultimate worthiness of reality and the people and things that mostly make it up.' Quotes from Jonathan Sacks and Victor Havel are used to support this point. Moreover Halpin says that 'there is an abundance of common-sense evidence to suggest that when people find themselves in dire and difficult circumstances they can help to sustain themselves by bringing to mind ideas of the Good Life. Courage, allied to persistence is the hallmark of such belligerence.'

Halpin does not elaborate on what the good life might be nor on ways of bringing it to mind. Here I consider briefly how Christian faith understands the good life and then the ways the tradition brings such things to mind.

The good life within the Christian tradition

The existence of the good and the yearning for it are central to the Christian tradition. Within this tradition the good exists because it inheres within the Trinity for whom and by whom humans (and their world) have been and are created. One is reminded of the famous words of St Augustine: 'our hearts are made for thee and are restless till they find their rest in thee'. The goodness of God and the divine initiative (imperative?) to create and extend this goodness means that our universe is of worth despite so much that might make us think differently. This is spelt out after each separate act of creation in the first book of the Bible with the words – 'and God saw that it was good' -. The first chapter of John, in language that reflects the first chapter of Genesis insists that 'the light shines in the darkness and the darkness has not overcome it'. (John, chapter 1, verse 1) Furthermore, the Bible indicates that creation is moving forward to an ultimate fulfilment. Paul's depiction of the redemption of creation in Romans, chapter 8 underlines perhaps more than any other passage in the Bible both the worthwhileness of the created order and its future destination: 'the creation waits with eager longing for the revealing of the sons of God; for the creation was subjected to futility, not of its own will but by the will of him who subjected it in hope; because the creation itself will be set free from its bondage to decay and obtain the glorious liberty of the children of God. We know that the whole creation has been groaning in travail together until now; and not only the creation, but we ourselves, who have the first fruits of the Spirit, groan inwardly as we wait for adoption as sons, the redemption of our bodies. For in this hope we were saved. Now hope that is seen is not hope. For who hopes for what he sees? But if we hope for what we do not see, we wait for it with patience.' (Romans, chapter 8, verses 19–25)

Ways of bringing the good life to mind: The practice of hope

The implication of the above passage from Romans is that hope should sustain us through difficulties. This is very much Halpin's point and one where the Christian tradition has much to offer. The classic passage is this one, also from Paul's letter to the Romans: 'let us rejoice in our hope of sharing the glory of God. More than that, let us rejoice in our sufferings, knowing that suffering produces endurance, and endurance produces character, and character produces hope, and hope does not disappoint us, because God's love has been poured into our hearts through the Holy Spirit which has been given to us.' (Romans, chapter 5, verses 2–5) The practice of hope begins here with the recollection of a future lived within the glory of God. This recollection acts as an antidote to the sufferings that may beset us. The recollection of future glory does not deny the reality of present suffering but refuses to let it be the final answer. Liturgy acts in much the same way. At the time of writing it is the season of Advent when the church prepares for the recollection of the first coming of Christ at Christmas and focuses attention on his future coming. Hymns, prayers and processions, the making of wreaths for Advent are part of this tradition. It might call for the practices of meditation, prayer, drama and Bible-reading. One practice which schools could adopt is the reading of a particular passage at the end of the school year as my school did. We were read the following passage:

> 'whatever is true, whatever is honourable, whatever is just, whatever is pure, whatever is lovely, whatever is gracious, if there is any excellence, if there is anything worthy of praise, think about these things.' Philippians, chapter 4, verse 8

But is hope an illusion?

Halpin identifies cynics and fatalists as the enemies of hope and hopefulness. Clearly if one holds the view that there is no reason to believe in the worthwhileness of reality or if one cannot go along with Julian of Norwich that 'all will be well and all manner of things will be well' then hope is but a vain thing promising things that one can never be sure of. But you don't have to be a cynic to feel that hope is a suspect disposition. Aristotle called hope a waking dream and the Greeks viewed hope as an evil coming out of Pandora's box since by not conforming to a pattern that could be observed and understood it could lead people astray. Moltmann considers the major criticism of Christian hope to be that by insisting on straining towards future joys it gets in the way of present ones. He quotes Goethe: 'Why go chasing distant fancies? Lo, the good is ever near! Only learn to grasp your chances! Happiness is always here.' (Moltmann 1967, p. 21) One might point out that even in these words there is a sense of straining forward and looking out for a happiness that comes to us from the future.

How we live matters

Moltmann takes the criticism extremely seriously. In effect, his whole book is written in response to the challenge. He argues that any notion of attempting to locate happiness in the present alone is deeply unhistorical and relies on a concept of God deriving more from Parmenides than the Bible. It denies the reality of corporeal life and suffering and takes meaning away from the world as we know it. Hope for the future and straining for the good life are rendered worthless since the good lies here at hand in the presence of an eternally present God. Earthly strivings and indeed earthly life seem to lose their point. In contrast to this, Moltmann develops a theology that is based on the notion of promise and (future) fulfilment. He opposes any form of non-materialism whether that be understanding the faith in existentialist terms, or the idea that the future is somehow non-corporeal and exists only for disembodied souls. It matters what happens now and in this world – this is the world in which one must seek out and do the good. The life of the believer is to witness to the good life and the ultimate worthwhileness of creation.

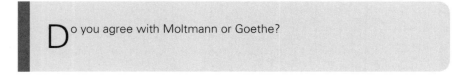

Do you agree with Moltmann or Goethe?

Because it is God who promises and who brings about the future fulfilment however it is possible to slip into a rather different form of fatalism or disengagement. If it is God who is going to bring about the denouement of everything in one final act at the end of time then does it really matter what human beings do in the meantime? Do our actions really count? Or is it OK if we just mark time and sing hopeful hymns? It might be if it were not that such a way of life is deeply antithetical to the nature of God, who does not stop working and calls human beings to be co-creators as sons and daughters. The Bible presents us with a picture of all of creation brimming with life and endeavour, moving towards a purpose that is characterized by movement and engagement. If creation is so called, then certainly human beings are called to engage and work for the good.

But the question might still be asked. Does all this endeavour matter? Does it achieve anything? Tom Wright forcefully rebuts this by arguing that what we do in the present 'will last into God's future'. He writes 'what you do in the present – by painting, preaching, singing, sewing, praying, teaching, building hospitals, digging wells, campaigning for justice, writing poems, caring for the needy, loving your neighbour as yourself – all these things *will last into God's future.*' Italics in original. (Wright 2007, p. 205).

Every good deed will find its way into the new creation that God will one day make. On the other hand 'Not to bring works and signs of renewal to birth within God's creation is ultimately to collude . . . with the forces of sin and death themselves.' (Wright, p. 220) Moltmann puts it like this: 'in all our acts we are sowing in hope . . . in love and obedience we are sowing for the future of the resurrection of the body.' (Moltmann, p. 213) Moltmann and Wright write from within Christian traditions. I particularly like the following words from an article published in *The Times* some time ago now by the Jewish Rabbi Arye Forta[3]:

> Judaism teaches that by living righteously, Jew and non-Jew alike imbue the world with spirituality and prepare it for its ultimate destiny. It is a sublime affirmation of the worth of the individual, recognising the capacity for moral and spiritual attainment within every human entity. It also endows the moral choices we make with cosmic significance and so confronts us with the awesome responsibility of our own humanity.

Utopias

My final pick up from Halpin is the theme with which he finishes his paper on utopias. He quotes extensively to illustrate the value of the utopian imagination. Utopias function to 'redirect our conservative attentions away from the taken-for-granted towards something new and innovative and progressive.' (Halpin, p. 9) Ernst Bloch thinks that utopianism defines what it is to be human. The psychologist Shelley Taylor writes: 'Normal human thought and perception is marked not by accuracy, but by positive self-enhancing illusions about the self, the world and the future.' (Halpin, p. 10) While pointing up the danger of framing one's hopes too extravagantly and leading to foolish risk-taking Halpin goes on to say: 'educators should not underestimate the degree to which the adoption of exaggerated perceptions of control and mastery over events can contribute to their ability better to engage in productive and creative work, even in circumstances where this is very difficult to achieve' (Halpin, p. 10).

False Utopias?

A cautionary note needs to be placed here regarding what it is that one hopes for. Plato's *Republic* (a form of state Utopia) with its rigid class system and related educational methods would not be what teachers would aspire to today. Dictators often come to power on the back of utopian visions which prove to be utterly evil and with long-lasting and devastating results as we have seen in the twentieth century, both in Europe with Hitler and Stalin and further afield in Cambodia and China.

The future of God

Christian faith aspires to something more solid than illusions. Rather than illusions about the self, the world and the future the language is that of hope of future realities. At the same time the Christian is alerted to the fact that we live in a world which is characterized by the 'not yet' as mentioned earlier. Christian faith offers a vision of the good, the charge to live by hope and work for change with the knowledge that perfection is not within reach – yet. But the question may be raised as to how one may know that such hopes are well-founded? Are they not just a remarkably extravagant example of the human propensity to create utopias? One might proceed, as Halpin does, to say that optimistic illusions are of value in themselves and that the vision of the good life presented to us in Christian faith is something that we 'recognise' and affirm. It may be taken-for-granted and not put into question by requiring justification in some rational way.

For Moltmann, by contrast, the event in the time of the resurrection guarantees what could never have been foreseen without it, the contingency and openness of our world. The future of God is still veiled but what was started in the resurrection must find fulfilment in the promise of a new heaven and a new earth, the 'glorious liberty of the children of God'. This gives present lives real importance and seriousness. It means we are accountable. We are not therefore at liberty to dream 'any dream' however productive or inspiring such a dream might be. Dream, yes, but dream with an eye to what is good and with faith in the coming renewal of creation. Illusions and utopias are unlikely to sustain hope and the life of faith for very long. It is because the Christian has real grounds for hope that hope becomes the sustaining force in difficult times. Moltmann writes: 'only an eschatology of promise . . . takes the trials, the contradictions and the godlessness of the world seriously in a meaningful way, because it makes faith and obedience possible in the world not by regarding the contradictions of no account, but by enabling us to believe and obey on the ground of our hope in the overcoming of these contradictions by God.' (Moltmann, p. 163)

Christian hope is directed to a future in which righteousness dwells, in which the final transformative work of the resurrection of Christ results in a new human being and a new (material) heaven and earth. The future of God (Moltmann's term) is not yet clear but glimpses of it are given to us.[4] Neither is the relationship between the day-to-day life of redeemed human beings clear but that there is some relationship is insisted on by the theologians such as Moltmann and Wright upon whose writings I lean in this chapter.

Are you convinced by Moltmann? What question, if any, would you put to him?

The Christian is called to witness to the life of righteousness and to strive to live that life which will one day be perfected.

Christian faith both extends and undergirds the insights that Halpin offers in his paper. It says that we are the sort of people who thrive on hope since we are moving towards a future which promises all the good we know of now and even more that we have not yet conceived of. We should not give up or accept that difficulties are the end of the story since all things are to be renewed and what we do now both witnesses to this fact and in some sense participates in it and anticipates it. We are the sort of people who are lit up by hope and visions because we are created in the image of the God of hope.

> How important are other virtues such as courage, faith and compassion to the maintenance of hope?

Not insignificant perhaps is the testimony of so many people of faith, who have held onto hope in the face of terrible difficulties. Indeed, it is those same difficulties that lead to the response of hope in God since in such circumstances only God can offer any help. Rod Garner (Garner, p. 127) speaks of 'the solidarity of the shaken' – the fact that so many have found consolation and help in time of need, mysterious and personal though that experience be. I knew a woman torn apart by the experience of an abortion she had undergone years ago. She found consolation in the conviction that God would, one day, restore to that child the opportunities denied by her decision. It did not take away her pain but it gave her hope. Less dramatic but perhaps expressing a widely held human perception are the simple words of a Breton fisherman's prayer:

> Protect me oh Lord for my boat is so small
> Protect me oh Lord for my boat is so small
> My boat is so small and your sea is so wide
> Protect me oh Lord

> (GGA 1984)

Notes

1 For a detailed (and contrasting) consideration of the virtue of hope, see the encyclical *Spe Salvi* written by Pope Benedict in 2007: www.vatican.va.

2 There, Cupitt concludes: 'You do your best – and you are but an unprofitable servant. You strive with all your might – in the knowledge that all your striving is but a jest. And you do not complain.' This intertwining of success and failure, he muses, is distinctive to the biblical and Judaeo-Christian tradition.

3 Rabbi Forta, in a telephone conversation with me in 2011, could not help me trace the date of the article.

4 See for example, 2 Peter, chapter 3, verse 13, Revelation, chapter 21, verse 4, 2 Corinthians, chapter 2, verse 18, and 1 Corinthians, chapter 15, verse 35ff.

References

Cupitt, D. quoted by George Pattison in the Church Times, 07 March, no 7514,' Liberalism's risky, moving staircase'.

Garner, R. (2006), *Like a Bottle in the Smoke*, Peterborough: Inspire.

Girl Guide Association (1984), *Songs for Tomorrow*. London: Girl Guide Association.

Halpin, D. (2003), 'Hope, utopianism and educational renewal', in The encyclopedia of informal education, www.infed.org/biblio/hope.htm. A fuller version of this paper was presented at Charterhouse School, Monday 6 January 2003.

Moltmann, J. (1967), *Theology of Hope*. London: SCM Press.

Wright, N. T. (2007), *Surprised by Hope*. London: SPCK.

CHAPTER TEN

Being temperate

moderating actions

Marius Felderhof

CHAPTER OUTLINE

This chapter seeks to re-establish the importance of the classical virtue of temperance by looking at various definitions. It also recognizes the importance of narrative and social context on the form that being temperate might take. Hence, using St. Augustine, it draws a sharp contrast between the classical and Christian view of the virtues in general and of temperance in particular. Christianity presupposes a love of God no matter how things go so ultimately consequences have no final bearing on the rightness of an action. Lastly, by drawing on the insights of the Danish Philosopher S. Kierkegaard, the chapter shows how sobriety and drunkenness can become extended metaphors on how we understand and live life in which being temperate and sober means to be wholly and fully invested in what we believe to be true and good. Being drunken is a form of anaesthesia or torpid lethargy where we fail to live what we believe and think.

Is temperance a virtue?

Of all the ancient world's cardinal virtues, (Wisdom, Justice, Courage and Temperance), temperance is the least convincing as a quality of character that we should cultivate and habituate. What is life without the insights of wisdom or for the ordinary person what is a life without the wisdom of plain common sense? What would society be like where there is no justice, for example, where socially inconvenient persons simply disappear or where social organization and policy depend on the exercise of power alone? What goals in life could be achieved where there is no courage to face difficulties and obstacles? *Prima facie* we do not need to argue for wisdom, justice and courage as virtues to be pursued. All that is required is to explicate their nature or to spell out what these virtues might mean in the complex reality of our modern world, that is, to show their sense now in our own times. With temperance it is evidently different. It is not only a case of showing more contemporarily what might be meant by it. First we need to be convinced that it is a virtue at all. Temperance suggests an ethos of restraint, control, sobriety and inhibitions and this does not fit well with the modern temperament. The latter, inhibition, for example, is sometimes depicted as a psychological handicap. Sobriety is dismissed as puritanical. Restraint and control, remind us of a class-ridden society or of the patriarchal family, where our lives were dominated by others (social superior, husband or father) and hence represent conditions from which we long(ed) to be freed. The supposition that temperance is a virtue, therefore, is by no means self-evident, a case has to be made for it.

Associating temperance with the ethos of restraint, control and inhibitions is certainly to be found in Plato's influential myth of the charioteer in his dialogue, *Phaedrus* (253Dff.). In this story, the essential human self is likened to a chariot. It is powered by a couple of horses, restrained and controlled by the charioteer, possibly representing 'reason'. The charioteer and horses are motivated by a 'love-inspiring vision' that energizes them. The picture of the charioteer and the two horses suggests a divided self. We are complex beings and what it is that empowers us to act is not always clear to us. Plato, however, captures the reality of human drives in his depiction of the horses, for we too recognize that sometimes our motivation is noble and at other times base:

> Now of the horses we say one is good and the other bad. . . . The horse that stands at the right hand is upright and has clean limbs; he carries his neck high, has an aquiline nose, is white in colour, and has dark eyes; he is a friend of honour joined with temperance and modesty, and a follower of true glory; he needs no whip but is guided only by the word of command and by reason. The other, however, is crooked, heavy, ill put together, his neck is short and thick, his nose flat, his colour dark, his eyes grey and bloodshot; he is a friend of insolence and pride, is shaggy eared and deaf, hardly obedient to whip and spurs. (253E – 254A)

The human self can be well intended and morally impressive but can also be recalcitrant and perverse such that it requires control and restraint. Kant put it in another way:

Moderation in emotions and passions, self-control, and calm deliberation are not only good in many respects but even seem to constitute part of the intrinsic worth of a person. (1993, p. 7)

Others might think such a person bloodless.

Thus, *prima facie* temperance invites images and appeals to restraint and self-control but we also saw that this needs to be more closely defined since it also generates reservations. Why should one not give free rein to one's impulses, provided it does not lead to undesirable consequences? Exhortations to 'live life to the full' or to 'enjoy life as much as possible' may appeal more to the modern person. Why restrain one's self? Let us eat, drink and be merry for tomorrow we shall die (conflating Ecclesiastes, chapter 8, verse 15 and Isaiah, chapter 22, verse 13). Why should one not pursue what we desire and enjoy it to the full? Plato's answer might be that we do not rightly know what we desire because of the divided self, or better, different parts of the self desire different and often incompatible objects and ends. We do not just wish to eat and drink. We also desire health and well-being. We may find that to satisfy the immediate craving for chocolate is only achieved at sacrificing the longer-term desire to remain slim and healthy. Or the desire to accomplish musical excellence can only be achieved by foregoing other desirable ends such as socializing or exercising for the sake of physical fitness. Given different interests and needs, temperance in this context might mean achieving a balance in life between our different goals and needs. Yet balance is not everything. One could respond that it is better to have developed some skill really well, even if like most Olympian athletes one is bound to give up on many other very desirable things in life to achieve this one end. One cannot be an Olympic gold medal winner, or even be an Olympic competitor, and live a balanced life. There is an element of real self-sacrifice in training hard. Thus, if temperance necessarily means a balanced life then it is not an obvious virtue for all people. Temperance may mean being clear about one's goal in life and being more single-minded in the face of other attractions.

We have begun to define temperance in three different ways: 1 self-control and restraint; 2 a balance in life; and 3 being transparent and clear. Which do you favour or do you have another definition that might show why temperance was always considered a virtue to be pursued?

Like Plato's depiction of a divided self with its good and bad impulses that need to be managed and controlled, the Christian tradition in its metaphors has maintained a similarly ambiguous view of human nature by insisting, on the one hand, that human beings are made in the image of God (and as such they reflect divine unity and perfection), and on the other hand, insisting that human beings are 'fallen' beings and to that extent have about them the air of being morally corruptible and corrupted, ignoble and base. Human beings are said to be aspiring, masterly creatures who live between heaven and earth, as the psalmist wrote: 'For you have made him a little lower than the angels, and have crowned him with glory and honour. You have made him to have dominion over the works of your hands; you have put all things under his feet' (Psalms, chapter 8, verses 5–6). Human beings may be heavenly beings like angels, but they are also earthly creatures, so what kind of ordered life is open to them? Is temperance on this imagery no more than the control and subordination of our lower nature to the higher?

Although sharing the judgement of human beings as fragmented, a difference between Plato and Christian tradition does emerge. Plato thinks the object of love and desire (eros) will be thought to be beautiful (though beauty here does not necessarily mean physical comeliness). Through the attraction of beauty, the human self can be put on the right path, guided through the soul's act of recollection, remembering its rootedness in the eternal, or in the realm of transcendence, where the true nature of beauty presented or presents itself. It is with the intellect's act of recollection, and in fear and reverence, that

> [the charioteer] is forced to pull the reins so violently backward as to bring both horses upon their haunches, the one quite willing, since he does not oppose him, but the unruly beast very unwilling. (254C)

Thus, with Plato's imagery an inspired reason, rooted in a transcendent vision of beauty, seizes control and tempers the different impulses in order to rise higher and to act more purposefully.

The Christian tradition is less sanguine about the capacity of reason to keep us temperate and on the right track. One cannot assume that reason already knows ideal beauty to guide it without beauty first being shown (or revealed) to it. Christianity perceives that human beings are enthralled by different objects and that misguided loves affect reason no less than the other elements of our nature. Solely taking thought, reflecting and 'making up one's own mind' – to echo some mantras of the RE world – will not do it. A right mind or the 'mind of Christ' is what is needed to live well. The difference between Plato and the Christian tradition in this regard gives temperance in each case a substantially different character. In Plato, a reason inspired by beauty orders and tempers the person by thinking rightly, developing his or her 'thinking skills', directing our instincts and controlling our impulses. In Christian thought, it is the 'mind of Christ living in us' – (one who had no comeliness about him for there is no beauty in suffering without a serious re-ordering and re-thinking of our values) – in the form of sacrificial love that brings about a temperate behaviour that is, by loving rightly and with the right 'object' in view. Augustine could therefore define temperance as love giving itself entirely (with all one's heart, mind and strength) to that which is loved – there is no hint here of restraint and limits.

Hence he writes about the cardinal virtues:

> As to virtue leading us to happy life, I hold virtue to be nothing else than the perfect love of God. For the four fold division of virtue I regard as taken from four forms of love. For these four virtues . . ., I should have no hesitation in defining them: that temperance is love giving itself entirely to that which is loved; fortitude is love readily bearing all things for the sake of the loved object; justice is love serving only the loved object, and therefore ruling rightly; prudence is love distinguishing with sagacity between what hinders it and what helps it. The object of this love is not anything, but only God, the chief good, the highest wisdom, the perfect harmony. (Augustine 1887, p. 48)

The words 'giving itself entirely', 'bearing all things', 'serving only', 'distinguishing with sagacity' stand out because there is no hint here of moderation, or anything that evokes a wishy-washy spirit where one is neither one thing nor the other. Once the proper object of love is identified, the person is expected to be passionate and single-minded in her loving actions. The definition of temperance therefore depends on the identity of the object of love. This will need to be explored further and illustrated with some of the narratives which help to define our objects and contexts in which we act.

> We are often inclined to see temperance as the way in which we do things but can that be characterized apart from the context and purpose for which we do it? Can you think of some concrete examples in teaching where context and goals affect the manner and method of teaching? How can one be a 'temperate' teacher?

Virtue qualified by narrative

As Plato's myths and Christian stories illustrate, the narrative imagery on which we rely can begin to affect the depiction of moral life in general and of temperance in particular. Of contemporary interest, we note that the religious and secular world may agree on the core virtues to be embodied while differing on their impact in life. K. E. Kirk for example notes how some of the major Christian theologians ignored certain scriptural starting points and

> on the whole [have] chosen to base [their] picture of the Christian ideal not upon any one of these scriptural foundations, but upon a pagan classification of virtue. . . . But Christian theology did not adopt them in any slavish spirit of imitation. It reinterpreted them and filled them with a Christian content, so much so that in the end it reversed those parts of their meaning which had a pagan, as distinct from a Christian outlook. (Kirk 1930, p. 33f.)

The capacity of taking the same virtues and giving them different content is possible only because the full meaning of these core virtues are tainted or redefined by their respective narrative contexts.

The degree to which the narrative context may lead to substantive moral differences may be deduced from Augustine who dismissed pagan virtues as 'splendid vices'. They are indeed splendid but nevertheless vices. Augustine's view was largely guided by the supposition that the pagan's pursuit of the moral life was in the final analysis a misdirected anthropocentric or ego-centric love. In his view, it is only by a love centred on the transcendent God that one is freed from a self that is turned in upon itself, that is, a person freed from selfishly pursuing the 'good' for her own benefit rather than for its own sake. The 'good' is put in quotation marks because a consequence of this condition of being turned in upon itself also leads to a misperception of what the proper object of love is and hence what the good is for human beings. Religiously speaking, only a faith in God, the transcendent, liberates one from such a self-enclosed existence and truly empowers a love of the proper object.

The impact of a narrative can be quite profound. Consider what happens to altruism – (which for someone like Augustine is the love and concern for our 'neighbour') – when, like R. Dawkins, one is solely dependent on the narrative of evolution for one's understanding of human beings. He needs an explanation for altruism since in evolutionary theory the reproductive mechanisms are so structured as to ensure the survival of a biological entity's own genes, not those of another. Care for another at the expense of one's own well-being or one's own existence is therefore an oddity or else a disguised practice that in reality serves the best survival of a shared set of genes, for example, a maiden aunt looking after her nephews and nieces. If there is a genuine case of altruism, Dawkins' supposition is that it is ultimately attributable to the 'selfish' genes malfunctioning; after all a 'good' gene is one that survives. It is not that Dawkins does not value altruism but the human default position is to be self-serving by looking to its own survival above all else. This colours temperance, for one can hardly be temperate about one's own existence. One cannot moderate existence with an element of non-existence. If existence is at stake, it is all or nothing. It is inconceivable that with the survival of the self at the core, one could 'define temperance as love giving itself entirely (with all one's heart, mind and strength) to that which is loved' if that love is for another. The religion that puts a love of the other at its core to the point of sacrificing one's life, on this secular humanist view, is 'unnatural', a malfunctioning nature, whereas the Christian before God would regard it as the most natural of all – natural in the sense of being what humans were created to be. In each case the narrative colours the moral judgement and hence the content of what the virtues, and in this case, what temperance might mean.

> To characterize temperance as a virtue is difficult to do in the abstract. It needed qualification by reference to our self-understanding, to the object of our love(s) in life, and to the possibility and reality of transcendence. These factors are sometimes best captured in an overarching narrative which, like life, is experienced in more concrete terms. Do we use one or many stories? Does historical narrative matter? Is there one overarching story that we can rely on?

I will now turn to the modern context which has had its impact on seeing the meaning of temperance in relationship to the abuse of alcohol and to one Christian effort at the redefinition of sobriety.

Temperance versus drunkenness

Modern perceptions of temperance are generally affected by the whole social movement spanning the nineteenth and twentieth centuries to curb excessive drinking so that we have lost our admiration for, and appreciation of, this pivotal classical virtue (Felderhof 2009). The young and the not so young enjoy their alcoholic drinks; they even enjoy getting drunk and being in a state of inebriation. As many birthday cards seem to illustrate, one is expected to drink to excess, most especially on such celebratory days. To celebrate has come to mean to drink to excess. Setting restrictions on this 'enjoyment' is not appreciated. Consequently, modern politicians seeking popular approval have found it advisable to lift many of the legal restrictions imposed by previous generations. The few 'dry' areas that remain, (where the sale of alcoholic beverages is not permitted), are under constant pressure from referenda to alter the regulations. The reverse case of 'wet' areas being subjected to referenda to prohibit the sale of alcohol is virtually unheard of today. Evidence demonstrating the longer-term damage caused to personal and social life by alcohol use does not suffice in the eyes of many to justify the restraint imposed on a majority when only a minority appears to suffer from it in any significant way. In fact, in our society, the power of alcohol to damage people, just as with smoking tobacco, is used as an argument for the legalization of all other forms of drug use. If one is permitted, why not the other? The lifting of the many legal restrictions on alcohol consumption appears to have made people even less tolerant of those who seek to exert social pressures to moderate drinking. They are dismissed as puritanical (in this context a term of abuse), wet-blankets, straight-laced and uptight. This social climate is simply not conducive to appreciating why temperance in the more traditional sense is an important virtue.

Can a liberal society be a virtuous society that includes being temperate? As an individual can one be liberal and temperate? Is it ever appropriate to set limits?

Yet some effort must be made to counter this social climate directly if the meaning of temperance is to be fully appreciated and valued; otherwise, this climate will always get in the way of grasping the attractiveness of this particular virtue. Generally, a case for restraint in alcohol consumption is reasonable given the potential effect on a person's physical and mental health, on family life, or on society through the disruption or intimidation caused by people under the influence of alcohol. Therefore, it is not too difficult to understand why some religious traditions, for example, Islam, ban the use of alcohol and other stimulants outright whether as a result of a divine command or as the result of an evaluation of the impact of alcohol use. However, to appreciate why alcohol is still indulged by many, despite the various attempts at prohibitions and awareness of the longer-term destructive consequences noted above, one must not underplay the considerable short-term pleasures it offers. The sociability, the desirable physical and sensual experiences are all part of the picture and have provided the reasons for permitting alcohol use. A balance must be struck between the pleasure enjoyed by many against the various adverse consequences for other individuals and society. The suggestion that striking a balance is a once for all decision is a mistake. The precise balance may well differ depending on the individual (and sometimes ethnic group) concerned as not everyone (or group) responds in the same way physiologically (some ethnic groups are less able to metabolize alcohol), or psychologically, to the consumption of alcohol (there may be psychological reasons why alcoholism is more of a problem in northern climes with long winter nights). The balance may also change over time through, for example, changing social habits caused possibly by the development of a cafe culture where the norm is to drink only moderately, or by changing perceptions of what is thought to be shameful. Also, the balance might reasonably be altered due to the development of new treatments for alcoholism or for cirrhosis of the liver. In effect, the search for a balance may need to be revisited again and again. Temperance in this context might mean the careful consideration of all the factors to arrive at a policy that maximizes goods and minimizes the disadvantages for all. Nevertheless, balance as we saw earlier is not everything.

There are some considerations that have perennially mattered in evaluating alcohol use that are not cast in such consequentialist terms. The drunken condition caused by alcohol may be thought to be an evil in itself. It has been thought that the peculiar dignity belonging to human beings is to be found in his rationality and self-consciousness. It is this that separates human beings from much of the rest of the animal kingdom. It is our rationality and self-awareness that enables us to see the real world for what it is. To impair that capacity is to reduce human beings to the level of other creatures and to undermine human dignity and thus become a cause for shame if it is wilfully done. With this in mind, temperance is the disposition that safeguards our rationality and avoids the escape from sense and self-obliteration in drunkenness. Kant writes about drunkenness (and about gluttony) in the following terms:

> Brutish excess in the use of food and drink is misuse of the means of nourishment that restricts or exhausts our capacity to use them intelligently. Drunkenness and gluttony are the vices that come under this heading. A human being who is drunk is like a mere animal, not to be treated as a human being. When stuffed with food he is in a condition in which he is incapacitated, for a time, for actions that would require him to use his powers with skill and deliberation. – It is obvious that putting oneself in such a state violates a duty to oneself. The first of these debasements, below even the nature of an animal, is usually brought about by fermented drinks, but it can also result from other narcotics, such as opium and other vegetable products. They are seductive because, under their influence, people dream for a while that they are happy and free from care, and even imagine that they are strong; but dejection and weakness follow and, worst of all, they create a need to use the narcotics again and even to increase the amount. Gluttony is even lower than that animal enjoyment of the senses, since it only lulls the senses into a passive condition and, unlike drunkenness does not even arouse imagination to an active play of representations; so it approaches even more closely the enjoyment of cattle. (Kant 1996, p. 180)

Seldom has Kant written in more censorious terms! Temperance is a duty to the self and in this context is preserving the powers to act, to deliberate, and the maintenance of one's intelligence and imaginative skills, not to do so is to become brutish.

Ethical theories are often divided into two groups: 1 teleological theories that consider consequences as defining the good and 2 deontological theories that consider duties. Do we need to choose between them to understand what we ought to do and what kind of persons we should strive to be?

The reference to the avoidance of shame raises other considerations. A sense of shame may be culturally determined but it is no less real for all that. In the Biblical creation and fall narrative, Adam becomes aware of his nakedness and out of shame covers himself. A subsequent story (Genesis, chapter 9, verses 20–27) tells of how Noah became drunk and was in such a state that his son, Ham, could see his nakedness. In the narrative it leads to the condemnation of Ham who looked at him, unlike Noah's other two sons, Shem and Japheth, who endeavoured to cover him while averting their eyes. In more recent times, a medical doctor upbraided a young girl in an accident and emergency unit because she had arrived drunk and in a state where they had to remove her clothes for her treatment. When she had recovered, the girl was asked, would she not normally be ashamed to be undressed by others? Or possibly to be sexually used or abused while insensate by strangers? They are rhetorical questions even though we live in a culture where there is much casual sex and where one encounters nearly everywhere on posters (and in life) various states of nudity. The supposition is that it is shameful and a cause for regret to be in a state where one might do the things that one would never do were one sober. It is clear that drunkenness generates a sense of impropriety and hence the need for personal and social measures to control the impulses, habits and practices that lead to it. It is all too easy, and possibly necessary, to associate temperance with this control and constraint in relation to alcohol.

But linking temperance to control and restraint, by no means exhausts its meaning as suggested earlier. For Plato, *sophrosune* (his word often translated as temperance) is more a knowledge of knowledge, that is, it implies a deep sense of self-awareness, and to be utterly transparent to oneself. This is directly the opposite of the self-obliteration and the state of unknowing exemplified and sought by some in drunkenness. On the other hand, there is an interesting link here to education for the goal of education since the classical age is said to be to 'Know thyself'. If this is the ultimate goal of education, then the goal of education is temperance. Schools can therefore not be indifferent to alcohol or drug abuse.

D o you think it is the business of schools to be concerned about pupils drinking after school hours or over the weekend? If not, why not?

Be ye therefore sober
(1 Peter, chapter 4, verse 7)

Sobriety features in various places in the Christian scriptures, for example, in the letter to Titus, especially its second chapter where the writer repeatedly exhorts his readers to be sober and alert. Thus in verse 12 '. . . live soberly, righteously and godly in this present world' and (verse 3) to be 'not given to much wine'; and Paul also writes

> Ye are all the children of light, and the children of the day: we are not of the night, nor of darkness. Therefore let us not sleep, as do others; but let us watch and be sober. For they that sleep sleep in the night; and they that be drunken are drunken in the night. But let us, who are of the day, be sober, putting on the breastplate of faith and love; and for a helmet, the hope of salvation. (1 Thessalonians, chapter 5, verses 5–8)

Drunkenness and sobriety become extended metaphors together with other metaphors (of battle and struggle) for two very different forms of life that are contrasted to each other.

Kierkegaard, the great nineteenth-century Christian thinker, plays with these metaphors (1941, pp. 107ff). Taking the exhortation from Peter's first letter to be sober, (Peter thus implying that his readers are drunken), and contrasting this exhortation with the accusation from mocking bystanders at Pentecost that 'these men [the disciples] are full of new wine' (Acts of the Apostles, chapter 2, verse 13), to which Peter had retorted, (Acts of the Apostles, chapter 2, verse 15) 'For these are not drunken as ye suppose, seeing it is but the third hour of the day' – that is to say, the accusation of drunkenness was not a fit explanation since it was far too early in the morning – Kierkegaard now elaborates and inverts the metaphor. The disciples aspire to be sober but are accused of being drunken, whereas the disciples 'regards the worldly mind as drunkenness' when the worldly persons think themselves to be sober realists; so Kierkegaard asks, 'Who exactly is it who is drunk and who is it who is sober?' 'What is it that makes these fit descriptions?' These are not questions of alcohol but of states of mind, of people's hold on reality or on the world in which they live, and the things for which they venture to live.

Kierkegaard depicts the person with the worldly mind as one who sticks to the facts, who looks for certainty, for proof, who knows his own interests;

who believes in common sense and being a realist. His venture in life is based on a precise calculation. Of course, there may be other worldly people who are prepared to be more adventurous; they may not require strict certainty but would be content with probability. Rational belief must at least be probable, they say; to venture on any other basis would be foolhardy. Yet according to the Christian spirit this is a form of being drunken. In contrast to the shrewd, calculating person, Kierkegaard claims:

> The man who never let go of probability never committed himself to God. All religious (not to say Christian) adventure is on the farther side of probability, is by letting go of probability. (ibid., p. 116)

This raises a new thought. There may yet be other rash and worldly men who are prepared not only to let go of certainty but also of probability and to venture out without any rational basis whatsoever – in modern times buying a lottery ticket with such a high degree of improbability of winning verges on this behaviour. Of the state of such people, declares Kierkegaard, 'both in a Christian and in a human sense this is drunkenness' (p. 117).

Would you define a person with faith in God as someone who believes without a proper basis for belief? What else could it be?

But is venturing forth in life without any rational basis not what the religious person does? Does he or she not claim to rely solely on God, to rely without evidence? The claim to rely on God would certainly change the picture and the story but it is not a claim that should be taken at face value. It needs to be tested.

> For to affix God's name to one's wishes, one's desires, one's plans, that too is easy, only too easy, for the lightly built; but from this it does not follow that their venture is in reliance upon God. (p. 117)

What then, one might ask, is the difference between a truly religious person and one who ventures forth without certainty, without probability, without anything to support him or her? Quite simply for this reason: when one wishes, desires, plans, one looks for gain or benefit, looks to triumph, or to be victorious, whereas in Kierkegaard's judgement, to the person who truly relies on God, it does not matter how things go, 'it is just exactly as possible that one will be victorious as that one will be defeated' (p. 117). Thus he goes on:

> Only when thou hast an understanding on this point, only then canst thou venture in reliance upon God. Thou hast let go of probability; to that

extent, humanly speaking, it even may be probable thou wilt be defeated. But in spite of that thou art determined to go forth, to go forward, to venture – in God's name. Good fortune attend thee! But it is true, is it not, thou hast an understanding with thyself that it was not to ensure thy victory thou didst invoke God, but in order that thou (if it should please God not to let thee be victorious . . .), that thou mightest be in good understanding with God, that He will strengthen thee to bear it if thou must be defeated in a good cause, in a venture made in reliance upon God. (Ibid., p. 117f.)

The success of any venture in life is not to be found in the outcome, whether certain, probable, or even improbable, but in it being the absolutely right thing to do. The religious consolation when one is defeated while doing the absolutely right thing is that one is 'in good understanding with God,' that is, one was on God's side.

Kierkegaard made a number of basic points:

1 If you are relying on probability or even on apparent certainties, you are not yet governed by what is absolutely good or evil, true or false, your interest is in the probabilities. The . . . '"maxim to a certain degree" is precisely what intoxicates, anaesthetizes, makes one heavy and lethargic and torpid and dull, pretty much like an habitual drunkard, of whom it is said that he falls into a state of drowsiness.' (p. 123) To accept things to a certain degree is the recipe for doing nothing or to act solely on the basis of a calculation without the question of moral responsibility. Such decisions contrast sharply with being bound absolutely before God and coming under judgement for doing or failing to do what is right and good.

2 If you literally forget yourself in the process of objective 'knowing and understanding, in thinking, in artistic production etc.' (p. 121f.) and have not invested yourself in them, in effect in doing so becoming a kind of spectator, if your knowledge and understanding is not utterly self-involving, that is a kind of absence, like the absence from reality and self of the drunkard.

'To become sober is: to come so close to oneself in one's understanding, one's knowing, that all one's understanding becomes action' (p. 130)

3 There is a difference between the incautious who calculatingly looks to God to bring him success in life and the person of faith who trusts in God no matter how things go, even in the face of defeat and failure. It is not the worldly outcome that matters; it is obedience and submission to the absolutely good and true that counts.

4   There is a great difference between Christianity and Christendom, a socially and politically convenient establishment. In the latter, one can preach and teach about doctrine and do so from a position of comfort without any self-sacrifice but in the former one can only teach and preach it by living it and possibly at great cost to oneself. It is by internalizing one's understanding where knowing becomes action that makes one truly sober.

In Kierkegaard's treatment the disposition to be temperate means integrity, being transparent to oneself, where knowing and understanding is doing. It is being resolute. Being sober or drunk has little to do with alcohol but everything to do with the way the self is invested in life. In this sense, temperance is not a negative but a positive disposition; it does not seek to prevent but to act positively to realize what is good and true.

Temperance has been differently defined as: 1 self-control and restraint, 2 balance in life, 3 being transparent and clear. The definition of the goal and context is shown to have had an impact on how we understand temperance. The modern acceptance of drunkenness gives a new context for understanding temperance, that is, as actually living what one knows to be true and good. Can you think of a better definition?

References

Augustine, St (1887), On the Morals of the Catholic Church, trans. R. Stothert, in *A Select Library of the Nicene and Post-Nicene Fathers of the Christian Church* Vol. IV.

Felderhof, M. C., (2009), 'Temperance, with a consideration of Evil, Violence and Pedagogy'. *Journal of Beliefs and Value* 30(2): 145–58.

Kant, I., (1993), *Grounding for the Metaphysics of Morals*, (1st published in 1785), trans. J. W. Ellington. Indianapolis: Hackett Publishing Company Inc.

—(1996), *The Metaphysics of Morals*, ed. by Mary Gregor. Cambridge: Cambridge University Press.

Kierkegaard, S., (1941), *For Self-Examination and Judge for Yourselves! and Three discourses 1851*, trans. W. Lowrie. Oxford: Oxford University Press.

Kirk, K. E., (1930), Plato, *Phaedrus* (1919) in Plato (Euthrypho, Apology, Crito, Phaedo, *Phaedrus*), trans. H. N. Fowler. London: Heinemann.

CHAPTER ELEVEN

Being wise

discovering the way

Joseph Houston

CHAPTER OUTLINE

This chapter explores wisdom and shows how it refers to both the making of wise judgements and to a body or school of wisdom. A wise person requires more than knowledge. He/She needs to be able to make connections and, through experience, be able to predict possible outcomes. The role of bad luck is discussed and the morality of imparting (or not imparting) wisdom is examined, particularly in relation to teaching. It is argued that the virtue of wisdom presupposes the objectivity of morals. The use of inspiring exemplars is recommended both as a way of overcoming weakness of will and conveying ideas of the good.

In the *London Times* of 9 April 2012, the leading Letter to the Editor was from Peter Green, the headmaster of Ardingly College. He concludes with a plea that those in authority (i.e. governments, curriculum constructors, examining boards, framers of university policy) should foster an education which should 'not simply impart information or provide training for economic benefit to society, but ... help form the human individual and impart wisdom'. The thought that schools (or universities about which Peter Green may also be writing) should, or might, 'impart wisdom' is not often found, certainly not expressed in these terms, either in public debate about education or in professional and academic literature. Taking up the thought is the purpose of this chapter.

There are wise judgements, wise policies, wise projects or actions, and wise people. The people are wise in that they, at least usually, make wise judgements and engage in wise actions when occasion or opportunity presents themselves. We shall shortly consider what that wisdom which is referred to in this paragraph might be. In addition, however, there is the wisdom which is a particular wisdom or a school of wisdom, understood as a body of teaching or a system of ideas or thought, or a guiding general principle, or even sustained, shrewd, perhaps pointed, comment on actions and events. Examples of a particular wisdom or school of wisdom would be: the wisdom of Confucius, or of Boethius, the teachings of the Old Testament 'wisdom' literature, the wisdom of Judaeo-Christian agapism, pacifist wisdom, and the conventional, received wisdom in a particular community, society, time and place. There is also the wisdom and wit of, say, Mark Twain or Woody Allen. Also to be noted here are those wisdoms which, paradoxically and/or ironically, advertise themselves as folly. Think of Paul (once of Tarsus), the Biblical author of 1st Corinthians Chapters 1–3, who says there that his message is a kind of foolishness, and of the wisdom of the Sufis, which is self-described as the *'Wisdom of the Idiots'*, and even of Erasmus's *In Praise of Folly*.

> For it is written, 'I will destroy the wisdom of the wise, and will bring to nothing the understanding of the prudent. Where is the wise? Where is the scribe? Where is the disputer of this world? For after that in the wisdom of God the world by wisdom knew not God, it pleased God by the foolishness of preaching to save them that believe.' (1 Corinthians, chapter 2, verses 19–21)
>
> What do you think St Paul meant here?

Plato and especially Aristotle on wisdom

As is to be expected Plato and Aristotle have telling, perceptive, even wise things to say about wisdom. Plato commends wisdom, saying that among the attributes, conditions and possessions, which are reasonably to be sought after and highly valued – such as wealth, health, power and status, and wisdom – wisdom is the only one which is always, in any circumstance, good to have. The others can be goods, good to have, but only if they are used wisely, as frequently they are not. Wealth, for example, can finance destructive addictions, or bribes; power can be used to oppress innocent people or destroy good things; frequently these goods are misused or employed in ways which do not contribute to human well-being even the well-being of their possessors. But wisdom is always good to have. Its employment in directing the uses of the other attributes will enable them to contribute to that 'happiness' (meaning not merely taking pleasure, or feeling good about things, but rather that well-being, or fulfilment, which has been expressed in the words: 'happy the person who . . .', e.g. . . . who finds her vocation . . . who can give it his best effort) which is our overall good. In relation to other virtues, notably courage, temperance and justice, wisdom (itself a virtue) again gives the virtuous person understanding of why these virtues are to be sought, why they are indeed virtues. So, courage, which Plato understood as holding true beliefs about what is to be feared, or justice, understood as the parts of the city or of the individual soul working together as they are properly fitted to do – such virtues are seen by the wise person to contribute to the welfare/happiness of the soul or the city, and so are to be valued. For Plato, then, wisdom operates in supervising the valuation and enjoyment of goods, and the appreciation of the virtues as truly virtues. The wise person, who by wisdom does these things, requires a good understanding both of the ways in which human lives turn out in the many sorts of circumstances which may be encountered, and of what is good for human beings individually and in society.

Notwithstanding differences between them, Aristotle would not have disagreed with Plato's high valuation of wisdom, any more than we are likely to do. Aristotle's own helpful discussion of wisdom gives more attention to what particular wise actions will consist of, what it is about them that makes them properly count as wise. His illuminating explication of wisdom in a wise action is helpful to us. It helps us to see more clearly what wisdom is and what, as an implication, will be involved in imparting wisdom. So, for Aristotle, wisdom is employed, when, in seeking to attain a valuable goal or gain a particular good, we make and utilize sound true judgements about what will happen or can be expected to happen in the conditions and circumstances which may unfold – particularly in view of actions which may be taken. The sound judgements will be based on experience – the experiences of the one who judges or of others' experiences which have been reported to him or her. And these experience-guided judgements will direct successful action, action which serves the good end which is aimed at.

Aristotle's requirement that the goal or end or purpose, which is successfully pursued by the wise person, should be a good one, is surely correct. Mere efficiency in securing a desired end by the course of action which you employ is not enough to qualify you as wise in this if the desired end is, say, the poisoning of a city's water supply. Suppose that the Nazis and their hugely efficient German war machine had, in the early 1940s, succeeded in their aims of the conquest and secured annexation of Europe west of the Urals with the extermination of all Jewish, and millions of Slav people. We would not recognize wisdom in their course of action notwithstanding its efficiency. Wisdom requires that the goal be good.

Knowledge and wisdom

Knowledge, information and understanding are necessary if there is to be wisdom. But what sort(s) of knowledge? If you have knowledge simply in that you know lots of bits of information with little grasp of their relations or connections (such as causal, historical-contextual, functional connexions) you will be unable to see how these distinct bits bear together on, (so as to provide guidance about), a practical issue or question. You will not be equipped merely by remembering all the daily tear-off calendar or diary factual-curiosity items of information ('Richard III, King of England, born today', 2 October) to understand what is likely to happen (or likely to have happened) in some circumstances of practical interest. Arguably such 'knowledge' hardly counts as knowledge at all if, as is maintained, there is no grasp of relationships or connections. One value of genuine knowledge is that it opens or generates understanding. Mere bitty, atomic, knowledge is insufficient for wisdom. That said, it is possible that awareness of a previously unrelated fact can, given a context and an awareness of its relevance, baulk a bad plan and prompt a better alternative. An increase in a person's knowledge and information, given an understanding of the significance of that knowledge and information for the way the world goes, should increase the range of matters over which wise judgement is made possible for that person.

However, the possession of lots of knowledge and information does not guarantee wisdom (some knowledge is a necessary condition but even lots of knowledge is not a sufficient condition of wisdom); the proviso above, 'given an understanding of . . .', is vital. The figure, who knows a great deal but who is not at all wise in the way the world works making bizarrely foolish decisions, may possibly be found in some neighbour in an academic community but almost certainly in its lore. Often such a person may actually be capable of wise decision-making towards a good, practical end in the fields about which she knows a lot, but be poorer at more commonplace planning – organizing a holiday, or a school open-day. It remains the case that someone's possession of much accurate information in a field does not alone guarantee wisdom in judgements in that field. Also required for the possession of wisdom is understanding of how at least a good deal of what he or she knows came to be the case and/or of what effects it had. He or she needs understanding of process.

Conversely, a person who is very meagrely informed may nonetheless possess valuable wisdom if he judges matters in fields where he has information with understanding of process. That understanding will have been formed by attentive awareness to his limited special experience and information. The native of Maggieknockater in the Spey valley, Scotland, who has been fishing in the river for 60 years and has talked often with his friends about their experiences is probably the man to give wise advice to you on how and where you can best spend your rare days fishing on the river, even if (improbably) he knows little about much else. Wisdom, then, is the effective utilization towards a worthwhile, good goal of knowledge about how the world goes. For example, the appropriate study of history – historical process – can surely facilitate wisdom.

Results of scientific work – from the natural and social sciences – may be utilized in the exercise of such wisdom; but wisdom is not to be identified with science. For one thing, even when wisdom does direct action by utilizing scientifically established expectations, wisdom is more than just the science. Wisdom determines that and how the science is utilized towards the desired and desirable ends. For another, although wisdom draws upon, is based on experience, very often it is experience which is quite non-deliberately unsystematically acquired, remembered, absorbed or reported to us. And it is mostly experience which is not deliberately and systematically noted, or sought in order to test general hypotheses; in brief, it is mostly experience of life. And, as indicated earlier, wise action, to be wise, has to be towards the securing of good ends, valuable outcomes, goods. But science is not (and sometimes takes pride in not being) evaluative. So, wisdom and science are not identical. And, obviously enough, many issues are wisely resolved without appeal to, or awareness of considerations we would call 'scientific': Should I buy this car from him? Should we move house?

A professor in a university chemistry department said (some years ago) that too many chemistry graduates left university thinking that because they knew what the chemistry text books said they were pretty fully prepared for their life's work. But if the firm which employed them thought it might introduce a new process, the text book chemistry they learnt would be the easy component in the decision making. Other urgent questions would be trickier: Will there be job losses? Redeployment? Pollution in the river or the air? Secure supplies of necessary raw materials and a growing demand for the product? Available investment for new plant? Room on the existing site?. . . . No doubt matters have improved today and graduates are keenly aware of the need for wisdom as they use their science.

The point here is not to down-value scientific knowledge (even if 'scientism' may well call for corrective attention). Scientific knowledge is surely a good; and we should employ wisdom to acquire it just as we employ wisdom to exploit it. But the scientific knowledge itself, acquired by wisdom and utilized by further wisdom, is not the same as wisdom.

Try to pinpoint the difference between having knowledge and being wise. Possessing knowledge does not make one wise but can one be both wise and ignorant? Think of examples.

Can the requirement for knowledge in making wise decisions mean that one can never be confident that one has made a wise decision?

How might a person be trained in scientific wisdom?

Bad luck

There is one feature of Aristotle's concept of wisdom that is reflected also in our usage of 'wise' and its cognates but which nevertheless seems to be at odds both with other intuitions about usage and with fairness. We do not call a course of action or a project wise if it fails to achieve its goal, if the good it is intended to secure is not secured. However shrewdly all the knowable relevant factors were fully assessed, all the knowable risks and dangers fairly and thoroughly evaluated and however reasonable the judgements that justified the going ahead with an operation or action, if, due to quite unforeseeable, unprecedented misfortune, it fails, we do not call it wise. This is surely problematic? Wisdom, we say, consists in (i) the justness of the judgement that a particular goal is a good goal, and (ii) the high quality of the due diligence undertaken in setting out to secure that good. Yet if, in a particular case, the goal is not secured due to outrageous misfortune, and even if both (i) and (ii) are satisfied, we will not say that the project was wise. It seems unfair to allow an unforeseeable danger or mishap to affect, let alone determine, our evaluation of a project and those undertaking it.

Suppose it is said that all factors that could possibly affect the outcome should have been considered before the project goes ahead, with the consequence that an unforeseen but calamitous thunderbolt (actual or metaphorical), which was always a possibility (since it happened), should have been considered and the project modified or abandoned. If that is said, and given the limitations on our knowledge, few if any plans or projects could be reckoned wise by this standard. Would not the spirit of enterprise die altogether among those who wish to be counted wise?

Our thought might go further, along these lines: (i) There will be consequences of inaction, or attempting little, too; and so the wisdom of those policies in a particular case, or generally, can be assessed; (ii) Risk assessments can attach weights of probability, and assist wise judgement, but the unforeseeable will always be with us. There is no space to pursue these points. Perhaps a more important point emerges: People who are successful in pursuing wise projects should be grateful, or at least glad, that the good they have achieved has come in ways not determined wholly by their meritoriously wise activity. Some sympathy for the unlucky might seem due.

How can one plan in an uncertain world?
Is the willingness to risk failure part of being wise?

Imparting wisdom

Even if the commonly experienced effects of luck (bad and good) do raise questions about the adequacy of Aristotle's writings on wisdom, the contention holds that a paradigm case of wisdom is one in which a good is secured by effective planning and action. Hence, it will help to think about imparting wisdom if we ask how people may be helped towards a disposition to recognize what is good, to desire it, and to find good ways of securing the aimed – for goods. If it is proposed that 'wisdom' be 'imparted', one obvious understanding of this (perhaps the most obvious) will be that some body of wisdom such as those mentioned earlier – the wisdom of Confucius, Judaeo–Christian agapism etc., (no doubt excluding Woody Allen) should be prescribed. This corpus of wisdom should be both described and recommended; then its adoption by those to whom it is imparted, so that it guides their actions, should be encouraged, or, (as may be possible) enforced.

At least some people self-identifying as liberals will baulk at this idea because (it will be said) the ones to whom the wisdom is to be imparted (the impartees, let's call them) should in a publicly supported education system have a range of the most obvious options presented, without favouring any in respect of recommendation let alone imposition. This is because (i) the public education system should not privilege some one particular body of what is believed or practised or advocated by many citizens, over others, also widely supported; and (ii) the autonomy of the pupil must be respected so as to exclude encouragement towards, let alone enforcement of, a distinct morality, a particular set of values, world view, religion, or 'wisdom'.

The attention given earlier in the paper to wisdom, understood not as a body of deep or important truths but as an intellectual virtue, should prompt at least two obvious rejoinders: (i) The 'imparting of wisdom' need not be simply, or at all, a matter of bringing pupils to accept and act upon some particular body of precepts by insistently asserting facts or beliefs and/or imposing prescriptions for behaviour. It can, in accordance with a principal classical conception of wisdom, be the enabling and encouraging of pupils to recognize and employ effective courses of action in order to achieve their good goals, so that they come to develop the capacity and disposition to do so. Before we move towards considering how such virtue can be fostered, it is worth pointing out, further: (ii) that any worthwhile school does, and must, commend and insist upon certain virtues, including and going beyond honesty, punctuality, respect for those different from ourselves, and self-respect. These further virtues – intellectual virtues – include open-mindedness, inquisitiveness, intellectual carefulness, thoroughness, humility to consider that one might be wrong and accept due correction, and at the same time include also a measure of confidence to persist with what one reckons one has good reason to believe, a readiness to apply oneself to study, fair-mindedness, balanced self-assessment. . . . The intention and hope will be that students come to desire and seek these virtues for themselves, exercising their autonomy in doing so; and as they do, they will expand their capacities, enlarging the scope for further exercising their autonomy. Aristotle holds that it is here rather as with many worthwhile activities, skills, and pursuits (perhaps, such as playing the violin, watercolour painting, taking regular exercise, speaking a new language) where you can find that these are good to do. You can come to know such things are good by being told that; but a better way is by engaging in them, where you will discover their worth, as well as enjoyment of a kind that is intrinsic to them. Analogously as you begin to be, say, careful and thorough in school work, as you are exhorted and required to be, you come to know for yourself that it is good to be careful and thorough, and to embrace for yourself what was at first required from you. Pupil autonomy matters; and good education will aim to enlarge the scope of pupil autonomy. But an argument simply from pupil autonomy to the exclusion, from the school, of specific ethical counsel, urging, exhortation, is at best too simple. Its prospects, indeed, do not seem promising.

If wisdom is the disposition to employ effective courses of action in pursuit and achievement of worthwhile goals, the imparting of wisdom will require: (i) a growing habitual recognition of, and desire to secure, good ends; and (ii) the enabling of the impartees to recognize, and the fostering of a disposition in them to employ, effective courses of action to attain these goals.

Think about the best teachers you have had. Would you say that they imparted wisdom to you?
How did they do this?

Subjectivism about what is good

An attempt to consider what will be required for (i) immediately turns into a problem, if what is good, and so which ends or kinds of ends, are good, is taken, properly understood, to be a subjective matter. The subjectivity might be held to be that of each individual, so that a person's attitude in favouring, or valuing, a state of affairs constitutes the goodness of that state. Or, differently, it has been held that it is the attitude of approval of a group (community, race, class, . . .) towards something, which constitutes the goodness of that thing, state of affairs, event. This suggestion introduces an 'objective' component into the attribution of goodness in that it is an objective, even empirically testable matter that the group does favour a particular thing, state, etc., whose goodness is constituted by that approval. (That 'objective' component may satisfy those who suspect that the account in terms only of an individual's subjectivity fails to do justice to an objectivity that value-judgements do appear to possess, e.g. 'health is good'.)

It is not appropriate here to try to enter far into the wider controversy about the objectivity or the subjectivity of (the) good. But our use of the concept of wisdom does seem to suppose an objectivist view. Suppose someone values something as a great good or is convinced that something is a great good. And suppose there is no dispute about the efficient means by which that something can be secured, but that nobody agrees with her that it is a good at all. Suppose she alone in the whole course of history considers it a good. The concept of the altogether unrecognized visionary, lone sage is not (it seems) incoherent. If we accept that, then neither form of subjectivism about the good can be maintained: If the goodness of someone is constituted by what some community, group, class or majority favours, then there cannot be a wise person whose (aimed-for or achieved) good is favoured by her alone.

And if the goodness of something consists in the approval of an individual who favours it, the possibility of being altogether, and always, an unrecognized sage runs into the problem that 'recognition' cannot have the meaning which is needed. Our usual concept of 'recognition of a sage about the good' collapses. If Jackson has long affirmed that some S is good, your coming to recognize that S is good will only be a matter of accepting that he, you, or someone, considers S is good. Once you first merely come to know of his thinking S good, there can be no question (given your consistency, sanity and awareness of what you are doing) of your denying that S is good, and so disagreeing with Jackson. 'Recognising' Jackson's sagacity in this matter becomes an empty recognition on the basis of this individualist subjectivism view of goodness. This kind of recognition should be compared with recognizing sound judgement in someone who maintains that S is good, meaning that S has a quality of being good which it possesses independently of his or her opinion about it or attitude to it. An unrecognized sage would, on the individualist subjectivism thesis, merely be someone whose evaluations of things were unknown. If the concept of the recognition of a person's good sense and wise judgement in making evaluations is to mean what we normally take it to mean, individualist subjectivism about the good is found wanting.

An 'unrecognised sage about what's good' is seeing something which is, so to speak, there to be seen for what it is, namely a good, and not merely someone who has what is logically akin to a unique personal taste or preference. The standard concept of being wise, then, is at odds with individualist subjectivism. We may still insist on being subjectivists here; but if we continue to think that there is such a virtue as wisdom, as usually understood, we will have to accept its objectivist implication.

Wisdom requires the recognition of what is good but what makes such recognition possible? Does the good have an intrinsic power to stimulate our love for it, or at least convey the sense that we ought to love it?

Communicating a vision?

None of the foregoing, however, resolves important questions about which goods are to be pursued. Some people will prioritize health, wealth, power, and the justified admiration of oneself (by others and oneself) – a rather Aristotelian view. Others will give clear primacy to love for, and service to, 'neighbour' (i.e. whomever we influence), aiming for usefulness above mere power, so that self-forgetfulness and even self-sacrifice might be called for.

A school might aim to commend and generate a particular set of goods, according to its distinctive vision. It will not only give a descriptive account of the goods it favours but do so in ways which seek to move pupils to embrace these for themselves. It will also, of course, and in a liberal society, give an account of alternative conceptions of what is good; and it will require this to be done in a fair-minded way not least because failure to present the other view in *optimam partem* will, in the longer run, make the school's own vision of the good vulnerable to the effective competition. Operating in a more or less liberal society puts pressure on anyone who wishes to commend a view or value to deal fairly with opposing views, both in exposition and criticism, in case misrepresentation or weakness in assessments becomes plain in due course. But also, where goods are being approved of, and commended to pupils with a view to these goods being sought after, it will, in fact, be a species of misrepresentation of such a good if its attractiveness is concealed, for fear of imparting undue pressure! Hence to present a good or a set of goods, for what they are, their attractivenesses are quite properly to be conveyed, brought out.

Do you think that teachers should be passionate about their subject? How (if at all) would you encourage a teacher to present their subject attractively if they are concerned about imparting undue pressure?

How honest should one be about alternatives?

An inspiring exemplar can reveal possibilities for living well which an individual's own experiences, and those of their acquaintance, would (very likely) not exhibit. A rightly inspiring exemplar can take us far beyond the horizons of our limited experience to reveal kinds of goodness together with ways of realizing those kinds of goodness, which common everyday experience would not present.

The defective will and the testing of exemplars

For the imparting of wisdom to be effective, in enabling pupils to be wiser in action than they would otherwise be, their will must be well disposed, in two respects. First, they must be ready, open, and willing to recognize what is good. By this is not meant that they should be easily browbeaten into submission, their critical faculties overridden by authoritarian insistence, or dulled by keenness to please. Wisdom is appropriated by autonomous, but sometimes guided, discovery, as we have seen. But autonomy can manifest itself as wilfulness and, in particular, as a wilful blindness or refusal to accept what is there to be acknowledged. (For secondary school teachers it will often be hard to distinguish between the critical care and caution proper to people who are trying to establish their own course in the world and mere bloody-mindedness. Bloody-mindedness is commonly a determination to gain space, elbow room in which care and thought can be given to what is heard or read.)

Second, when people do recognize and acknowledge the goodness of some worthwhile good goal, and they see a good, efficient way of achieving it, then in order to act wisely – in order to be wise in the matter – they must will to act accordingly and, then, they must so act. Here we meet the problem of *akrasia*, namely, the gap between on the one hand recognizing what is good, seeing how to attain it, plus wanting to do what is required to reach it, and, on the other hand, actually taking the required steps to secure that good. Sometimes this is called 'weakness of will' (*akrasia*): we do want to do what is needed to secure the acknowledged good, but we don't want that enough actually to do it. Overoptimistic progressivist educators can neglect the problem posed by *akrasia*. It is easier to recognize it than to deal with it; but it cannot be marginalized as a minor matter; it is endemic.

These two problems are not easily dealt with – and some would say that they will not be disposed of while human nature remains what it is. Having registered the problems of wilful moral blindness and *akrasia*, we shall explore ways of imparting wisdom, and return in due time to these problems with a particular approach to them.

D o you and can you encourage in others strategies for dealing with 'weakness of will'?

They say the road to hell is paved with good intentions, but how can good intentions be brought into effect?

To this point in the chapter, the imparting of (Aristotelian) wisdom has been thought of: (i) as the enabling, prompting, encouragement and coaching in the habit of drawing on experience to identify good, efficient ways of gaining good things, achieving good ends; and, going in step with that, (ii) as helping in the acquisition of at least a modest body of information and understanding about well-tried, effective ways of gaining particular sorts of good ends. The process of acquiring such wisdom – the virtue and the set of known ways of gaining good goals – has been presented as gradual habituation and accumulation.

But there is a further complementary possibility whose existence holds the promise of countering wilful or willed blindness to the good, and against akratic weakness of will, this is another, and valuable, way whereby wisdom in action is elicited, guided, shaped, instructed and inspired by an exemplar. A saint, leader, or an admirable community's life can act as an inspirational exemplar. An exemplar can present itself influentially and powerfully so that its attractiveness engages, draws, enthrals and provides an inspiring model for a way of life. Though it is adaptable, the agent, the person influenced, starts from that paradigm or model, and can apply it to the circumstances encountered, rather than starting from the circumstances and figuring out a way of arriving at the good goal. An inspiring exemplar provides motivation towards good action as well as direction, guidance as to what is good. Wilful blindness and *akrasia* can be countered and overcome by the power of the exemplar. Moreover, an exemplar, once embraced, can give stability to our love of the good and our quest towards it. And an exemplar can give concrete exemplification of a new way of living, by living it out, revealing its difficulty, no doubt, as well as its possibility and attractiveness. The exemplar's inspiration derives in large part from its (her's, his) going beyond what we could have imagined for ourselves or independently set up as our own aspiration. But this does not entail that our critical faculties are suppressed and that our autonomy is infringed any more than the budding pianist who is taken to hear Daniel Barenboim play and is swept away by the experience, seeing possibilities never previously imagined, has his critical powers suppressed or his autonomy infringed.

Think of stories or episodes from history which can be used to convey to younger children the value of wise planning and/or action to achieve a good thing. Some of Aesop's fables might be useful: The Eagle and the Fox, The Birds, the Beasts and the Bat, The Horse and the Loaded Ass, even the Hare and the Tortoise.

Being captured/enthralled by an exemplar or ideal has some parallels in finding a hypothesis (in science, or history-research, or detecting a culprit) attractive, even 'eureka' – evoking, and convincing. The enquirer is aware of a coming together of experiences into an intelligible configuration (experiences of respectively different kinds: sense experience, reported or actually met in the lab, in the case of a scientific hypothesis, or of historical data, clues, human lives' being lived well, in the case of the exemplar). There is a meaningful relating of such experiences to one another with a conviction of understanding them much better now that they are subsumed, revealed in their true light, by the illuminating hypothesis or exemplar. Both hypotheses and exemplars can be tested or will have been tested, respectively, against sense experience in the case of the hypothesis, and against our individual judgements about what is wise action, what sorts of behaviours are wise in accordance with the rather Aristotelian conception of wisdom we explored earlier, in the case of the exemplar. Employing that conception of wisdom we can ask whether an exemplar (Socrates or Jesus Christ, Avicenna, Francis of Assisi, or Kagawa of Japan, for examples) reveals, or even perhaps creates, goods that its way of life will at least help us reliably to secure.

This is a time of moral pluralism or fragmentation or scepticism, in which pupils may lack shared starting points (or any starting point?) for the discussion of morality or wisdom. To make good a lack of a shared moral inheritance the presentation of some proven-to-be inspiring, worked-out moral vision, especially one that is embodied in a particular life, offers a way ahead. By that approach at least a starting place for critical appropriation can be found, and maybe, at the same time, even provide some inspiration and motivation towards caring about the good, and searching for ways to secure it. Finally, the prospects for the recognition and appreciation of, and allegiance to, a coherent, valuable body of wisdom, are surely better on this approach than on most others.

References

Adams, R. M. (2006), *A Theory of Virtue*. Oxford: Oxford University Press, chapter 12.

Urmson, J. O. (1988), *Aristotle's Ethics*. London: Blackwell, chapters 6 and 7.

CHAPTER TWELVE

Being faithful

trusting beyond

Jeff Astley

CHAPTER OUTLINE

In this chapter, religious faith is first analysed in detail, including such issues as faith and reason and grace and virtue, before moving to the concept of faith as a component of human relationships. Faith is an expression of the human heart which is traditionally the deepest sense of the self, the source of thinking, feeling and willing. As such, faith is not reducible to mere content (or beliefs) but is an activity or process of knowing, valuing or meaning-making that relates us to what we take to be our ultimate environment, in the form of trust and loyalty. This leads to a discussion of other distinctions within faith that also apply to relationships between human beings, for example, between 'believing in' and 'believing that', and faith as vision. The question as to whether faith is a valuable human virtue is then addressed.

Introduction: Getting to the heart of faith

The Old and New Testaments employ many words that are translated by the English word 'heart', especially the Hebrew *lêb* (which occurs 589 times) and the Greek *kardia* (160 times). In these Scriptures, the heart is seen in some way as the essence of human nature: its spiritual, intellectual, moral and ethical centre. The Lord 'does not see as mortals see; they look on the outward appearance, but Yahweh looks on the heart' (1 Samuel, chapter 16, verse 7; cf. 2 Corinthians, chapter 5, verse 12). It is in their hearts that fools say 'there is no God' (Psalms, chapter 14, verse 1). Those who are pure in heart will be blessed – or are already blessed – and will 'see God' (Matthew, chapter 5, verse 8). The heart is the source of decisions – for good or for ill (Joshua, chapter 14, verse 8; Proverbs, chapter 6, verse 18; Isaiah, chapter 13, verse 7; chapter 65, verse 14; Jeremiah, chapter 5, verse 23; Mark, chapter 7, verses 21–22; Romans, chapter 6, verse 17; Luke, chapter 12, verse 45), and a centre of emotions such as joy, sadness and rage (Deuteronomy, chapter 28, verse 47; 1 Samuel, chapter 25, verses 36–37; Nehemiah, chapter 2, verse 2; Job, chapter 29, verse 13; Psalms, chapter 34, verse 18; chapter 69, verse 20; chapter 105, verse 3; chapter 143, verse 4; Acts of the Apostles, chapter 7, verse 54).

But the heart is also a metaphor for deep-seated belief: 'one believes with the heart and so is justified' (Romans, chapter 10, verse 10; cf. Mark, chapter 11, verse 23; Luke, chapter 24, verse 25). Religious and moral conversion requires a change of heart: 'I will remove from your body the heart of stone and give you a heart of flesh' (Ezekiel, chapter 36, verse 26). In every sense, then, it is from the heart that there 'flows the springs of life' (Proverbs, chapter 4, verse 23).

In his book, *The Heart of Christianity: Rediscovering a Life of Faith*, New Testament scholar and Christian apologist Marcus Borg writes:

> [T]he twin notions that being Christian is about 'believing' in Christianity and that faith is about 'belief' are a modern development of the last few hundred years.... Prior to the modern period, the most common Christian meanings of the word 'faith' were not matters of the head, but matters of the heart. In the Bible and the Christian tradition, the 'heart' is a metaphor for a deep level of the self, a level below our thinking, feeling, and willing, our intellect, emotions, and volition. The heart is thus deeper than our 'head', deeper than our conscious self and the ideas we have in heads. Faith concerns this deeper level of the self. Faith is the way of the heart, not the way of the head. (Borg 2003, p. 26)

This resonates with the now classic argument of Wilfred Cantwell Smith (1997), that the original usage of the verb 'believe' was associated with trust and fidelity; it signified love and to give allegiance, to be loyal and to value highly – that is, to set one's heart.

The concept of religious faith

In religious language, the word 'faith' is used both of an object or content (*fides quae creditur*: the faith which is believed) and of a human activity, process or faculty directed towards that object (*fides qua creditur*: the faith by which it is believed). The former usage, as in the phrase 'the Christian faith' or even 'the Faith', refers to a religion or more often its teachings, particularly teachings about its values and beliefs. However, faith as a process must be our theme here, and this is thought of as directed either to this human object, 'the religion's teachings', or to the divine realities of which these speak – in Christianity, the triune God, Christ, the Church, and so on.[1]

The distinction between faith as content and faith as process has been developed by James Fowler. He understands religious faith as faith directed to specifically religious centres of value and power, and religious 'master stories'. Fowler's main interest, however, is much wider than this, for he insists that we all share a generic human faith. Everyone who is not about to commit suicide believes in something or someone; everyone therefore possesses some 'faith in'.

Human 'faithing' is described by Fowler as 'an integral, centering process, underlying the formation of [the] beliefs, values and meanings' that all humans embrace; it is something that gives coherence and direction to their existence, and helps them face their lives and their deaths. Although he often speaks of 'faith-knowing', Fowler does not restrict faith to cognition alone but commends a 'logic of conviction' that represents a more holistic notion than any 'logic of rational certainty'. In this more inclusive sense, faith is our activity (or state) of knowing, understanding and valuing whatever it is that we take to be of ultimate significance in our lives.[2] Human faith is thus our 'way-of-being-in-relation' to whatever is ultimate for us – whatever we take to be our 'ultimate environment' – and it therefore plays a central role 'in shaping the responses a person will make in and against the force-field of his or her life'. (Fowler and Keen 1978, p. 25; Astley and Francis 1992, p. 5; Fowler 1996, p. 56.)

In addition to these elements of thought and feeling, some scholars regard the overt, 'outer' expression of these 'inner' responses as a further 'lifestyle' element in (or type of) faith. Thus, Thomas Groome includes 'a lived life of agapé' as one of faith's 'essential and constitutive dimensions' (Groome 1980, pp. 57–66, 73–7). In today's terms, the faith of which Jesus spoke engages people's 'beliefs, relationships and commitments', their 'heads, hearts and hands – their entire way of being in the world' (Groome 2011, p. 26).

> H ow would you summarize the way faith is being understood so far?

This faith as doing lies close to the traditional notion of *fidelitas*, understood as the lived-out loyalty and faithfulness expressed through our behaviour – particularly our fealty to whatever we recognize as our Lord, but also to our friends. It includes the virtue of constancy. In this sense, God is pre-eminently the faithful one. Depending on the context, 'faith' and 'faithfulness' both translate the Greek New Testament's word *pistis*. Faithfulness is 'faithful obedience to God's will' (Dunn 1992, p. 27).

Exploring the theological vocabulary further, we note that *fidelitas* is the active expression of faith as *fiducia*. *Fiducia* is faith as trust, which is an attitude directed to a person rather than a set of doctrines; faith is here understood as a 'perseverance in trust in the guiding and covenanting Lord' (Buber 1951, p. 10). Its opposite is mistrust or distrust. St Paul, Luther and Protestantism in general have stressed this species or component of faith. This attitudinal interpretation of faith is often distinguished from the traditional Catholic analysis (expressed particularly by St Thomas Aquinas) of faith as *assensus*: that is, assent to propositions. On that view, faith is essentially an intellectual conviction, a conversion to a body of beliefs, particularly truths about the existence and nature of God. Luther called this merely 'historical faith'. It is most often nowadays described as belief, and its opposite is disbelief or doubt.

Fiducia usually goes along with a commitment to, and a positive evaluation of, the object of faith. In theistic religions, the religious believer is 'for' God, evaluating God as one who possesses supreme worth and therefore worthy of worship. Again, this is a matter of the heart rather than the head, involving affective ('feeling') attitudes (Price 1969, p. 452). Faith is therefore often viewed as an orientation towards whatever it is in which we have faith (see Cunningham 2008, pp. 112–17, 160–1, 309–14).

But we should return to the language of belief. Faith as *assensus* is belief that some proposition is true, whereas faith as *fiducia* is belief in a person – or in some value, ideal or institution. Belief-that (or belief-about), understood as a propositional or cognitive state or disposition relating to what is the case, may be clearly distinguishable from this wider notion of faith as belief-in. However, this distinction is often ignored, not least by the designers of questionnaires! Simply to believe that God exists is compatible with having no trust in God whatever, no sense that God is supremely valuable and no commitment to fulfilling God's will. Believing in God, by contrast, understood properly, includes these additional elements. (The same distinction applies to other objects of faith. Asked, 'Do I believe in baptism?' the grumpy interviewee would be missing the point if he replied, 'Of course. I've seen it done.') According to the Epistle of James, 'even the demons believe' that there is one God (James, chapter 2, verse 19), but this is not enough to make them believers in God. They do not deny God's existence, but they refuse to take the extra, truly religious step of worshipping God, or engaging in the works that faith requires as a response. Faith as belief-in is thus more than a factual belief. It is belief-that plus: belief-that 'with attitude', and accompanied by appropriate behaviour.

For most people, however, a belief-in usually implies some belief-that, unless it is a belief in a hoped-for and yet unrealized ideal (world peace, for example, or Christian unity). Certain theological 'non-realists' apart, belief-in God usually presupposes that God exists 'in fact'. Hence, the more

Protestant concept of faith in God is something that itself involves a belief that God exists. And Catholic theology has always recognized the importance of submitting one's will – as well as one's intellect – to the revealing God. (For Aquinas, to love God is more excellent than just knowing God, and 'love is perfected by the lover being drawn to the beloved': *Summa Theologiae*, I–II, q66, a6.) For both Catholics and Protestants, therefore, religious faith involves 'saying "amen" to what God speaks' and to whom God is (Immink 2005, p. 245; see also Lee 1990, chs 6 and 7; Swinburne 1981, 2005, ch. 4).

Some analyses of the concept of faith see it more as a way of seeing. 'Faith as visio' is how Borg puts this (Borg 2003, pp. 34–7). The philosopher of religion John Hick developed the idea of religious faith as the interpretative element within religious experience, arguing that it is the element by which religious people experience the world as God's world, 'life as divinely created and ourselves as living in the unseen presence of God' (Hick 1983, p. 47; cf. 2008, ch. 2). This is close to what Donald Evans called 'onlooks'. An onlook is more than an intellectual opinion or 'view', and implies more commitment than an 'outlook' or 'perspective' (Evans 1963, p. 125). 'I look on the world as' something or other: as a home, as a road to God, as a gift. Its opposite may be said to be unfaith, seeing reality as hostile or indifferent (Borg 2003, p. 36); compare, 'I look on death as the mockery of human hopes'. To switch from one perspective to the other may require some sort of conversion that involves 'a characteristic emotional shift, allowing the world to be seen differently' and in its true meaning (Cottingham 2009, p. 123).

D o you find this analysis of faith helpful? If so why; if not why not?
     What would you say is your way of 'looking on' the world?

For many analyses of the religious concept of faith, the link with the notion of evidence is important. Positive accounts of the relationship between faith and reason have been offered by many. Some have even argued that some sort of faith is a necessary prerequisite for all reasoning, and therefore that faith undergirds science and common sense; while others hold the less radical view that (some aspects of) religious faith may be reached through reason. But Protestants have often drawn a sharp line between faith and reason, insisting that faith is a direct gift of God's grace that surpasses or even destroys our fallen reason, because unaided human thought can only delude us concerning the saving truths of God. It seems natural for those who hold this view to argue that a 'leap of faith' is required for religious commitment; and that true faith is focused on what will often seem to be absurd in terms of worldly reasoning.

Yet the very idea of religious faith seems to involve our believing, trusting or acting towards God in ways that 'go beyond', and may even run in the face of, the available evidence. In this sense, all faith – including faith in our friends – is 'the assurance of things hoped for, the conviction of things not seen' (Hebrews, chapter 11, verse 11; see also 2 Corinthians, chapter 5, verse 7). Richard Swinburne defines the overt expression of religious trust as a person's acting on certain assumptions about God's meeting our needs, 'when evidence gives some reason for supposing that [God] may not' (Swinburne 1981, p. 115). For many, the fact that religious faith is not based on evidence in the way that the sciences are, is enough to condemn it. However, the rationality or reasonableness of religious faith, which is inherent in the claim that the faithful have good reasons or grounds for their faith – that is, that it is 'justifiable', has been vigorously defended by many philosophers of religion in a wide variety of ways.

Why do you think that the relationship between faith and reason has been so keenly contested? Is this debate a good thing or not, and why?

Faith as a human interaction

Not every feature of the concept of faith outlined above relates to faith as a component of human relationships. But many do, including this last element. It is by no means obvious that it is irrational to continue to trust in someone or something in the presence of evidence that appears to undermine that trust. Rather, this dimension of faith is almost a defining characteristic of what it is to be fully human, and certainly of what it is to be in a steadfast, loyal relationship with another person. Faith, therefore, lies at the heart of friendship (see Astley 2007, ch. 4).

Should our trust in friends go 'beyond the evidence'?
Are our friendships formed on the basis of evidence? If so, what sorts of evidence?
If our lives appear to be undermining our credibility, would we hope that our friends would give us the 'benefit of the doubt'? Should we give them the same benefit?

In what I have said above, I have rather passed over the thorny theological debate over the relationship between human faith and God's grace – 'faith as gift' over against 'faith as achievement'. One reason for this lapse is that

I want an analysis of faith in God that can most readily map onto interpersonal faith. Where Christians talk of faith as one of the 'divinely infused virtues' and of the 'light of grace', or something similar, most educators will want to change the subject – or even to make their apologies and leave.

We should, however, explore the issue further here. Protestants traditionally stress grace wherever they can, and often object to virtue language on the grounds that it seems to make the Christian life a kind of human achievement, even a sort of self-justification (see Hauerwas and Pinches 1996, p. 14). For Karl Barth, 'it is the part of the divine will to precede and the human to follow, of the former to control and the latter to submit'. He would countenance, therefore, no 'harmony of the divine and human wills' (1957, p. 644). However, although Catholic theology talks of the cardinal virtues as naturally acquired strengths that make us fit for human society, it also acknowledges our need for grace on account of our human sinfulness, in order for us fully to attain the goals to which these virtues are directed. Catholics further insist that extraordinary grace is absolutely necessary for the exercise of the theological virtues (faith, hope and love), which best characterize the divine nature and make us fit for a divine communion, because attaining such a state is inevitably beyond any natural human capacity. It can therefore only come by the infusion of God's grace (Freddoso 2005). Religious faith is being thought of here as something that requires cooperation between free human activity and the assisting grace of a benevolent God. However, many Protestants would also warmly concur that faith is both a gift of God and a human act, 'both gift and choice' in the sense that 'true faith is a gift that is freely accepted' (Tilley 2010, p. 55) – and may be 'cultivated' (Wright 2010, pp. 170, 176).

> Consider the story of the man whose son was healed by Jesus (Mark, chapter 9, verses 17–27). Jesus told him that all things were possible for those who believe. The man replied, 'I believe, help my unbelief'.
>
> How might this story help us to understand the relationship between faith and grace?

It may be argued, however, that the need for extraordinary grace is more a function of the orientation of faith towards God than it is of the intrinsic nature of faith (or of love and hope) when these virtues find their objects and application within human society. Of course, special gifts of grace are welcome everywhere, but they are surely only needed where God's ordinary grace – expressed in God's creative, sustaining and providential care through and in Nature – is insufficient to realize God's ends. In any case, we cannot seriously write a curriculum for the community school, or any other 'non-faith school', that is dependent for its delivery on special dispensations of grace.[3] Armed with these excuses, I shall say nothing further about the relationship between faith and grace.

The central premise of this whole discussion, of course, is that religious faith is not the only species of faith. As Robert Solomon put it, 'one can place his faith in other people, in the fortunes of the weather or the Massachusetts state lottery, or in himself' (Solomon 1983, p. 310). Having faith in people (parents, friends, teachers) is part of what makes us human. We are rightly encouraged, at least to a degree, to 'believe in them' (see Cunningham 2008, p. 113). And 'accepting something on faith' (that is, being willing to assume it be true, and therefore holding a belief-that about it), on the basis of the authority of teachers, books and even web pages, would appear to be an essential feature of any effective general education. Alfred Freddoso suggests a further dimension of interpersonal faith, when he writes of 'filial friendship' as including a desire in children 'to see the world as their parents see it out of love for them' (Freddoso 2005, p. 181). Here we again meet faith as *visio*.

However, I intend in this chapter to place most of my eggs into another basket, by understanding interpersonal faith as *fiducia* (plus *fidelitas*).

Virtuous faith?

In what sense is faith a virtue? And is it one that should be taught in the community, common or non-religious school?

Regrettably, my Anglican background is not much help here. Books on Anglican moral theology understand faith solely as a theological virtue. The older ones hold to a traditional Catholic line. For Kenneth Kirk, faith 'considered as a theological virtue' is 'the consecration of the mind to the service of God' (Kirk 1921, p. 80). Bishop R. C. Mortimer (Mortimer 1947) is even more volitional and Thomistic: the virtue of faith is believing something that God has revealed because God has revealed it, though this act is only possible because God assists the will to assent. Herbert Waddams retains the volitional element, although he does treat faith as more than intellectual assent. For Waddams, faith is our choice to trust God, and to surrender to God through an 'act of the will which takes Jesus as. . . . Saviour and Lord'. Hence, there is no one 'who cannot have faith if he wills' (Waddams 1972, p. 113). Tom Wright treats faith solely as a theological virtue, defining it – in a phrase that neatly combines *fiducia*, *fidelitas* and *assensus* – as 'the settled, unwavering trust in the one true God whom we have come to know in Jesus Christ' (Wright 2010, p. 175). However, we shouldn't restrict human faith to the religious domain.

I am also unhappy with too volitionalist an interpretation of faith. Certainly, I take the view that belief (belief-that) is only indirectly under the control of the human will, in that 'believing itself is not an act, [but] our acts determine the sort of beliefs we end up with' (Pojman 1986, p. 180).

We are therefore only indirectly responsible for our beliefs; for although we have some control over the pathways to belief, our final response is beyond our control. And it must be, if it is to count as a belief. Beliefs should reflect evidence or argument, and we must therefore be willing to acknowledge that our beliefs are forced on us by these factors. We can't simply will them to be true. (And we can't anyway: try it, and see for yourself!) Our pupils like ourselves may only be said to be culpable, therefore, if they believe lazily: without seeking out and attending to appropriate evidence, or examining the logic of their arguments carefully enough.

According to Robert Adams, the religious 'sin of unbelief' is 'not a refusal to assent intellectually to theological truths, but a failure to trust in truths to which we do assent' (Adams 1987, p. 17). Richard Swinburne also allows no freedom of belief, but he acknowledges a meritorious faith in the sense of actively relying on our beliefs about God. Where trust is thus interpreted as 'active faith', this seems reasonable. Where, however, it is taken to be an inner attitude or disposition (or valuation), I am not clear that the will is involved – except, again, indirectly. I do not think that we can 'by an act of will directly add an inch to the stature of our pro-attitude towards God, or cause our trust in God to grow' (Astley 1994, p. 202; cf. Astley, 2012 and Cunningham 2008, pp. 310–1). And the same applies when this virtue is considered in relation to human beings.

Are any virtues under our direct control? It is not, David Hume writes, in a person's power 'by the utmost art and industry, to correct his temper, and to attain that virtuous character to which he aspires' (*The Sceptic*, 1742). This is too extreme, but such a view at least allows us to recognize that lives live people as much as people live lives (Kupperman 1991, p. 57). It is never always or our entire fault whether we are virtuous or not; and we must acknowledge that some people find acquiring virtue easier than others. Which is not to say that the others cannot do it. It is to allow that the virtues we most readily acquire are those that run along the grain of our natures, rather than across it.

Yet don't we find fault with people's vices, even holding them responsible for their characters? Well, saying that I ought to be less selfish (or more trusting) does seem to make sense; although it isn't quite like saying that I ought to act more kindly to people (which would be entirely proper). The reason blame seems plausible in such circumstances may be that criticizing my character can make me less likely to do selfish acts, which is where my real freedom lies. And that is how we change our virtuous habits – by practising them: 'Only an utterly senseless person can fail to know that our characters are the result of our conduct' (Aristotle, *Nicomachean Ethics*, bk3, chs 2, 5). If blame works, it is justifiable. If it works. But again, it works better with some people than it does with others.

Note that I am not saying that we cannot acquire virtue (eventually) by our own efforts. I would argue, however, that: (a) this is an indirect freedom, not a direct one; and (b) that we need to be less simplistic in our judgements about people's characters – including our own, and those of our pupils (and our children). Who I already am strongly affects how and how much I can change; individual psychological differences matter in this area. This is not a level playing field.

Like some theologians, the atheist philosopher André Comte-Sponville includes neither faith nor hope among the eighteen virtues he surveys in *A Small Treatise on the Great Virtues*. He omits them on the grounds that neither has any other plausible object than God (Comte-Sponville 2001, p. 287). But he does not list 'trust', either. Yet when we talk of having 'faith in people' – as we do – it is this element that is all-important. For Donald Evans, by contrast, trust is fundamental. It is at the heart of the eight 'attitude-virtues' that he sees as the pervasive, unifying stances underlying morality as well as religion; and which he holds to be not only intrinsic values ('good-in-themselves') but also constituents of human fulfilment (Evans 1979). We are better and – in a deep sense – happier, more fulfilled people when we possess them. (And we are also then better placed to experience God.)

What are the similarities and differences between faith in God and our trust and loyalty towards another person?
Can one distinguish between (a) a trust that may be earned (or lost) and (b) a 'basic trust' that is always warranted or, to put it another way, one that life demands from one?

Evans' complete list of attitude-virtues comprises basic trust, humility, self-acceptance, responsibility, self-commitment, friendliness, concern (both pastoral and prophetic) and contemplation; the last three being interpreted as species of love. I take all these to be essentially spiritual virtues, in the sense adopted by Charles Taylor when he writes of the spiritual as constituting a 'background picture' of strong evaluation that incorporates, but points beyond, the moral and personal. Spiritual concerns connect here with our ultimate ideals and our deepest sense of what makes life meaningful and generally worth living – in short, what we take to be 'the good life'.

> While it may not be judged a moral lapse that I am living a life that is not really worthwhile or fulfilling, to describe me in these terms is nevertheless to condemn me in the name of a standard, independent of my own tastes and desires, which I ought to acknowledge. (Taylor 1989, p. 4)

Interestingly, in a Christian–Humanist discussion group convened in the 1980s by the Christian Education Movement, both sides accepted Evans' list as a proper basis for a general spiritual education in all schools (see

Lealman 1986). Evans treats all eight attitude-virtues as neither exclusively theological (as having God as their object and source) nor exclusively moral (as being human achievements rather than divine gifts). He rightly notes that in a proper doctrine of the relation of creation to grace, trust directed to other human beings may be seen as 'a particular expression of trust in God, the constant and primary focus of trust' (Evans 1979, pp. 168–9).

For Evans, trust is fundamental to the other attitude-virtues, each of which depends on it but also goes beyond it (p. 109). He analyses trust itself into five elements: assurance (which can foster the other four elements),[4] receptivity, fidelity, hope and passion. Their opposing vices are anxiety, wariness, idolatry (understood here as craving for a substitute good, to be contrasted with a faithful commitment to 'the source of the essentials for life', p. 61), despair and apathy.

What Evans writes about these attitudes may readily be defended as an account of what it is to be a fulfilled and balanced human being, open to others and the world – but not naively or dangerously so.[5] And that is surely what we want for our pupils, as well as our children and grandchildren, and fellow members of our society.

As such, faith-as-trust may be regarded as a proper part of education for human maturity.

What forms might a 'basic trust' take?
What might be involved in nurturing a 'basic trust'?
Does education presume a 'basic trust' that needs to be respected?

Notes

1 Religious believers often baulk at treating God as an *object* of any human activity. However, 'to designate a god as the object of faith is simply to designate whatever it might be that one has faith in. To say faith *has* an object is to say that faith is *transitive*' (Tilley 2010, p. 34).

2 In Paul Tillich's famous definition, 'faith is the state of being ultimately concerned' – whether about God, or about the 'gods' of success, social standing or economic power, or whatever is 'experienced as ultimate' (Tillich 1957, pp. 1–4, 9).

3 As such dispensations are unpredictable, they cannot be guaranteed even in faith schools.

4 For Evans' profound distinction between 'satisfaction-assurance' and 'reality-assurance', with reference to Matthew, chapter 6, verses 25–27, see Evans 1979, pp. 23, 39–40 and Astley 2003.

5 It is usually argued that faith, viewed as a *theological virtue*, is not a mean
   between two vices – for there is no vice in having unlimited faith in God.
   However, as an *interpersonal virtue*, faith or trust can be taken too far or not
   far enough, as may such virtues as courage and humility also.

References

Adams, R. (1987), *The Virtue of Faith: And Other Essays in Philosophical
   Theology*. New York: Oxford University Press.
Astley, J. (1994), *The Philosophy of Christian Religious Education*. Birmingham,
   AL.: Religious Education Press.
—(2003), 'Spiritual Learning: Good for Nothing', in Carr, D. and Haldane, J. (eds),
   Spirituality, Philosophy and Education. London: Routledge Falmer, 141–53.
—(2007), *Christ of the Everyday*. London: SPCK.
—(2012), 'Can we Choose our Beliefs?', in Parker, S., Freathy, R. and Francis, L. J.
   (eds), *Religious Education and Freedom of Religion and Belief*. Bern:
   Peter Lang, 81–93.
Astley, J. and Francis, L. J. (eds) (1992), *Christian Perspectives on Faith
   Development: A Reader*. Leominster, UK: Gracewing Fowler Wright; Grand
   Rapids, MI: Eerdmans.
Barth, K. (1957), *Church Dogmatics*, vol. II/2. Edinburgh: T. & T. Clark.
Borg, M. (2003), *The Heart of Christianity: Rediscovering a Life of Faith*.
   New York: HarperSanFrancisco.
Buber, M. (1951), *Two Types of Faith*. London: Routledge & Kegan Paul.
Comte-Sponville, A. (2001), *A Small Treatise on the Great Virtues: The Uses of
   Philosophy in Everyday Life*. New York: Holt.
Cottingham, J. (2009), *Why Believe?* London: Continuum.
Cunningham, D. S. (2008), *Christian Ethics: The End of the Law*. London:
   Routledge.
Dunn, J. D. G. (1992), *Jesus' Call to Discipleship*. Cambridge: Cambridge
   University Press.
Evans, D. D. (1963), *The Logic of Self-Involvement*. London: SCM Press.
Evans, D. (1979), *Struggle and Fulfillment*. Cleveland, OH: Collins.
Fowler, J. W. (1996), *Faithful Change: The Personal and Public Challenges of
   Postmodern Life*. Nashville, TN: Abingdon.
Fowler, J. W. and Keen, S. (1978), *Life Maps: Conversations on the Journey of
   Faith*. Waco, TX: Word Books.
Freddoso, A. J. (2005), 'Christian Faith as a Way of Life', in W. E. Mann (ed.),
   The Blackwell Guide to the Philosophy of Religion. Oxford: Blackwell, 173–97.
Groome, T. H. (1980), *Christian Religious Education: Sharing our Story and
   Vision*. San Francisco: Harper & Row.
—(2011), *Will there be Faith? Depends on Every Christian*. Dublin: Veritas.
Hauerwas, S. and Pinches, C. (1996), *Christians among the Virtues: Theological
   Conversations with Ancient and Modern Ethics*. Notre Dame, IN: University of
   Notre Dame Press.
Hick, J. (1983), *The Second Christianity*. London: SCM Press.
—(2008), *Who or What is God?* London: SCM Press.

Immink, F. G. (2005), *Faith: A Practical Theological Reconstruction*. Grand Rapids, MI: Eerdmans.

Kirk, K. E. (1921), *Some Principles of Moral Theology and their Application*. London: Longmans, Green and Co.

Kupperman, J. J. (1991), *Character*. New York: Oxford University Press.

Lealman, B. (1986), 'Grottos, Ghettos and City of Glass: Conversations about Spirituality'. *British Journal of Religious Education* 8(2): 65–71.

Lee, J. M. (ed.) (1990), *Handbook of Faith*. Birmingham, AL: Religious Education Press.

Mortimer, R. C. (1947), *The Elements of Moral Theology*. London: A. & C. Black.

Pojman, L. P. (1986), *Religious Belief and the Will*. London: Routledge & Kegan Paul.

Price, H. H. (1969), *Belief*. London: Allen & Unwin.

Smith, W. C. (1997), *Belief and History*. Charlottesville, VA: University Press of Virginia.

Solomon, R. C. (1983), *The Passions*. Notre Dame, IN: University of Notre Dame Press.

Swinburne, R. (1981, 2005), *Faith and Reason*. Oxford: Clarendon Press.

Taylor, C. (1989), *Sources of the Self*. New York: Cambridge University Press.

Tilley, T. W. (2010), *Faith: What it Is and What it Isn't*. Maryknoll, NY: Orbis Books.

Tillich, P. (1957), *The Dynamics of Faith*. New York: Harper & Row.

Waddams, H. (1972), *A New Introduction to Moral Theology*. London: SCM Press.

Wright, T. (2010), *Virtue Reborn*. London: SPCK.

PART THREE
Exemplars

Exemplars

Introduction

Part 3 contains examples of how teachers can approach the teaching of virtues in the classroom. Each exemplar is related to one of the chapters in Part 2 and has been inspired by it. No exemplar or group of exemplars attempts to cover all the points made in the chapters. Teachers too will inevitably be selective. We offer exemplars for all keystages grouped accordingly, beginning with Keystage (KS) 1.[1] Exemplars are sometimes designed as a short series of lessons and sometimes as stand-alone. Each chapter of Part 2 has at least one exemplar here. They are exemplars rather than fully developed lesson plans and it is our hope that students and teachers will be inspired by them to think about what is possible and appropriate for the classes they are responsible for. One idea in one lesson might spark a particular train of thought and become the basis of a whole series of lessons. Although the exemplars are keystage related, it is possible that an idea contained in an exemplar for one keystage may be developed suitably for use with a different keystage. Good teachers will always think carefully about the children in their classes and tailor lessons to suit.

The authors have all had experience in the classroom. Jo Anderson was a teacher of RE in secondary schools. Ranjit Singh Dhanda was Principal Designate responsible for the development of Nishkam schools and is currently developing curriculum materials and teaching Faith Studies in the Primary and Secondary Schools in Birmingham. Penny Thompson was a teacher of RE in secondary schools in Sefton. Brenda Watson taught RE in secondary schools including sixth-form and went on to teach in Didsbury College of Education. We are grateful to Elizabeth Ashton for her insightful comments on the exemplars. Elizabeth was for over nineteen years a classroom-based primary teacher and latterly appointed to the University of Durham in the School of Education as Lecturer in Religious and Moral Education.

Exemplars for Keystage 1 (ages 5–6)

The first 3 exemplars are about learning to be wise.

Exemplar 1

Learning to be wise

Lesson Objectives:

- Understand the difference between being clever and being wise
- Practise using knowledge to achieve something good
- Learn about someone who has used their knowledge to bring about good

Discussion

Show a picture or tell a story about a jackdaw that likes to collect bits and pieces. Are people like jackdaws, collecting bits and pieces of information? Get children to suggest places/people from whom we get information.

Does collecting bits and pieces of information make you clever? If someone is clever, they do more than just collect facts. They can arrange them in a sensible way; they can see relationships between facts and use them to achieve something.

Activity

Give children 5 or 6 cards with pictures of familiar objects on them. Ask the children to arrange the cards so as to tell a story showing how the objects can be used to good purpose. For example, paper/card – crayons – wrapping paper – child drawing – flowers - Mum.

Story

Tell the story of someone like Christopher Columbus who was able to use facts and link information together so as to do something really useful with it.

Exemplar 2

Lesson Objectives:

- Consider further examples of differences between wise and merely clever people

Discussion

Recap: ask the children what purpose they have in finding out about things and doing things with the knowledge they've got? Is it to show off? Is it to try to be top dog? Is it to help other people? Is it to do harm to other people? Is it to try to make the world a better, or a worse, place? Explain that to be wise a person must want something good and helpful and be able to see how that can be best achieved. Thus, we would call Dr Ludwig Guttmann who was the founder of the Paralympics clever and wise, but Hitler we would call clever but not wise. Would you call the wolf in 'Little Red Riding Hood' wise or simply clever? The Prince in the 'Sleeping Beauty?' 'Rumplestiltskin?' 'Aladdin?' What other examples can children think of? What about the cult of celebrity?

Activity

Set up a wall display about 'only clever people' and 'wise people'.

Exemplar 3

Lesson Objectives:

- Understand about being quiet and listening to our inner voice.

- Realize that wisdom can help us make good choices.

- Identify ways we already use wisdom in our daily life and how we can use it better as we grow.

- To experience using wisdom in the classroom

Discussion

- It is important that we listen quietly to the little voice inside us; it is a soft voice. We call this conscience.

- This voice can guide us and helps us understand things.

- Explain that sometimes we hear this voice in our hearts, sometimes we hear it in our heads, sometimes we feel it in our stomachs.

- Help them identify times they may have listened to the little voice, such as telling the truth, or going over to help someone without being asked.

- Highlight examples when our voice has helped us to stay safe, for example, reminded us not to run after a football that has gone into the road.

- Wisdom can help to realize answers to important questions we may have.

- Wisdom can help us to know what is good and what is right.

- Wisdom helps us live by our values, even when we have a strong urge to do something differently.

- Wisdom is not about trying to be clever or showing off.

- Encourage them to always listen to the voice of wisdom within them

Story

Read the following story to the whole class, asking questions to emphasize the key messages.

Bhagat Puran Singh's father died at an early age; his mother was very poor and she brought him up by working as a servant. He was not able to complete his basic education, and soon his mother also died.

At a young age he became homeless and penniless. He survived by doing voluntary work in places of worship. One day, someone fell from the roof of the Gurdwara (Sikh place of worship); Bhagat Puran Singh rushed him to hospital. After helping the injured man, he felt an inner joy. He began helping those who had no one, the abandoned, beggars and the injured. He would wash their dirty clothes, look after their wounds and try to find food for them. He also helped abandoned and stray animals. He was often seen clearing glass and rubble from the road to avoid injury to animals. He wrote pamphlets and would talk to people about looking after the environment.

He lived outside railway and bus stations helping others. Many people would turn away from him because he looked ragged, frail and hardly had any clothes. Later he became a well-known figure, who shared all he had with others, carrying the disabled on his back, and comforting the abandoned and dying at the road side.

Slowly many people started to contribute to his efforts and Bhagat Puran was able to build a care home for the sick and disabled, a sanctuary for animals and initiated tree plantation campaigns.

Discussion

- Highlight the fact that during Bhagat Puran Singh's time there was no government support for the poor (such as hospitals, care homes and welfare).

- People had to pay for everything they needed.

- Sometimes a few very rich people would help the poor. Bhagat Puran Singh was very poor.
  - Why do you think he decided to help?

- Did he always take the injured people to the hospital or did he help in other ways?

- Why was he able to help the poor when most other people may think they cannot help?

- Discuss differences between knowledge, understanding and wisdom.

Activities

Ask pupils to sit quietly and listen to their inner voice. Ask them to think about how they can help poor people without giving them money or giving them other things (for example, being kind and talking to people, spending time with people, telling good stories to people).

Ask pupils to give examples of when their inner voice has helped them. The story of St Francis of Assisi is a good example of listening to an inner voice. There should be some discussion of how we can distinguish the voice of conscience from other voices within us which may seek to condemn or lead us astray.

The following exemplar is about learning to be faithful:

Exemplar 4

Learning to be faithful

Lesson Objectives:

- Learn more about belief, trust and faith.

- Realize that each one of us has a natural tendency to trust and be faithful.

- Identify ways we already use trust in our daily life.

- See how trust and faith can help us to be happy.

Discussion

- What and who we believe in – our parents, our inner voice and our close friends.

- Explore how our trust in our parents grows (starting from holding onto our parent's finger and going onto playing independently)

- Examples of trust and faith – holding hands at school, being helped to cross the road by a supervisor.

- Name people we trust (shopkeepers, bus drivers etc.)
- How does it feel when we have trust and faith in people?
- How does it feel when we do not have trust and faith in people?

Story

Read the following story to the whole class, asking questions to emphasize the key messages.

A long time ago, a rich man called Bhai Lehna had a wish to find God and serve people. He had heard a lot of wonderful stories about a holy man called Guru Nanak Dev; so he decided to join Guru Nanak Dev and learn from him.

Although Bhai Lehna was a very rich man, he served under Guru Nanak Dev with love and devotion. He would do anything that was needed, even if the work was dirty and very hard. He would work on the farm in the day time and serve food to the congregation in the evening. Bhai Lehna was also a very good teacher and children loved to be taught by him.

Once during a heavy rainfall a neighbour's wall had fallen down. Guru Nanak asked his two sons and other Sikhs to build the wall quickly. Everyone made excuses and wanted to build the wall the next day. Bhai Lehna started to build the wall immediately although it was late in the evening, and very cold and dark. Bhai Lehna always wanted to make Guru Nanak Dev happy.

One day Guru Nanak Dev's pot fell into a dirty ditch. Guru Nanak asked his two sons to fetch the pot. One of his sons refused, the other made excuses and offered to buy a new pot instead. Bhai Lehna at once went into the ditch to get the pot and cleaned it.

Guru Nanak Dev asked Bhai Lehna 'When there is something difficult to be done, other people make excuses, why do you always do those things gladly?'

Bhai Lehna replied: 'I am your servant, I always want to be at your side and make you happy.'

Bhai Lehna loved Guru Nanak so much that he became like Guru Nanak Dev. Guru Nanak Dev changed his name to Angad (which means a limb from my limb). Guru Nanak also said Bhai Lehna would be the next Guru (prophet) of the Sikhs.

Discussion

- Who did Bhai Lehna trust most?
- How did he show his faith in Guru Nanak Dev?
- Discuss how having faith helped Bhai Lehna.

Activity

1 Privately reflect and recall a time when they experienced trust and faith.
2 How did they feel in trusting the other person or thing?
3 Ask pupils to draw a picture or write a story about friendship, trust and faith.

Exemplars for Keystage 2 (ages 7–11)

The first example is about learning to be compassionate, the second about learning to be faithful and the third about learning to be wise.

Exemplar 1

Learning to be compassionate

Lesson Objectives:

- Learn more about compassion, kindness and forgiveness.
- Realize that each one of us has a natural tendency to be compassionate.
- Identify ways we already use compassion in our daily life.
- See how applying compassion can enrich our lives.

Discussion

(The teacher should be ready with examples here)

- What is compassion?
- What actions show compassion?
- How does it feel when we are compassionate?
- How is compassion linked to kindness and forgiveness?
- Sometimes we find it very difficult to be compassionate.
- When we understand and care about how another person feels, that's compassion.
- Stress that we all feel and use compassion every day.
- Compassion is showing kindness as well as feeling it empathetically.
- It is as important that we act with compassion to ourselves as well as being compassionate to others. Why is this?

Story

Read the following story to the whole class, asking questions to emphasize the key messages.

Bhai Kanhaiya was born into a wealthy family and from a very young age he showed remarkable compassion and love for the poor. He gave money to the poor; as he grew older he helped labourers by carrying their heavy loads over long distances. His parents were a little annoyed at seeing their son doing manual work. Bhai Kanhaiya replied that he was unable to see the suffering of others and wanted to alleviate some of their hardships even for a short moment.

He left home at a young age in search of spiritual enlightenment and peace, and he continued serving those in need. He was initiated as a Sikh by Guru Tegh Bahadur (the ninth Sikh Guru) who also guided him to carry out Nishkam Sewa (service of others without expecting any reward or recognition).

During the reign of Guru Gobind Singh (the tenth Sikh Guru) Bhai Kanhaiya was visiting the holy Sikh City of Anandpur, when it was attacked and surrounded by the Mughal army. The enemy also cut off food and water supplies to the City. During the fighting that followed, Bhai Kanhaiya was often seen comforting, resuscitating and serving water to all injured and dying solders, without discriminating between the Sikh and the Mughals. His acts of compassion drew stern criticism among fellow Sikhs, who eventually complained to Guru Gobind Singh.

Guru Gobind Singh summoned Bhai Kanhaiya. 'These brave Sikhs are saying that you won't stop serving the wounded enemy soldiers and they recover to fight again – is this true?'

Bhai Kanhaiya replied: 'Yes, what they say is true. My Lord, when I looked into the eyes of the injured I saw no Mughal or Sikh, I only saw the light of the One Creator from within every soul.'

The Guru smiled and blessed Bhai Kanhaiya. 'You have understood the true message of the Sikh scriptures and religious teachings.' The Guru also gave Bhai Kanhaiya ointment, bandages and other medical supplies to complete his role in delivering care to all the wounded, friends and foes alike.

Discussion

- Talk about the importance of forgiveness as an aspect of compassion.

- How might being compassionate help us to be happy and healthy?

Activities

Privately reflect and recall a time when they noticed that another person was sad, sorry, hurt, embarrassed, angry or confused, and they felt what that person was feeling.

1 Did they want to help?

2 Was it a situation in which they could help in some way?

3 Did they offer any comfort or help?

4 Do people sometimes gain secret satisfaction from seeing others in trouble? Why is this?

5 Identify at least 8 ways to be compassion towards other people, animals, the earth and oneself.

6 Ask pupils to do one, small, individual 'random act of kindness' to a friend or a family member, and keep it a secret.

Background information A brief introduction to Bhai Kanhaiya: http://tuhitu.blogspot.co.uk/2007/07/sakhi-series-58-bhai-kanhaiya-singh-ji.html

Exemplar 2

Learning to be faithful

Lesson Objectives

- Learn that faith in God calls for obedience
- Consider that faith in God does not guarantee right action
- Think about what matters and what should matter to them

Read the story of Daniel from the book of Daniel in the Old Testament – Chapter 6. A modern translation will be best.

Discussion

Ask children where faith occurs in the story. Note that the story does not say that Daniel had faith that God would save him from the lions. Oddly enough it is the King who believed that this was the sort of thing that a powerful God could do (see verse 16). And the King even spoke words of encouragement to Daniel, assuring him that his God would save him! So the King had faith and the events of the story increase this faith (verses 26–27). The narrator says that Daniel's faith has saved him (verse 23) yet Daniel says that it was because he had done nothing wrong, either to God or the King.

In this story, faith and obedience are very close. Daniel was committed to a life of prayer and service to his God and nothing was going to deter him from this course, certainly not the jealousy and scheming of his fellow courtiers. Faith requires obedience and has consequences, something Daniel was well aware of. The King had faith too but one wonders about his new law (verse 26)! One could bring in other stories about those who have acted in faith regardless of consequences for themselves and family.

Activities

1   'What really mattered to Daniel?' Draw a picture, cartoon or use sentences.
2   Ask the children to think about the question 'What really matters to me?' and,
3   'What should matter to me?' Draw a picture, cartoon or use sentences.

Some background[2]

The story fits into a genre of 'courtier stories' whereby a courtier (often foreign) comes into conflict with others and/or is involved in a contest in which his intelligence and wit saves the day for the King. The story of Joseph is an example of this. There is a similar story in Assyrian literature about a high official called Ahikar. Such stories were told sometimes for entertainment and sometimes to warn or give moral encouragement. It is likely that the book of Daniel was written to encourage Jews to keep their faith at a time of great crisis in national life. The genre means that it is likely that we have here a fictional story rather than a historical account. The punishment given is severe, even by the standards of the time (although the Greek historian Herodotus records one such event) and may be intended as a warning to those imposing their will on the Jewish diaspora. The story is situated in Babylon at the end of the sixth century BC. The narrator presents us with Daniel and his friends, part of the group of Jews who had been exiled from Judah to live in Babylon and who had so impressed the authorities that they were given important positions in the court of the King. Daniel is appointed as one of three rulers in charge of the large area that Darius the king had conquered. Daniel is going to be in sole charge and to avoid this, a group of the rulers, jealous of Daniel, attempt to discredit him. Daniel did not worship according to the customs of the Babylonians but continued to practise the faith of his forefathers, nurtured in the Temple in Jerusalem. They hatch a plot which will use his faith to bring about his downfall.

This may be the place to discuss different types of narrative in the Bible and the role of fiction in conveying truth.

Exemplar 3

Learning to be wise

Lesson Objectives

● Hear the story of the rich young man and Jesus
● Argue for and against the wisdom of his choice not to follow Jesus
● Make a resolution to cultivate wisdom

Story

Tell the children the story of the rich young man coming to Jesus and going away sorrowful. He didn't want to give up living in a nice house and watching his business grow to follow Jesus who was living with very few belongings – more like a tramp.

Activities

In groups discuss whether he made a wise decision. Share their views with the class and have a vote. Perhaps hot-spot the rich young man asking him why he chose as he did and whether he thinks it was a wise decision and other questions that occur to the children.

Discussion

Many people today are clever at getting rich and staying rich. What would they need to be or to do to be wise as well? Hopefully the children will suggest that giving money to help make other people happier would mean they are wise as well as clever. This would be because instead of being selfish with money they value being kind and good as more important. So the money would be put to a really good use. Bill Gates (ex-Microsoft) is a good example. His foundation employs people to work on humanitarian projects in the developing world. Ask children to think about a time when they were clever but not wise and a time when they were both clever and wise. Perhaps they can put this in their diary or make a resolution to cultivate wisdom.

Keystage 3 (ages 11–14)

The first three exemplars are about learning to be courageous and form a unit on the theme. The second three exemplars are about learning to be temperate and also form a unit. One exemplar follows on learning to be hopeful and one on learning to be honest.

Exemplar 1

Learning to be courageous

Lesson Objectives

- Consider the link between courage and character
- Think of the types of risk that require courage
- Reflect on the difference between being courageous and being foolhardy

Discussion

What is courage?

Ask for words describing courage: brave, plucky, daring, bold, foolhardy, heroic, audacious, adventurous, etc. What is the opposite of being courageous? Being timid? Weak-willed? Cowardly? Unadventurous? Would standing up to a bully be more courageous for someone who is fearless or for someone who is timid and shy?

It is said that we live in a risk-free society. Ask for examples. Is this true? Is it a good thing? What kind of risks should we try to avoid, and what kind of risks should we have the courage to take?

List types of risk:

- to risk physical injury

- to risk making a mistake

- to risk the disapproval of people in authority especially in a repressive regime

- to risk censure by one's peers

- to risk losing face with one's friends

- to risk having to say sorry

- to risk doing badly in tests at school

Activity

In pairs write a one-sentence definition of courage. Class could then vote on the best definition and write it up in their exercise book/work diary.

Research

If we are not prepared to take risks there are many things we shall never achieve. Think of Scott of the Antarctic and of Shackleton. Make a study of Scott's final expedition and of Shackleton's Endurance expedition. Think about their respective motives. How far would a motive such as competitiveness mean that risk-taking is likely to be immoral? Would pupils say that they were both equally courageous or was Scott foolhardy and not quite so meritorious as Shackleton who was more careful not to take risks endangering the lives of his men? Scott's concern for forwarding his scientific project was a major reason for the loss of his and his companions' lives, while Shackleton drew back in time and so didn't lose one life on the fateful expedition.

Exemplar 2

Aspects of courage

Lesson Objectives

- Think about different situations which call for courage
- Enter imaginatively into situations requiring courage

Discussion

What kind of courage is shown in these statements? Discuss and ask pupils to give examples either from their own experience or from that of others:

- He had the courage of his convictions.
- Although a red-hot socialist Tom let his friendship with liberal-minded Kevin change his attitude on some matters.
- She had the courage to admit she had been wrong.
- She coped with failure magnificently making it a triumph in itself.
- Ella never got far in speaking French because she was so afraid of making a mistake and being laughed at.
- He never tried because he was afraid of failing.

Activity

Pupils to role play (in threes) one of the above situations.

Exemplar 3

Courage and religious faith

Lesson Objectives

- Reflect on the link between religious faith and being courageous
- Find out about individuals whose faith in God has given them courage
- Realize that being courageous sometimes results in failure

Discussion

- What does it mean to have faith in God?
- Does faith in God give people an inner strength?

- Why might this be?
- Can pupils give examples from their own or another religion?

Story

A striking example of courage aided by religious faith was Shackleton in the 1916 expedition referred to above. The Endurance having been broken up by the ice, he left 22 men on Elephant Island while he and 5 others in a makeshift boat travelled to get help. They eventually landed on South Georgia Island only to find they had to trek over mountains to reach the whaling stations 22 miles away. Shackleton with Crean and Worsley managed this heroic walk through uncharted land. Shackleton had a real Christian faith, and he said afterwards that it seemed as though there were a fourth person walking with them giving them strength.

Research

Pupils could research the story of Jesus in the Garden of Gethsemane or before Pilate. Or they could research a story of courage from their own or another religion. Write a short piece about the sort of courage shown, what risks were involved and how faith in God played a part.

Finally, have a class discussion on how far they agree with the following statement of Libby Purves, referring to the newly set-up Speakers for Schools organization: 'I hope that some of them are willing to include stories of failure, slog, disappointment and pratfall on the way. Because that's where courage grows, and ambition, and new ideas.' ('However high you aim, try not to look down,' *The Times*, 29 October 2012)

Exemplar 4

The following three exemplars are about learning to be temperate

Learning to be temperate

Lesson Objectives

- Begin to understand what being temperate means
- Learn that being temperate applies to actions and opinions
- Consider the story of the temptations of Jesus and how his actions and words expressed temperance

Discussion

Ask pupils for examples of dictionary definitions of the word 'temperate'

- Exercising self-restraint (in pleasures)
- Being abstemious
- Not self-indulgent

Explain that being temperate may apply to both actions and opinions – so a person can be

- moderate in opinions such that they are open to the views of others
- restrained in action and expression
- Not violent or excessive about views or opinions
- Not adopting extreme standpoints or expressing them through force

A person might then be said to be equable, have an even temperament, be patient/composed/serene. Can pupils give examples of people they know who exhibit these qualities?

Activity

Pupils to think of how the above qualities could be expressed.

1 Of persons: give an example of when someone might show self-restraint
2 Of ideas and opinions: give an example of someone expressing an opinion in a peaceful way
3 Of climate: give an example of a country in which the climate is described as temperate

Role play in groups one of these situations/draw a cartoon/or write a short sketch.

Pause for thought

Is it always a virtue to be temperate?

Story

Tell the story of the Temptations of Jesus (Matthew, chapter 4, verses 1–11)

Discussion

- How did Jesus exercise self-restraint in this story?
- Where did he avoid excessive behaviour?
- How did he turn away from the use of power as a means of establishing his leadership?
- Was it difficult for Jesus to be temperate in this situation?
- Why? (Or Why not?) Was it the right thing to do? Why? (Or Why not?)

Pupils need to know that Jesus had just submitted to being baptised by John (Matthew, chapter 3, verse 13 to end) at which a voice was heard saying 'this is my beloved Son with whom I am well pleased'.

Exemplar 5

Lesson Objectives

- Understand that being temperate does not always require self-restraint
- Consider the story of Jesus cleansing the Temple and ask whether such action was intemperate or not
- Compare this story with that where Jesus restrained a disciple from using violence

Discussion

Remind pupils of the question from the last lesson: Is it always a virtue to be temperate? See if they can give examples where self-restraint might not be appropriate. Tell them that there was a time when Jesus was anything but temperate in the sense discussed in the last lesson.

Story

1) Tell the story of the Cleansing of the Temple (Mark, chapter 11, verses 15–19)

Why did Jesus show no restraint in the Temple? Was it appropriate behaviour on this occasion? Is there anything in current events which mirrors this action?

What were the likely consequences? (see verse 18)

2) Tell the story of the disciple in the garden of Gethsemane who drew a sword (Luke, chapter 22, verses 47–53).

Why did Jesus dissuade the disciples from their intentions? What did this show about his attitude? (violence is never the answer – going to the Cross was part of God's plan)

Discussion

- Why do you think Jesus himself used force in the temple while telling his disciples to desist?

- Would it be correct or incorrect to describe Jesus' actions in the temple as intemperate?

Challenge

Can you think of a definition of being temperate that includes Jesus' actions in the temple?

Exemplar 6

Lesson Objectives

- Learn that being temperate is often applied to alcohol

- Find out about Alcoholics Anonymous

- Consider the idea that temperance is sticking by one's values

- Act out a situation where temperance is shown

Temperance is often spoken of in a narrow way in terms of conduct, especially eating or drinking. A temperance movement aims at restricting intoxicating drink. Anyone joining the AA (Alcoholics Anonymous) programme admits he or she has become powerless over alcohol and that life has become unmanageable. This might be the place to discuss the issue of drinking as pupils of this age may already be involved.

Research

Find out about The American Prohibition Act in the United States from 1920 to 1933

Key Question: Why was this Act a dismal failure?

Official control by the state through raising the price of alcohol, or even by means of the influence of others is ineffective. Only if someone wants to work towards a life in which he or she lives according to his or her true values can temperance be discovered and sustained.

Activity

Devise short role play/sketch on the theme: 'Being temperate means . . .'.
Topics could be bullying in the playground or through social media, speaking
out for a strongly held opinion, an incident of road rage.

Exemplar 7

Learning to be hopeful

Lesson Objectives

- Consider the idea that hope can be present in the most hopeless of
  situations

- Learn how Job's hope in the goodness of God provoked discontent
  with suffering

- Ponder the sense we have that life must be leading somewhere
  beyond death

The story of Job

Tell the basic story – Job is a good man with a rich lifestyle and a big
family. Satan challenges God: your friend Job is good only because he has
everything going for him. Take good things away from him and he will
turn against you. God allows Satan to bring all kinds of troubles upon
Job, including disfiguring boils! Job is visited by friends who advise Job to
repent. Job refuses to believe that his suffering is a punishment, or, if it is,
that God must be an unjust God and thus not worth much. He rails against
his fate and against God, dismissing his friends as false comforters. In the
end God speaks to Job and this personal revelation satisfies Job and comes
as a reward for his integrity.

Story – Job Chapter 14

Pupils should read this carefully, in groups or individually. The New King
James version is very direct and retains the poetic feel of the original Hebrew.
The New Living Translation may be easier for some to understand. Point
out that there are sections, each presenting a different thought/s. Use the
following questions as prompts for reflection:

Section 1. Verses 1–6. What picture of the human condition does Job
present here? What is Job asking God for here? Try to think up a phrase to
sum up Job's request (e.g. Give us rest).

Section 2. Verses 7–12. Here Job reflects on aspects of nature where renewal is a built-in feature. Yet for human beings, he says, there is no possibility of renewal. Ask pupils to think whether Job's words are entirely hopeless. Human beings are said to sleep, the question is asked, 'Where are they?' If there is hope for a tree, the argument might develop, surely there must be hope for humankind.

Section 3. Verses 13–17. This section does develop into a cry for something better. What does Job hope for here? (being brought back to life, being restored to a relationship with God) What prompts Job to think that God might restore him?

Section 4. Verses 18–22. Here we find Job sinking back into hopelessness. It is God himself who 'destroys the hope of man'. There is a sense of anger that a man cannot even rejoice over the success of his sons or give help to family in a time of crisis.

Activities

1   Divide the class into four groups. Each group is to take a section each and work out a way of presenting their section to the class. Probably it is best to say that the section must be read out loud but may be edited for dramatic effect. For example, the words 'you destroy the hope of man' may be repeated. Then do a class performance.

2   Write a short piece answering the question, 'What hopes do you have?' Or, write a monologue in which Job argues that it is only hope that keeps him going. Or, draw and caption a diagram charting the different emotions Job goes through in this chapter.

Exemplar 8

Learning to be honest

Lesson Objectives

- Think about what it means to be honest

- Learn that there may be a cost to being honest

- Consider that there may be times when it is not easy to decide whether to be honest or not

- Think about the consequences of practising one's faith openly

Story

Daniel disobeys the law of the Medes and Persians.[3]

Read the story from the book of Daniel Chapter 6. Usually a modern translation will be best.

Discussion (1)

What sort of character is Daniel?

List some adjectives: exceptional, capable, intelligent, loyal, trustworthy, careful to avoid offence, decisive, honest, thorough and devoted to God above all else. Not exactly too good to be true but getting near to it.

What sort of character is Darius?

Administratively wise but perhaps naive (not seeing the trouble it might cause to appoint a foreigner), too trusting, not independent-minded enough, easily trapped, but able to admit he was wrong and decisive after the event.

Discussion (2)

Is it always right to be open and honest? Ask for examples from children's own experience.

Read Daniel's response to the new law (verses 10 and 11). Could his reaction be termed provocative? Could he not have waited 30 days before praying in public? Could he not have closed the windows and prayed without people noticing? Perhaps he could have gone to the King and explained the motive for the new law. Is prayer not something best done in private? Here prayer becomes a political act. Is it right to disobey a law that was passed without proper debate and seems unjust?

Activities

1   Ask children to debate one or more of these questions in small groups or pairs and report back to whole class. Hand out workcards with questions written on them.

2   In pairs take turns to be Daniel answering the question, 'Why did you not just close the windows and save everyone trouble?' The other member of the pair takes the role of interviewer.

Keystage 4 (ages 15–16)

There is one exemplar for keystage 4. It is about learning to be just

Learning to be just
Lesson Objectives

● Think about the relation between justice and compassion

● Reflect on the fact that religious rules can obstruct justice

- Consider the example and motives of some who have fought for justice in society
- Realize that rules in themselves do not always lead to just outcomes

Discussion

In an address to a gathering of bishops in Rome marking the 50th anniversary of the Vatican II Council, Rowan Williams, then Archbishop of Canterbury, summarized what is at the centre of all religion in the phrase 'the silent gazing upon God that is the goal of all our discipleship'. Through such gazing we 'learn what we need so as to live truthfully and honestly and lovingly . . . how to see other persons and things for what they are in relation to God, not to me. And it is here that true justice as well as true love has its roots'.
What might this mean?

Story

Read the story of the Good Samaritan (Luke, chapter 10, verses 25–37)

Examine the motivation of the Samaritan. Why did he act as he did? It would have been very inconvenient for him – he might be late arriving where he was going; it cost him money; even more, it could have been dangerous for him to help. The man had been mugged, and that could have happened to him too.

Then examine the motives of the priest and levite, respected religious officials. Were these just common human failings of not bothering, not noticing, lacking courage, not willing to take initiative? There was more – the impact of the purity rules of their religion. If they infringed these by touching blood they would be ritually defiled, and there was a long complicated procedure to go through to become clean again to perform their functions in the Temple.

Religion here gets in the way of doing the decent, humane, just thing. And this was Jesus' point. He was attacking both political and religious conventions of the time: the inherited hatred between Jews and Samaritans, and the abject failure to be human of religious leaders. It makes a most arresting distinction between moral awareness and amoral religious obligation. Can religious belief blind people to a proper sense of compassion and justice?

Research

Pupils should research examples of religious people who have taken the lead in fighting injustice. What was it about the religion of people like William Wilberforce that responded so strongly to the need to work towards justice? Other examples might be Martin Luther King, Gandhi, Florence Nightingale, Josephine Butler, Terry Waite, etc. Very interesting work could be done on the work of Canon Andrew White who has brought warring factions together and who has made friends among all the religious groupings in the Middle East. (See The Vicar of Baghdad.[4] He brings leaders of all the religious groups together, so that they can meet each other as persons. And the Church in Baghdad deals with the injustice of poverty, malnutrition, lack of health care, etc by running a medical centre where people of all religions are treated for free, and where both Sunni and Shia Muslims work alongside Christians in serving the poor.)

Activity

Pupils should give a short presentation on their chosen person and comment on the following questions:

1   What is it about being religious that enabled this person to become more humane rather than less humane?

2   How far is it true that the ethic of justice and the ethic of care are the same? (refer to the quote above of Rowan Williams)

3   How can society or school ensure that rules do not get in the way of justice?

Pause for thought

Here is an example where obedience to rules ended up in injustice. Rotherham Council, obeying the rule of no hint of any possible bias against ethnic minorities, took three children away from foster parents because the latter were members of UKIP (UK Independence Party) which some people wrongly believe to be a racist party. This is in fact the Good Samaritan story in reverse. The foster parents had a good record in looking after the children entrusted to their care, and these children were happy, but a rule had been transgressed and so the trauma of taking the children away from where some stability and love was being shown towards them happened.

Keystage 5 (ages 17–18)

There is one exemplar for keystage 5 and it is about learning to be compassionate.

Learning to be compassionate
Lesson Objectives

- Think about the impact of a compassionate person

- Realize that there may be a cost to being compassionate

- Consider that a person who is compassionate in public may not be so in private

- Reflect on the compassion of God and how this has inspired followers

Students could read one of the Sansom books, for example, *Dark Fire*. They will find it riveting reading – extremely good prose style. They'll get a vivid glimpse of life in Tudor England, and there is plenty in the book, as in most detective stories, on character, motives, and the distinction between what people say and do in public and what they are in private. It would provide excellent material for discussion and for asking provocative questions concerning the difference that compassion can make in difficult situations, and how to bring together benevolent intention with benevolent consequences in action.

The character of Master Shardlake who tells the story is one of truth-seeking integrity and genuine compassion, accompanied always by sharp-eyed perceptiveness of motives and character.

It is relatively easy for us today with hindsight to see what went wrong in the world he inhabited: papist/reformist wars and violence which so signally lacked compassion. We can see how people got caught up in it because of the cultural milieu in which they were being brought up and consequent inability to distinguish what is essential from what is not or indeed what is harmful. Can we do better today?

Students can be encouraged to think of modern parallels to the examples of compassion Shardlake gives. Thus, he is prepared to risk his life to correct corruption in high places when he sees the disgusting conditions in buildings cheaply provided by a fellow lawyer Bealknap out of newly acquired monastic property; he earns a powerful enemy as he tries to get justice in the courts for the poor people involved. In his imperfections, Shardlake presents a good role model. Thus, when a colleague points out that he is treating his assistant Skelly roughly for being slow and untidy, not realizing that Skelly has terrible problems with his eye-sight, he tries to make amends by personally paying for Skelly to get some glasses.

There are also nuggets of sheer theological gold hidden in the book, for example, this short discussion giving perhaps the best response possible to the problem of evil: the powerful compassion of God towards the victims of evil.

Shardlake talking to his apothecary friend Guy on the wall of whose room hung a crucifix – Guy was an ex-monk from Granada of Moorish background who had converted to Christianity. His dark appearance was the frequent butt of racist gibes:

> 'I don't distrust you, Guy. God's wounds, I think you're the only one left I do trust.'
>
> Guy looked at the cross. 'There is the only one you need to trust and follow.'
>
> I shook my head sadly. 'Where was Christ when that poor girl and her brother were being cut to pieces last night?'
>
> 'Watching, in the sorrow you see there in his face, as men use the free will God gave them to do terrible evil.' (p. 393)

An interesting real-life example of such 'suffering-with' could be explored: Etty Hillesum whose experience of God in the Nazi concentration camps enabled her to rise above and help others to rise above all the sordidness and evil around them. See for example, Chapter 26 of Rowan Williams's book *Faith in the Public Square* (Bloomsbury 2012).

Notes

1   In schools in England and Wales KS1 refers to children aged rising 5 to 6. KS 2 refers to children aged 7–11, KS 3 to children aged 11–13, KS 4 to children aged 14–16 and KS 5 to pupils aged 16–18.
2   This story is also the basis for lesson activities below p. 190.
3   This story also forms the basis of a lesson exemplar on faith, see above p. 199.
4   Monarch Books 2009.

APPENDIX: THE BIRMINGHAM RELIGIOUS EDUCATION SURVEY

Penny Jennings

CHAPTER OUTLINE

The results of a pilot study into how pupils in Birmingham schools in the UK view RE are given and a comparison made with an earlier study of pupils in Cornwall. Pupils in Birmingham who responded to the survey tend to have more positive attitudes to religious values than those in Cornwall.

Introduction

The introduction of a radically different religious education syllabus for Birmingham (UK) called for a systematic means of assessing its impact on teachers and pupils alike. It was decided to set up a wide-ranging research project, building upon the large body of research that has, over several decades, studied children's and young people's spirituality, values, attitudes towards Christianity, moral attitudes, and various aspects of religious education. The research would take account of the body of empirical research that has examined relationships between provision for the subject, curriculum content, teaching methods and pupil attitude towards the subject. By using insofar as practicable the same research methods and content and comparing the resulting Birmingham data with those from similar studies, it was thought that it would be possible to compare the impact of the new Birmingham syllabus on teacher and pupil attitudes with that of more traditional syllabuses. The research would, however, also include new material relevant to the new syllabus.

Research design

A number of meetings took place from 2009 to 2011 between Dr Marius Felderhof, Agreed Syllabus Drafting Secretary, University of Birmingham, Simone Whitehouse, RE Adviser to Birmingham City Council, Ryan Parker (University of Birmingham) and Dr Penny Jennings, (PhD University of Wales, Bangor). The overall aims of the research were identified thus:

1   To demonstrate that the use of the 2007 Birmingham RE Syllabus fulfils government's aims for religious education.

2   To provide a means of assessing provision for RE, teacher and pupil attitudes towards RE, teaching approaches and lesson content, and pupils' spiritual and moral attitudes, suitable for replication in Birmingham's rolling programme of monitoring RE every 5 years.

3   To provide a means for assessing the possibility that the 2007 Birmingham Agreed Syllabus for Religious Education provides for pupils' spiritual and moral development more effectively than more traditional syllabuses used elsewhere.

It was decided that the research would be both quantitative and qualitative, involving primary and secondary school teachers and pupils. The quantitative element would take the form of questionnaire surveys, and would be followed by semi-structured interviews with teachers and pupils, thus providing a qualitative element.

The quantitative element would build upon questionnaire surveys carried out in Cornwall in 1995/96 (Jennings 2003, unpublished PhD dissertation) and 2004/05, (Jennings 2006, research report to Cornwall's SACRE). These surveys took account of the then governments' aims for religious education but also built upon research studies relating to various aspects of school religious education and the spiritual and moral development of children and teenagers, studies carried out in the United Kingdom over several decades, most notably by Professor Leslie Francis, formerly at the University of Wales, Bangor, currently Professor of Religions and Education, University of Warwick.

The advantages of questionnaire surveys are as follows. They can gather very large amounts of information from very large samples on single occasions that take up a relatively short amount of time. They can also allow for the mapping of trends, they can provide for constant measures across a wide range of participants and they can examine similarities and differences between groups of participants. Provided that samples are representative of whole populations, generalizations about the populations can be made with some degree of confidence. Questionnaire surveys carried out with the necessary guarantees of confidentiality enable both teachers and pupils to be open and honest in their responses. They also provide an opportunity for all pupils, including the least vocal, to express their views.

Questions are pre-coded to allow for computer analysis. While this type of questionnaire may fail to give respondents the opportunity to express the full range of their views, it provides for objectivity, in the sense that the administration, instructions and scoring procedures are standard, whatever the composition of the sample or the biases of the administrator. Inter-related questionnaires for both pupils and teachers would give a full picture of what is happening in schools.

The qualitative element of the research, consisting of a series of semi-structured interviews with teachers and pupils, would allow for the expression of views not covered by the questionnaires, and would enable interviewers to expand upon and clarify issues raised by the questionnaire responses.

It was decided that initially, a relatively small number of schools would be involved in a pilot study. The aims of a pilot study are to discover whether the planned large-scale study will provide answers to the research questions, and to identify possible problems with data gathering, such as difficulties pupils might experience in completing the questionnaires or teachers might find in administering them, or problems in running the statistics.

Questionnaire design

As noted earlier, the present Birmingham research builds upon earlier research studies that examined relationships between various aspects of pupils' religious education, their attitude towards the subject, and their spiritual and moral attitudes. Yet it differs from earlier studies in that most of these, in light of the legal requirements for locally agreed syllabuses to 'reflect the fact that the religious traditions in Great Britain are in the main Christian' and carried out in mainly monofaith contexts, have focused largely upon material relating to the teaching of Christianity, whereas the Birmingham questionnaires, in light of the authority's relatively high numbers of pupils with 'other faith' backgrounds, add in more multifaith material. Additionally, most earlier research studies have included established personality measures, whereas the Birmingham questionnaires use items to measure the dispositions identified in the new agreed syllabus.

Teacher questionnaires

Two teacher questionnaires were developed, one for primary school teachers, one for secondary school teachers. Each will provide information on the cultural/faith context of the school, provision for religious education in terms of time allocation, staff numbers and specialist qualifications, teaching content, method and resources, and teacher attitudes towards the new approach to RE. From this information schools can be categorized and grouped according to, for example, different cultural contexts, or differences in teaching approaches, thus enabling identification of the factors most likely to influence pupils attitudes towards their religious education and their spiritual and moral attitudes.

Each questionnaire contains mainly pre-coded questions offering a definite range of possible answers. A small number of questions are open-ended, giving teachers the opportunity to express more fully their views on the disposition-based approach, thus allowing for some qualitative data.

The primary teacher questionnaire asks for information on the ethnic/faith population of the school, size, location, staff training experience, use of the agreed syllabus, time allocation for RE, number of religions taught, resources. It also asks for any problems with teaching RE, and to what extent completing the questionnaire has been useful.

The secondary teacher questionnaire, using much of the material used in the Cornwall surveys, is longer than that used for primary teachers, asking for more detailed information on lesson content, with specific references to the nine faiths most likely to be taught in Birmingham's schools, and the spiritual and moral attitudes teachers consider that RE should promote. These sets of questions use Likert-type scales to measure teachers' attitudes. Agreement or disagreement with each statement is rated on a five-point scale, ranging from 'agree strongly', through 'agree', 'not certain' and 'disagree' to 'disagree strongly'.

Pupil questionnaires

As with the teacher questionnaire, the pupil questionnaire consists almost wholly of pre-coded or closed questions, employing multiple choice or Likert format, and offering a definite range of possible answers. This allows pupils to work quickly through the questionnaire.

The primary questionnaire seeks to establish each pupil's sex, time spent on after-school activities, time spent watching television/using computers, religion-related activities, attitude towards school lessons and, in more detail, religious education, religious beliefs including attitude towards Christianity, spiritual experience, how personality is expressed in relation to the dispositions, and a range of moral values relevant to this age group, such as 'right and wrong' and care for the environment.

The secondary pupil questionnaire extends the primary questionnaire, seeking additionally to establish pupils' academic ability, religious allegiance and practice, parental religious practice, relationships with other people, and attitudes towards sex and drugs.

The pilot study

The main aim of the pilot study was to identify and overcome unforeseen problems; hence, the procedures planned for the main study were followed as closely as possible. The sample was to be drawn from a population similar to that of the main study and large enough to allow for a variety of opinions. The pilot questionnaires provided space for respondents to make comments about the questionnaire itself so that they might indicate any ambiguities and whether provision should be made for responses that are not included in the questionnaire. The pilot study was to show whether the measures to be used in the main study would provide the required answers to the research questions, identify difficulties pupils might experience in completing the questionnaires; and identify difficulties teachers might find in filling in their own questionnaires or administering the pupil questionnaires.

Sample

The impact of religious education on pupil attitudes can be best assessed by examining the responses of the pupils who have spent the longest time in school. In the case of primary schools, the questionnaires were designed with Year 6 pupils in mind. However, it was decided not to ask for access to final year secondary school pupils in view of examination pressures. Instead, questionnaires were given to Year 9 pupils. With regard to the teachers, questionnaires were distributed in primary schools to the religious education coordinator, and in secondary schools to the subject leader for religious education.

It was decided that in order to gain representation of the cultural/religious diversity of Birmingham's schools, eight primary schools should be involved and four secondary schools - Church of England, Muslim, 'multifaith' and 'secular'. Within these, the head of RE/subject leader would be invited to participate, and Year 6 and Year 9 pupils, respectively. Head teachers would first be approached for permission for their schools to participate in the research. In accordance with established ethical standards for research in the social sciences, school and pupil confidentiality would be protected by the use of numbers instead of names.

In practice, just 6 primary schools and three secondary participated. Of the 6 primary schools half are community and half voluntary aided schools (two being Church of England schools). Two serve a majority of pupils from a white British population and one school has a population of African black heritage and small white population. Three schools serve a mixed range of minority ethnic groups; including one school where 16 different ethnicities make up the pupil population. Of the three secondary schools, two are community schools and one has foundation status. One of these schools has a smaller than average minority ethnic population; of the other two schools three quarters of their population is of minority ethnic groups.

Data analyses

In order to compare the influence of different factors on pupils' spiritual and moral attitudes, schools will be categorized in relation to each chosen factor. Tests for statistical significance will be carried out to determine whether differences between groups could have occurred by chance. It is hoped that Likert-type attitude scales can be developed, enabling comparisons to be made of the dispositions of pupils in schools that are categorized differently. For example, the dispositions of pupils in faith-based schools might be compared with those in 'secular' schools.

Preliminary analysis of pilot study data

Since the samples are so small it has not been practicable to carry out advanced statistical procedures, but the following findings are given to illustrate the kind of data that are likely to emerge from the Birmingham questionnaire surveys.

Teacher responses

Of the Year 6 teachers in the six participating primary schools, only four completed the questionnaire. Of these, three followed the Agreed Syllabus very closely (one, fairly closely), all found it fairly easy to use, three said that their school followed the exemplar schemes of work very closely (one, not at all), with three teachers finding them very useful (one, not sure), one found the training sessions very useful (two, fairly useful, one, no response), one found the 'Faith Makes a Difference' films very useful (three, fairly useful), three found the website very useful (one, fairly useful), two have a detailed scheme of work for RE (two not), and finally, all teachers said that their school used resources other than those provided by the city a lot.

Of the Year 9 teachers in the three participating secondary schools, only two completed their questionnaire. One followed the Agreed Syllabus very closely (one, fairly closely), one found it very easy to use (one, fairly easy), one said that their school followed the exemplar schemes of work occasionally (one, not at all), with one teacher finding them very useful (one, of limited use), one teacher found the training sessions very useful (one, not sure), one found the 'Faith Makes a Difference' films very useful (one, fairly useful), one found the website very useful (one, fairly useful), and one of the teachers said that their school used resources other than those provided by the city a lot, (one hardly at all). The secondary school teachers were asked further questions. Both stated that the majority of RE teachers prefer the thematic (as opposed to systematic) approach to teaching RE, both have reworked existing schemes in devising work for the new syllabus, neither have had to purchase new resources, one had had his/her choices influenced by the religious background of the pupils (one not), one had asked their Pupil Voice what they would like to learn through the disposition based approach (one not), one had seen an impact from teaching through dispositions on pupils' attitudes (one not), one had changed or modified the assessment policy and manner of assessing pupils (one had not) and both had undertaken some evaluative work on the impact of the dispositions approach.

This example of teacher responses to the syllabus indicates how, for example, the dispositions of pupils in schools where the new syllabus is followed very closely might be compared with those in schools where it is followed only occasionally.

Pupil responses

In a preliminary non-statistical perusal of the data, Ryan Parker, a final year theology student who input the data, made a number of general observations.

Parker observed that in Year 6 religious education was considered one of the least enjoyable subjects by most pupils. However, the position was reversed in Year 9, where religious education was considered the third most enjoyable subject, bettered only by PE and games lessons.

Regarding moral values, Year 6 pupils were almost unanimously positive in their responses relating to 'How I feel about our world', with concern for the environment and animals high. There was a wider range of responses relating to keeping animals in zoos, killing for food, and using animals for experimentation. Responses to items relating to environmental issues were also positive for the large majority of Year 9 pupils, but with differing responses as above and also to the question of hunting animals for sport, and recycling.

A more detailed analysis of some of the pupil data follows.

The following are mainly responses to items used in the Cornwall surveys in a Likert-type attitude scale, indicating pupil attitudes towards their RE lessons. Agreement or disagreement with each statement is rated on a five-point scale, ranging from 'agree strongly', through 'agree', 'not certain' and 'disagree' to 'disagree strongly'. For the sake of brevity, in the following summary the figures for 'agree' and 'agree strongly' are combined, as for 'disagree' and 'disagree' strongly. Figures are rounded up to the nearest whole number. Responses are given in percentages.

Of the Year 6 pupils, 100 pupils were asked to complete the questionnaire. Almost all pupils responded to each item.

A total of 84 per cent agree that 'RE helps me to understand what people think God is like' (3% disagree, 16% not sure), 90 per cent think it important to know what different faiths believe (3% disagree, 17% not sure), 66 per cent enjoy learning about different religions (14% disagree, 19% not sure), 73 per cent agree that 'RE helps me to find rules to live by' (9% disagree, 17% not sure), 75 per cent agree that 'RE helps me to understand my beliefs better' (13% disagree, 11% not sure), 48 per cent agree that 'RE helps me to sort out my problems' (26% disagree, 27% not sure), 60 per cent enjoy discussing problems in RE (21% disagree, 18% not sure), 66 per cent agree that 'RE helps me to think about who I really am' (21% disagree, 13% not sure), 70 per cent agree that 'RE helps me to lead a better life' (15% disagree, 16% not sure), 63 per cent enjoy debates in RE (19% disagree, 18% not sure), 76 per cent like their RE teacher (10% disagree, 13% not sure), 72 per cent find studying holy scriptures interesting (9% disagree, 13% not sure), 69 per cent agree that 'RE helps me to think about why I am here' (11% disagree, 18% not sure), 64 per cent agree that 'RE helps me to believe in God' (20% disagree, 17% not sure), 43 per cent like best RE that is just about facts (37% disagree, 21% not sure), 59 per cent like best RE that is relevant to their life (14% disagree, 27% not sure).

Of the Year 9 pupils, 56 pupils were asked to complete the questionnaire. Almost all responded to each item.

68 per cent agree that 'RE helps me understand God' (9% disagree, 22% not sure), 76 per cent enjoy learning about different religions (4% disagree, 21% not sure), 61 per cent agree that 'RE helps me make sense of my life' (11% disagree, 28% not sure), 38 per cent find RE enjoyable when not GCSE (General Certificate of Secondary Education) subject (25% disagree, 38% not certain), 15 per cent agree that 'RE wastes time I could spend on exam subjects' (62% disagree, 23% not sure), 45 per cent agree that 'RE helps me find rules to live by' (21% disagree, 34% not certain), 87 per cent find it interesting to learn about life after death (none disagree, 13% not sure), 30 per cent agree that 'RE helps me to choose a faith to live by' (43% disagree, 26% not sure), 34 per cent agree that 'RE helps me to sort out my problems' (36% disagree, 30% not sure), 32 per cent agree that 'RE provides relaxation in a busy timetable' (38% disagree, 30% not sure), 64 per cent enjoy discussing moral problems in RE (13% disagree, 23% not sure), 55 per cent agree that 'RE helps me to think about who I really am' (23% disagree, 23% not sure), 65 per cent think that RE is fun (12% disagree, 23% not sure), 45 per cent agree that 'RE helps me lead a better life' (19% disagree,

36% not sure), 85 per cent think it important to know what people of other faiths believe (2% disagree, 15% not sure), 76 per cent like their RE teacher (13% disagree, 11% not sure), 70 per cent enjoy debates in RE (9% disagree, 21% not sure), 15 per cent enjoy studying sacred texts (45% disagree, 40% not sure), 66 per cent agree that 'RE helps me to think about why I am here' (8% disagree, 26% not sure), 60 per cent agree that 'RE helps me to believe in God' (8% disagree, 32% not sure), 34 per cent 'like best RE that focuses on facts' (23% disagree, 43% not sure), 60 per cent like best RE that is relevant to their life (9% disagree, 30% not sure).

As a general observation, Parker noted that many of the pilot study pupils were from faith backgrounds, and of these, the majority were Muslim or Christian. He observed that for the former, responses were predominantly positive for almost all questions regarding faith, religious education and spirituality; for the latter, responses were also predominantly positive, but to a lesser extent. Pupils' faith backgrounds will therefore need to be taken into account when analysing the data from the large-scale surveys.

Although aware that comparisons cannot be made without the relevant statistical analyses and unless samples are comparable in size and composition, Parker noticed that the responses to some sections of the Birmingham pilot study differed greatly from those in the earlier Cornwall survey on which the present research was based. For example, Birmingham's Year 9 pupil responses to items examining attitudes to 'spiritual' experiences appeared to be predominantly positive, whereas Cornwall's Year 9 and 10 pupil responses in this section were predominantly negative.

As further examples, with regard to sexual behaviour, a set of items only included in the secondary school questionnaire, responses showed that around 80 per cent of Birmingham's Year 9 pilot study pupils saw adultery as wrong, compared with just under 50 per cent of Cornwall's Year 9 and 10 pupils, just over a half of Birmingham's Year 9 pilot study pupils thought it wrong to have sex under the legal age, compared with just 20 per cent of Cornwall's Year 9 and 10 pupils, but only a third of Birmingham's Year 9 pilot study pupils thought it wrong to have sex before marriage, compared with just 6 per cent of Cornwall's Year 9 and 10 pupils. Similar results were observed in relation to the use of illegal drugs. However, as noted above, such comparisons have no statistical legitimacy. They merely serve to encourage the hope that the disposition-based approach in religious education will make a major contribution to promoting positive spiritual and moral attitudes in pupils at both primary and secondary levels of schooling.

Conclusion

As noted above, the primary aim of a pilot study is that it reveals problems that are likely to occur in the main large-scale survey. No problems were reported, although it has been noted that such surveys take far longer to complete than might be expected, and due to heavy work-loads, schools may need more enticements to encourage participation.

The benefits of carrying out the pilot study are numerous. The findings reported here should enable those with stakeholder interest in the research to make any necessary adjustments prior to the large-scale surveys, ensuring that the research questions will provide the needed answers. Once finalized, the same questionnaires can be used in future years, providing constant measures of pupil and teacher attitudes and values in the context of social and cultural change. The findings should also provide a basis for those devising the questions for the semi-structured interviews that are to follow.

Yet perhaps the greatest value in the pilot study lies in the fact that it points to the range of information that can be generated, information to be used not only, in the ensuing large-scale surveys, to assess the value of the Birmingham Agreed Syllabus, but also with the potential to be used by other local councils to assess the value of their own syllabuses of Religious Education.

INDEX